KNOWLEDGE, POWER AND EMANCIPATION:
FROM MARX TO THE OCTOBER REVOLUTION

Alexander A. Chryssis

MINERVA PRESS
LONDON
MONTREUX LOS ANGELES SYDNEY

KNOWLEDGE, POWER AND EMANCIPATION: FROM
MARX TO THE OCTOBER REVOLUTION
Copyright © Alexander A Chryssis 1997

All Rights Reserved

No part of this book may be reproduced in any form,
by photocopying or by any electronic or mechanical means,
including information storage or retrieval systems,
without permission in writing from both the copyright owner
and the publisher of this book.

ISBN 1 86106 331 8

First Published 1997 by
MINERVA PRESS
195 Knightsbridge
London SW7 1RE

Printed in Great Britain for Minerva Press

KNOWLEDGE, POWER AND EMANCIPATION:
FROM MARX TO THE OCTOBER REVOLUTION

To my parents

About the Author

Alexander A. Chryssis was born in Athens in 1958 and he is now teaching Philosophy at the Pantheion University of Social and Political Studies (Athens, Greece).

Contents

Introduction

The Theoretical Background of the Problem   11

I   Philosophers En Route to the Communist League   43

     1. A Young Philosopher in the Realm of History   45
     2. Philosophers and their 'Discovery'
        of the Proletarian World   54
     3. Intellectuals and Proletarians: Marx, Engels
        and the Proletarian Vanguard of the 1840s   64
     4. Intellectuals and Proletarians in and around the
        League of the Just   74
     5. Marx and Engels in the Communist League   83
     6. Proletarian Self-Emancipation or Intellectual Elitism?
        A Critical Reconsideration   94

II   Intellectuals and Proletarians in the International
      Working Men's Association.   109

     7. Marx, Engels and the International
        – Motives and Tactics   111
     8. Intellectual Leadership and Proletarian
        Self-Emancipation: the Aristodemocracy Question   120
     9. Bakunin and the International
        – Motives and Tactics   124
   10. The Marx/Bakunin Controversy:
        Knowledge, Organisation and Authority   132
   11. Marx and Bakunin: Philosophy and Emancipation
        – a Critical Summary   143

III Intellectuals, Intelligentsia and Proletarian
    Self-Emancipation – a Debate within the
    European Proletarian Movement   151

    12. Intellectuals and Proletarians: From the Paris
        Commune to the International's Dissolution   153
    13. Marx, Engels and European Social Democracy:
        Intellectuals and Workers' Parties   158
    14. Intelligentsia: an Attempt to a Definition   166
    15. Intelligentsia, Emancipation and Russian Populism   173
    16. Intelligentsia, Emancipation and Russian Marxism   187

Conclusion

Intellectual Leadership and Proletarian Self-Emancipation
from the 1905 to the 1917 Russian Revolution   217

Bibliography   229

Public opinion therefore deserves to be as much respected as despised – despised for its concrete expression and for the concrete consciousness it expresses, respected for its essential basis, a basis which only glimmers more or less dimly in that concrete expression.

Hegel's *Philosophy of Right*
§ 318

Introduction
The Theoretical Background of the Problem

The adequacy of Marxism as a programme of social and political emancipation is strongly questioned in our days, especially after the fall of the so-called 'existing socialism'. From our point of view, however, the connection between Marxism and 'existing socialism' cannot be sufficiently examined, unless Marx's own analysis of the theory-practice relationship is critically studied and evaluated. More specifically, the Marxist principle of the unity of theory and practice (a fundamental thesis of a socialist theory of revolution) demands a direct approach of the philosopher's role in the revolutionary practice. Such an approach is exactly the object of this research, which will be developed and promoted in the field of Marxist political theory.

According to Marx's well-known *Eleventh Thesis on Feuerbach*, 'the philosophers have only interpreted the world in various ways; the point, however, is to change it.' An unbiased interpretation of this thesis leads us to the obvious conclusion that 'Marx's point is not that we must stop thinking, but that one cannot change the world through thought alone: revolutions are made not in the philosopher's study, but in the real world.'[1] (Hoffman's emphasis). In any case, the philosopher's concrete role in the revolutionary process still remains an open question and deserves a detailed examination within the frame of analysis of the highly controversial relation among the 'men of knowledge', on the one hand, and political power, on the other.

From this point of view, however, it is worth realising as well that this relation constitutes in itself one of the most crucial philosophical problems from ancient years until modern times. That is why it

---

[1] J. Hoffman, *Marxism and the Theory of Praxis*, London, Lawrence and Wishart, 1975, p.31.

proves to be necessary, before proceeding to the way Marx himself faces the connection of philosophy with politics, to present the pre-Marxian philosophical background of this complicated issue.

It is now the time, therefore, to write down the fundamental questions concerning the philosopher's relationship with political power and emancipation.

1. What is the role of the philosopher within a concrete political society as regards his (or her) contribution to the formation and realisation of a particular programme of emancipation? Ruler, adviser, educator, legislator are only several of the answers provided by the history of philosophy, answers which we are going to present a little later.

2. What is the relation among the 'men of knowledge', on the one hand, and the masses, on the other, in order to achieve a specific kind of social and political emancipation? Strictly connected with this question lies the problem of people's self-emancipation.

3. Given the analysis of these questions, how should education, on the one hand, and democracy, on the other, be confronted with regard to their respective impact on people's self-emancipation?

Philosophers in the realm of politics

Bearing directly on the first of the above mentioned questions, Plato's thesis, according to which Reason ought to rule not only in the personality of the individual, but in the state as well, seems to be a rather interesting starting point of analysis.[2] In a similar line of argument Aristotle proceeds to an equally interesting remark distinguishing between the rule of a master and that of a statesman, in other words rule by command and rule by persuasion.

> The living creature consists in the first place of mind and body, and of these the former is ruler by nature, the latter ruled [...]. The rule of soul over body is like a master's rule, while the rule of intelligence over desire is like a statesman's or a king's.[3]

---

[2] See Plato, *The Republic*, Harmondsworth, Penguin Books, 1974, 441d, e.
[3] Aristotle, *Politics*, Harmondsworth, Penguin Books, 1981, 1254a, 1254b.

Therefore, ascribing to Reason, the ruling power within both man and the state, Plato and Aristotle admit and defend not only the necessity of ruling in general, but also the exercise of ruling by the specific agent of Reason as such. The concrete consequences of this position as regards the philosophers' political role can, however, be effectively grasped through different ways and towards different directions on the basis of Plato and Aristotle's political philosophy.

According to the well-known Platonic formulation, the role of the philosopher and that of the ruler must be combined in and expressed by the same person.

> There will be no end to the troubles of states, or indeed [...] of humanity itself, till philosophers become kings in this world, or till those we now call Kings and rulers really and truly become philosophers, and political power and philosophy thus come into the same hands [...].[4]

The unity of philosophy (true knowledge) and political power as personified by the *philosopher-king* represents, therefore, Plato's thesis as regards the role of philosopher in the life of a republic. Only he who knows best has the right and duty to decide and act in the field of political power. Putting aside for the moment the highly questioned relationship between philosophers and the people, it must be stressed, however, that, according to Plato, genuine philosophers are not especially those agents of knowledge who are confined to the interpretation of the world, but those who are powerfully and selflessly intervening in the shaping of the new state and whose only reward will be not to be governed by men worse than themselves.[5]

At this point, it is worth mentioning that Plato uses the analogies of captain, shepherd and doctor in order to express his views on the authority of 'men of knowledge'.[6] In, for example, his critique of the rebellious crew of a ship, Plato argues as follows:

---

[4] Plato, *The Republic*, 473d.
[5] op. cit., 347c: '[T]he worst penalty for refusal is to be governed by someone worse than themselves.'
[6] For Plato's use of the analogy among statesman and captain, see op. cit., 342d ff. For Plato's use of the analogy among statesman and doctor see op. cit., 342a ff. For Plato's use of the analogy among statesman and shepherd see op. cit., 343b ff. in connection with Taylor's interesting remark in A. E. Taylor, *Socrates*, Westport, Connecticut, Greenwood Press Publishers, 1975, p.158 ff.

> They have no idea that the true navigator must study the seasons of the year, the sky, the stars, the winds and all the other subjects appropriate to his profession if he is to be really fit to control a ship; and they think that it's quite impossible to acquire the professional skill needed for such control [...] and that there's no such thing as an art of navigation.[7]

The conclusions which can be directly drawn from the above political analogy, often used by political theorists in modern times as well, are the following:

1. A republic cannot live without a ruler.

2. Such a ruler cannot be the people themselves, but the true agents of knowledge, this means the men (and women), who really know the art of navigation, i.e. the art of ruling a state.

It is, moreover, important to notice that during the period of the European Enlightenment Jean-Jacques Rousseau – in the first phase of his work – came close to Plato's position as regards the philosopher-ruler. While fighting against the phoney intellectuals of his time – the 'lovers of opinion', enemies of the true 'lovers of wisdom', according to Plato's distinction[8] – Rousseau proceeds to the following conclusion.

> But so long as power alone is on one side, and knowledge and understanding alone on the other, the learned will seldom make great objects their study, princes will still more rarely do great actions, and the peoples will continue to be, as they are, mean, corrupt, and miserable.[9]

In other words, by defending the 'man of knowledge' *qua* adviser or ruler, there is no doubt that the young Rousseau himself was actually

---

Finally, for a presentation and critical attack against Plato's above-mentioned analogies see R. Bambrough, 'Plato's Political Analogies' in G. Vlastos (ed.), *Plato, II, Ethics, Politics and Philosophy of Art and Religion*, Doubleday Anchor, 1971, pp.187–206.

[7] Plato, op. cit., 488e.

[8] op. cit., 480.

[9] J.J. Rousseau, 'A Discourse of the Arts and Sciences' in J.J. Rousseau, *The Social Contract and Discourses*, London, Dent, 1975, p.26.

attracted, up to a certain point, by the Platonic model of the philosopher-king.

Aristotle's analysis, however, seems to move in a rather different direction. According to Aristotle, and contrary to Plato, the argument that the people must be sovereign, rather than the best but few, contains a germ of truth in it.[10] The way he is trying to substantiate such a view is the following:

> [I]t is possible that the many, no one of whom taken singly is a sound man, may yet taken altogether, be better than the few, not individually but collectively [...] For even where there are many people, each has some share of virtue and practical wisdom; and when they are brought together, just as in the mass they become as it were one man with pairs of feet and hands and many senses, so also do they become one in regard to character and intelligence.[11]

From this point of view, such a 'collective personality' may become a more adequate agent of the (ruling) Reason in comparison with the individual experts of knowledge. There is no doubt, therefore, that such an analysis denies the validity of the Platonic model of the philosopher-ruler/king.[12] Aristotle's approach, however, makes way for the construction of the model of the *philosopher-governor,* a model which is compatible with his own approach to a *polity* as a mixture of oligarchy and democracy.13 As he himself acknowledges, to let the mass of the people share in the highest offices is a great risk;[14] on the other hand, it is equally risky to reject any kind of people's participation in the political life of the

---

[10] Aristotle, op. cit., 1281a.
[11] *ibid.*
[12] There is no doubt that this position contradicts not only Plato's views on this issue, but the young Rousseau's analysis as well. According to Rousseau's approach, as exposed in his *Discourse of the Arts and Sciences*, knowledge is always a privilege of a few distinguished personalities.

For an interesting critical presentation of Rousseau's rejection of 'popularised science', see L. Strauss, 'On the Intention of Rousseau', in M. Cranston and R.S. Peters (eds), *Hobbes and Rousseau: A Collection of Critical Essays*, New York, Anchor Books, 1972, especially pp.263-269.
[13] Aristotle, op. cit., 1293b and 1294a ff.
[14] op. cit., 1281b.

state.[15] Being excluded from the governing function of the state – a function successfully promoted by the wisest citizens[16] – the mass of the people, 'provided it is not too slave-like',[17] may be, however, a better judge than the expert himself. Finally, 'there are tasks of which the actual doer will be neither the best nor the only judge, cases in which even those who do not possess the skill form an opinion of the finished product.'[18]

Nevertheless, the question which Aristotle does not succeed in answering is the following: under which conditions, and by which methods may the people be able to choose the best, that is to say the wisest and most virtuous among them, to govern their polity?[19] Taking for granted that the people are not 'slave-like' does not seem an effective and sufficient presupposition for such a demanding choice. Moreover, if the mass of the people is considered able to judge and elect the wisest to govern, one may wonder why such a people must be excluded from the polity's higher offices. Anyway, we will return to a more detailed discussion of this issue later on.

It is worth mentioning, however, that a similar objection can be raised to Rousseau's analysis, as this is expressed in his *Social Contract*. Actually the 'Citizen of Geneva' – during the second phase of his work – seems to move away from the Platonic model of the philosopher-ruler in order to endorse the model of the philosopher-governor within an *elective aristocracy*.

Given his well-known anti-intellectualism, while rejecting democracy as well as a type of government suited to Gods and not to men,[20] Rousseau does not hesitate to defend his elective aristocracy,[21]

---

[15] *ibid.*
[16] In regard to this issue, see Aristotle's interesting remarks concerning the Carthoginian aristocratic constitution: Aristotle, op. cit., 1273a, b.
[17] op. cit., 1282a.
[18] *ibid.*
[19] According to Aristotle, op. cit., 1292a, 'when states are democratically governed according to law, there are no demagogues, and the best citizens are securely in the saddle; but where the laws are not sovereign, there you find demagogues.' However, Aristotle does not give a direct answer to the following question: how will people succeed in protecting themselves from the demagogues, even if they are not too 'slave-like'?
[20] J.J. Rousseau, *The Social Contract*, Harmondsworth, Penguin Books, 1984, p.114.
[21] op. cit., pp.115–116.
In regard to Rousseau's reference to elective aristocracy see the following analyses:

the affinity of which to an aristocratic version of the Aristotelian polity is quite evident:

> Aristocracy [argues Rousseau] has not only the advantage of distinguishing between the sovereign and the government, it has also the advantage of selecting its magistrates [...]. It is the best and most natural arrangement for the wisest to govern the multitude, if we are sure that they will govern it for their advantage and not for their own.[22]

It becomes obvious, therefore, that according to Rousseau the philosopher-ruler should give way to the elected wise governors, a group of men distinguished not only in the field of knowledge and wisdom, but also in that of virtue.[23] At the same time, however, the Rousseauist aristocrats of mind and virtue are actually controlled by the people, who remain the indisputable sovereign body. Thus, the mixture of aristocracy and democracy, which Aristotle suggested through his *polity*, finds its modern extension in Rousseau's *elective aristocracy*.

Nevertheless, it was not only Aristotle and later Rousseau who kept their critical distance from the Platonic model of the philosopher-king. Another distinguished representative of the European Enlightenment, Immanuel Kant, openly rejects Plato's thesis as regards the ruling role of philosophers.

---

a) M. Cranston, *The Noble Savage, Jean-Jacques Rousseau 1754–1762*, Harmondsworth, Allen Lane, 1991, pp.308–309.

b) B. de Jouvenel, 'Rousseau's Theory of the Form of Government' in *Hobbes and Rousseau, A Collection of Critical Essays*, pp.484–497.

[22] J.J. Rousseau, op. cit., p.115.

[23] As regards Rousseau's confrontation of knowledge, Ernst Cassirer in *The Question of Jean-Jacques Rousseau*, London and New Haven, Yale University Press, 1989, p.57, proceeds to the following comment of neo-Kantian origin: 'Knowledge – that is the insight which Rousseau had now achieved – is without danger as long as it does not try to raise itself above life and to tear itself away from it, as long as it serves the order of life itself. Knowledge must claim no absolute primacy, for in the realm of spiritual values it is the ethical will that deserves primacy.' From this point of view, Rousseau's wise magistrates should dispose not only knowledge but virtue as well; knowledge is absolutely connected with ethical will. At this point, Rousseau's ideas are in irreconcilable opposition to any kind of technocratic authority of experts. Experts devoid of virtue are real enemies of human community and must never be allowed to govern.

> It is not to be expected [argues Kant] that kings will philosophise or that philosophers will become kings; nor is it to be desired, however, since the possession of power inevitably corrupts the free judgement of reason.
> Kings or sovereign peoples (i.e. those governing themselves by egalitarian laws) should not, however, force the class of philosophers to disappear or to remain silent, but should allow them to speak publicly.[24]

As is obvious, however, from Kant's position quoted above, the German thinker rejects not only Plato's model of the philosopher-ruler, but that of the philosopher-governor as well. Possession of power and the philosophical judgement of reason, according to Kant, must be clearly separated. The corrupting influence of political power on man's freedom of thinking can be avoided only through such a separation. Does this mean that philosophers or theorists must keep themselves out of the realm of public affairs? At this point, Kant seems to adopt and defend the model of the *philosopher-public speaker* and *adviser* of political rulers. Especially, as regards the advisory role of philosophers, it must be mentioned that, in complete opposition to the young Rousseau's analysis, separation and not unity of power and philosophy is, according to Kant, the necessary condition for the philosophers' success in their reforming work. Moreover, by making public use of reason, philosophers may and must act as the true enlighteners of the people. In this twofold way, Kant really believed that the state of enlightened despotism of his own time would proceed towards its gradual reform. Besides, it is a kind of *moral imperative* that urges the 'man of learning' to move in a direction like this. So, through his moderate way of arguing, Kant insists that

> [philosophers], on account of the very freedom which they allow themselves are a stumbling block to the state, whose only wish is to rule; they are accordingly given the appellation of 'enlighteners', and decried as a menace to the state. And yet they do not address themselves in *familiar* tones to the people (who

---

[24] Kant, 'Perpetual Peace: A Philosophical Sketch' in Kant, *Political Writings*, H. Reiss (ed.), Cambridge, Cambridge University Press, 1991, p.115.

themselves take little or no notice of them and their writings), but in *respectful* tones to the state, which is thereby implored to take the rightful needs of the people to heart.[25] (Kant's emphasis)

Reviving, therefore, in modern times, the Socratic portrait of the *philosopher-horsefly*, stuck upon the state in order to make it move in the right direction,[26] Kant defends the consultative role of the 'men of knowledge' towards the rulers themselves and their enlightening role towards the subjects of the state, so as to make them conscious of their rights and duties. In both cases, however, the philosopher, according to Kant's own position, should be carefully kept apart from any direct intervention in the exercise of political power, both in the form of ruling and that of governing as well. Hence, such a philosopher does not seem to incarnate a real menace to the state; he is rather a saviour of the state through the smooth and gradual reform of mind he himself promotes by making public use of his reason.

It is in a different cultural context, however, revealing a *romantic* influence, that the young Fichte's analysis of the vocation of the scholar (*Gelehrter*) - a person who devotes his life to the process of learning[27] - unfolds. First of all, as his own lectures to his students at the University of Jena definitely show, Fichte does not aim at persuading the rulers of his time to adopt a programme of enlightenment. Being a scholar himself, he feels completely oriented to society.[28] As a result, he turns the axis of analysis towards society itself and defines the 'man of knowledge' as the 'educator of mankind'.[29] In other words, according to Fichte, philosophers or

---

[25] Kant, *The Contest of Faculties*, p.186.
[26] The description of the philosopher-horsefly is expressed in Plato's *Apology of Socrates*, 30e.
[27] Fichte, 'Some Lectures concerning the Scholar's Vocation' in Fichte, *Early Philosophical Writings*, Ithaca, Cornell University Press, 1988, p.172.
[28] op. cit., p.173: 'The scholar is especially destined for society. More than any other class, his class, insofar as he is a scholar, properly exists only through and for society.'
[29] On the portrait of the 'scholar-educator of mankind', see Fichte, op. cit., p.175, where Fichte insists that such an educator 'may employ none but moral means to influence society . He will not be tempted to use compulsory means or physical force to get men to accept his convictions [...]. But neither should the scholar employ deception [...]. In each of his actions he ought to be able to think of himself as an end and ought to be treated as such by every other member of

scholars are not mere thinkers or passive agents of Reason; they are, above all, 'men of action' or, in his own words, 'priests of truth'.[30] From this point of view, the moral duty of the scholar, as underlined by Fichte, leads him not to the courts of despots and princes, but towards the common members of society, whose teachers he and his students should become.[31] Consequently, one can rightly argue that Fichte's portrait of the scholar is that of a *philosopher-agitator,* not only mentally, but also morally devoted to his own goal, i.e. to the education of mankind and finally to advancing the human race towards a society, within which one may achieve 'the highest good [...] the complete harmony of a rational being with himself.'[32]

Furthermore, strongly attached to a struggle for the total liberation of humanity,[33] the young Fichte describes the vocation of the scholar as follows:

> The purpose of all human knowledge is to see to the equal, continuous and progressive development of all human talents. It follows from this that the true vocation of the scholarly class is *the supreme supervision of the actual progress of the human race in general and the unceasing promotion of this progress.*[34] (Fichte's emphasis)

It is, therefore, self-evident that, according to Fichte such a 'man of knowledge' is steadily oriented not towards the interpretation of the past, but towards the active participation in the shaping of humanity's own future. The *philosopher-priest of truth,* as Fichte portrays him, does not come on the scene too late, as Hegel insists a few decades

---

[30] society. A person who is deceived is being treated as a mere means to an end.' (Fichte's emphasis). The Kantian flavour of Fichte's remark as regards the educator/mankind relation as an end in itself is self-evident.
op. cit., p.176: 'Within my special area the culture of my age and of future ages is entrusted to me. My labors will help determine the course of future generations and the history of nations still to come. I am called to testify to the truth. My life and destiny do not matter at all, but infinitely such depends upon the results of my life. *I am a priest of truth.* I am in its pay, and thus I have committed myself to do, to risk, and to suffer anything for its sake.' (our emphasis).
[31] op. cit., p.174.
[32] op. cit., p.151.
[33] op. cit., pp.167–168.
[34] op. cit., p.172.

later.³⁵ The philosophers, according to Fichte, are not the theorists who understand and interpret what has already happened; they are men, for whom thought and knowledge are means to action and struggle.

> Act! Act! [Fichte prompted his students]. That is what we are here for. Should we complain that others are not as perfect as we are, as we ourselves are only more perfect than they are? Isn't our greater perfection precisely this calling we have received to work for the improvement of others? Let us rejoice over the prospect of the immense field that is ours to cultivate! Let us rejoice because we feel our own strength and because our task is endless!³⁶

At this point, however, Fichte's position pushes us to proceed to the second level of analysis, coming, therefore, face to face with the fundamental question of the philosopher/masses relation. Rulers or governors, advisers of despots or enlighteners of the masses, horseflies upon the state or priests of truth devoted to the education of mankind, philosophers, in the broad sense of the term, directly or indirectly, exert their influence not only on the mechanism of political power, but above all on the masses' social and political consciousness and practice.

---

[35] Hegel, *Philosophy of Right*, Oxford, Oxford University Press, 1967, pp.12-13.
[36] Fichte, op. cit., p.184.

Philosophers and Masses: a Controversial Relation

It seems beyond any doubt that a significant number of distinguished thinkers, from the ancient until the modern times, describe the philosopher/masses relationship, at least during the transitional phase between the old and the new social/political order, as a relation marked by intensity and power-asymmetry. Actually, Plato is one of the first political philosophers who comes face to face with the problem, following the steps of his beloved teacher Socrates.

> So philosophy [argues Plato] is impossible among the common people [...]. And the common people must disapprove of philosophers.[37]

Whether such a verdict was final as regards Plato's views will be discussed a little later; from another direction, however, Aristotle as well expresses a similar disapproval, rejecting for example the ability of (manual) workers to become citizens,[38] even though he himself believes that 'man is *by nature,* a political animal.'[39] (our emphasis). According to Aristotle,

> what we have called the virtue of a citizen cannot be ascribed to everyone, nor yet to free men alone, but *simply to those who are in fact relieved of necessary tasks.*[40] (our emphasis)

Following, to a certain extent, this tradition in modern times, Voltaire, one of the most eminent representatives of the French Enlightenment, does not hesitate to note that 'the populace always remains in the profound ignorance to which it is condemned by the need to gain its livelihood...'. In fact, Voltaire doubts whether 'that order of citizens will ever have the time and the capacity to instruct themselves; they will die of hunger before they become philosophers...'. Thus, it is on the basis of such a consideration that

---

[37] Plato, op. cit., 494a.
[38] Aristotle, op. cit., 1277b–1278a.
[39] op. cit., 1253a.
[40] op. cit., 1287a.

Voltaire orientates his 'philosophical propaganda' not to 'shoemakers and servants', but to the 'enlightened middle order'.[41]

Even Rousseau, despite his very romantic view of the people, supposedly less affected by the 'virus' of arts and sciences, does not ascribe the role of the founder of the new society to the people themselves, but to an extraordinary man, a kind of a demigod, the wise and virtuous Legislator. The reasoning of such a view is revealing:

> How can a blind multitude, which often does not know what it wants, because it seldom knows what is good for it, undertake by itself an enterprise as vast and difficult as a system of legislation? [...] Individuals see the good and reject it; the public desires the good but does not see it. Both equally need guidance. [...] Hence the necessity of a lawgiver.[42]

Moving in a similar direction, the young Fichte, though recognising that 'all men have a sense for what is true', nevertheless concludes:

> Such a sense of feeling for truth is not sufficient to lead the uneducated person to all the truths that he needs; but [...] it is always enough to permit him to recognise the truth *after another has guided him to it* [...][43] (our emphasis)

Given these positions, a preliminary conclusion may already be reached: philosophers, those true lovers of wisdom, are due to act directly or indirectly, one way or another, as guides of the people, at least during the transitional phase of the new society's foundation. However, a general remark like this undoubtedly deserves further consideration and critical analysis.

Starting once again from Plato's *Republic,* it should be mentioned that Plato himself proceeds to a further analysis in order to underline the philosopher's duty towards the community and its members. From this point of view, it is worth noting that those men (and women) – 'the best minds' as Plato calls them – who succeed in

---

[41] All the aforementioned extracts are included in P. Gay, *Voltaire's Politics, The Poet as Realist*, New York ,Vintage Books, 1965, p.222.

[42] J.J. Rousseau, *The Social Contract*, p.83.

[43] Fichte, op. cit., p.174.

getting out of the cave and becoming agents of the true knowledge, are, according to Plato, *obliged* to return to the cave and help the ignorant prisoners understand what is really going on. Contrary to Homer's Ulysses, who *uses* his rowers in order to reach his own Ithaca, Plato's philosopher approaches his fellow men in order to *help* them and *free* them from the darkness of ignorance; this is the way which leads to the construction of his beloved Republic:

> You must therefore [urges Plato the philosophers-future rulers of the republic] each descend in turn and live with your fellows in the cave and get used to seeing in the dark; once you get used to it [continues Plato], you will see a thousand times better than they do and will distinguish the various shadows and know what they are shadows of, because you have seen the truth about things admirable and just and good.[44]

Consequently, knowledge is not the exclusive privilege of philosophers; it is a matter of duty towards community. The republic itself, as it has been presented by Plato, is not a state promoting 'the special welfare of any particular class';[45] it is the philosophers' work to help free their fellow citizens from ignorance and it is these citizens' sense of discipline to accept the ruling power of philosophers. This means that common people are not definitely condemned to ignorance; moreover, people themselves will not be for ever in conflict with philosophers.[46] Learning to distinguish between lovers of opinion and lovers of knowledge, i.e. authentic philosophers, the 'common run of men' will change their minds and recognise the social and political role of those distinguished agents of reason as regards the future construction and ruling of a just and self-disciplined state. In a state like this, everyone will act according to his (or her) specific talent and philosophers shall rule not in favour of their particular interest, but in favour of the common good.

At this point an obvious question arises, concerning the methods by which a republic like this may be founded and survive so as to avoid any kind of political degeneration. Education, as we are going to argue later on, seems to play a crucial role in the whole process. For

---

[44] Plato, op. cit., 520c.
[45] op. cit., 519e.
[46] op. cit., 499e ff.

the time being, it is worth noticing, however, that the philosophers' ruling activity within the Republic is not an end in itself. Their real target is to prepare their fellow men to achieve freedom and live in justice.

> [Having] educated the best in them to be their guardian and ruler and to take over from the best in us: *then we give them their freedom.*[47] (our emphasis)

Given such an analysis, however, it must be pointed out that Plato's thesis, according to which political power must be exercised in favour of the common interest and not for the rulers' own sake, is applied by Aristotle in his well-known classification of correct and deviated constitutions.[48] Hence, from Aristotle's point of view, democracy is considered a deviation from polity, given the fact that popular rule promotes only the people's particular interests and not the interests of the whole community. On the contrary, within a polity which combines democratic and aristocratic elements, common men and citizens distinguished in terms of wisdom and virtue share the same ideal, in other words the pursuit of the community's interest. In such a polity, therefore, the exercise of political power – following the Aristotelian way of approaching the best men/common people relationship – is the *dialectical outcome* of different ways to accede to virtue. Practical wisdom of the masses interacts with the theoretical wisdom of the *gnorimoi;* it is through such an interaction that a polity is created and governed wisely by those who are superior in terms of intellectual and moral virtue. The cornerstone, however, of such a polity is the fruitful combination of two forms of equality, already distinguished by Plato; *numerical equality and equality of value.*[49]

> There are two kinds of equality [says Aristotle], the one being numerical, the other of value. I use 'numerically equal' to cover that which is equal and the same in respect of either size or quantity, and 'equal in value' for that which is equal by ratio.[50]

---

[47] op. cit., 591a.
[48] Aristotle, op. cit., 1279a, b.
[49] See:
  a) Plato, *Republic*, 558c.
  b) Plato, *Laws*, 757b, c.
[50] Aristotle, op. cit., 1301b.

The impact of this distinction on the theory of democracy, and more specifically on the philosopher/people relationship we are here dealing with, is obvious.

Besides, it is exactly from this point that Aristotle, lover of the golden rule of *mesotes* (μεσότης), distances himself from Plato's condemnation of democracy. Aristotle's polity represents an attempt to transcend dialectically two apparently contradictory principles: the *principle of number* and the *principle of value;* it is from this point of view that the combined use of equality of number and equality of value is undoubtedly fruitful, especially in connection with the 'men of knowledge' – common people relationship. Aristotle himself is very lucid in his own choice.

> To lay it down that the equality shall be exclusively of one kind or the other is a bad thing as is shown by what happens in practice: no constitution that is constructed on such a basis lasts long [...].[51] *Therefore we must make use both of numerical equality and equality of value.* (our emphasis)

Contrary to Plato, whose exclusive preference for the equality of value is indisputable and harmoniously co-exists with the nomination of philosophers *qua* rulers of the Republic, Aristotle orientates his analysis towards a very balanced use of principles. As a result, he is led to an equally symmetrical approach of the relation among wise men, on the one hand, and their fellow citizens, on the other.

As far as philosophy of modern rimes is concerned, however, one may point to Voltaire's analysis of the issue during the end of his life and Rousseau's thesis as this is expressed in his *Social Contract.* It is in fact Peter Gay, one of the most eminent experts on the Enlightenment's philosophy, who proceeds to the following consideration:

> [Voltaire] never wholly gave up his distrust of the masses; his remarks, even of his last years, sometimes betray petulance and caprice. But to a surprising extent he overcame the tenacious social prejudices of his youth. By the time he began to devote himself to the Genevan

---

[51] op. cit., 1302a.

Natives his social philosophy was more radical than most liberal bourgeois thought of his century.[52]

This means that, according to Gay, even Voltaire whose *aristocratic arrogance* towards the populace has already been underlined, actually became the adviser and protector of the common people; during the natives' struggle in Geneva, the central aim of which was the achievement of political rights, Voltaire stood by them and helped them with all the force of his wisdom. Although some of them did not trust him and others refused to follow his advice, 'in these annoying circumstances, the aristocratic general [concludes Gay] showed more patience with his democratic troops than anyone might have expected.'[53]

The well-known fact of Voltaire's failure to convince an enlightened despot or a king to act as a genuine philosopher – an attempt equally unsuccessful as compared with efforts of other modern and ancient philosophers, like Diderot and Plato – did not, however, lead Voltaire to a retirement. He chose instead to promote a very creative coalition with common people. As he himself argues in his philosophical essay under the title *A,B,C,*

> it pleases me that my mason, my carpenter, my blacksmith, who have helped me to build my lodging, my neighbour the farmer, and my friend the manufacturer, all *raise themselves above their trade and know the public interest better than the most insolent Turkish official.*[54] (our emphasis)

Nevertheless, it must be admitted that expressions, as sentimentally charged as the above, should not obscure the fact that in Voltaire's as well as in Rousseau's references to the pursuit of the public interest, the role of the wise and virtuous men is constantly considered important. Actually, the public interest cannot be grasped and promoted by the people themselves without the guiding role of enlightened personalities.

Especially, as regards Rousseau, however, one must distinguish between the foundation period of the new state and the period which

---

[52] P. Gay, op. cit., p.226.
[53] op. cit., p.228.
[54] op. cit., p.236.

follows the transition from the old to the new social order. During the foundation period, the guiding role of the Lawgiver, as has already been mentioned, is absolutely necessary and decisive. It is during this particular phase that the power asymmetry between the wise Legislator and the common people is proved beyond any doubt.[55] This wise demigod is confronted with a tremendous social and, ultimately, political task, the realisation of which deserves even the change of human nature.[56] It is worth noting, however, that, among other difficulties which the Legislator should overcome, Rousseau highlights the following one:

> The sages who insist on speaking in their own language to the vulgar instead of in the vulgar language will not be understood. For there are thousands of ideas which cannot be translated into the popular idiom.[57]

At this point, Rousseau touches one of the most serious problems of the sages/masses relation, the problem of communication. According to the 'Citizen of Geneva', neither force, nor argument are adequate means as regards the Legislator's effort to orientate the masses towards a new type of social and political life. Hence, Rousseau's appeal to divine authority.[58] Speaking in the name of God, the wise Legislator succeeds in persuading the masses to follow 'the

---

[55] As Maurice Cranston points out: 'Rousseau limits the intervention of the Lawgiver to the founding phase of the republic: once it is set up the Lawgiver will disappear, and the people will rule themselves [...]. And although the people does not govern itself in Rousseau's sense of "govern", it will elect the magistrates who do govern [...]. Such a system he can call aristocratic in the true classical sense of that word: government by the best.' (M. Cranston, op. cit., p.309).

[56] See Rousseau's presentation of the wise and virtuous Legislator in *The Social Contract*, pp.84-85.

[57] op. cit., p.87.

[58] As Judith N. Shklar, 'Rousseau's Images of Authority' in *Hobbes and Rousseau, A Collection of Critical Essays*, pp.343-344; points out, 'Rousseau was never able to draw a very convincing portrait of the great legislator [...]. Of all Rousseau's images of authority this is the least well-drawn and the least convincing figure. How could it be otherwise, since the legislator is a miracle, a superhuman genius, who, though he knows our nature thoroughly, does not share it? His tasks and his powers have nothing in common with the more usual forms of political authority. He neither coerces, nor argues. Everything is done by the force of personality. A magnetic personality transforms lesser men [...]. In all this the guiding bond must remain hidden. To rule over public opinion one must not only be above it, but out of its sight.'

basic rules of statecraft', as he himself conceives them.[59] In other words, the wise and virtuous personality of the Lawgiver should attract not only the mind, but above all the soul of the common people. It is in relation to this position that Rousseau concludes, as well, that religion and politics have the same purpose among men; it is simply that at the birth of nations, the one serves as the instrument of the other.'[60]

As soon as the new state is founded, however, the wise men/common people relation is approached by Rousseau within the political context of an elective aristocracy. Within such a context, the power asymmetry diminishes and a fragile division of power among wise magistrates and sovereign people appears. The transformation of the *will of all*, however, into the *general will*, as well as the pursuit of the public interest, never cease to demand the guiding role of enlightened and virtuous personalities.[61] At this point, it is worth mentioning Rousseau's following aphorism, as quoted from the preface of his *Discourse on Inequality:*

> Above all, I would have fled from a republic, as one necessarily ill governed, where the people, believing themselves either to do without magistrates altogether or to allow their magistrates only a very precarious authority, foolishly kept in their own hands the administration of civil affairs and the execution of their own laws.[62]

---

[59] J.J. Rousseau, op. cit., pp.86–87.
[60] op. cit., p.88.
[61] At this point, Leo Strauss's comment, in Strauss, op. cit., p.283, seems very interesting as regards the transformation of the will of all to the general will: 'Now [argues Strauss], according to Rousseau, this problem cog can only be stated by political philosophy; it cannot be solved by it; or, more precisely, its solution is endangered by the very political philosophy that leads up to it. For its solution is the action of the legislation or of the "father" of a nation, that is, of a man of superior intelligence who by ascribing divine origin to a code which he has devised, or by honoring the gods with his own wisdom, induces the citizen body to submit freely to his code' (our emphasis). What one may add, however, to the above comment is that the transformation of the will of all to the general will is not a process corresponding only to the founding period, but an everlasting educative and political process.
[62] J.J. Rousseau, *Discourse on Inequality*, Penguin Books, Harmondsworth,, 1984, p.60.

On the other hand, it is self-evident that, for the people to be sovereign, they must exercise legislative power and at the same time control and recall, whenever they find it necessary, their own magistrates. To do this, however, common citizens must be adequately educated and prepared; it is, therefore, exactly at this point that the wise magistrates/common people relationship proves to be directly linked with and grounded on *transformative education*.

Philosopher-Educator: a Journey from Aristodemocracy to the People's Self-Emancipation?

From ancient until modern times, people's social and political self-emancipation is usually approached not as the direct/spontaneous outcome of actuality, but as the realisation of one, among others, objectively given possibility. In Hegel's own words, 'Actuality is first of all *Possibility* [...]. Possibility is what is essential to reality, but in such a way that it is at the same time only a possibility.'[63] (Hegel's emphasis). In terms of political theory, an approach like this means that what really matters is not merely what people are, but what they can become. Such a transformation, however, presupposes a special kind of social and political education, the realisation of which depends upon the socio-political role of the 'men of knowledge' and the educational role of the state as well.

From this point of view, it becomes easily explicable why Plato himself lays such an emphasis on the educational system of his *Republic* and the ideological intervention of the philosophers as well.

> It is not only [argues Plato] to the poets therefore that we must issue orders requiring them to portray good character in their poems or not to write at all; we must issue similar orders to all artists and craftsmen, and prevent them portraying bad character, ill-discipline, meanness or ugliness in pictures of living things, in sculpture, architecture, or any work of art, and if they

---

[63] Hegel, *Logic*, Oxford, Oxford University Press, 1975, p.143.

are unable to comply they must be forbidden to practise their art among us.[64]

And even Aristotle, a philosopher often regarded as the true founder of the liberal political tradition, does not hesitate to link education directly with political power. In a way followed in modern times almost word for word by the French Enlightenment philosopher Helvétius,[65] Aristotle insists that

> education must be related to the particular constitution in each case [...]. Since there is but one aim for the entire state, it follows that education must be one and the same for all and that the responsibility for it must be a public one [...]. In matters that belong to the public, training for [the children] must be the public's concern.[66]

In other words, the agents of political power are responsible for the intellectual formation of the common citizens, especially in relation to these matters which are the main objects of the public interest. However, such a process cannot be promoted and completed, unless philosophers or 'men of knowledge' themselves play their own educational and, in the last analysis, political role.

There is no doubt that the methods and the desired extent of such an intellectual/political intervention have been questioned and criticised, as in the often quoted and amply used distinction between liberal and totalitarian political thought. As regards, however, the object of this particular research, it is sufficient to mention that the philosopher/people relationship, a relation political in essence, may take different shapes and forms according to the respective ways 'men of knowledge' or wise magistrates conceive their own educational stance towards the people. On the other hand, political rulers and governors, either totalitarian or liberal, cannot remain indifferent with regard to the intellectual formation of their subjects or fellow citizens.

As an example of what is usually characterised as a totalitarian kind of modern political thought, one may point to Hobbes's analysis of the problem in his well-known *Leviathan*. From his own philosophical point of view, Hobbes seems quite clear:

---

[64] Plato, *The Republic*, 401b.
[65] Helvétius, *De l'Esprit*, Paris, Editions Sociales, 1968, p.181.
[66] Aristotle, op. cit., 1337a.

> [The Actions of men proceed from their Opinions; and in the well governing of Opinions consists the well governing of men's Actions in order to their Peace and Concord [...]. It belongs therefore to him that has the Sovereign Power, to be Judge, or constitute all Judges of Opinions and Doctrines, as a thing necessary to Peace [...].[67]

Despite Hobbes' totalitarianism, however, his specific statement that the well-governing of men's actions presupposes the well-governing of their opinions, is equally valid from a liberal point of view as well. It is beyond any doubt that even in the most liberal version of the European Enlightenment, the *transformative* dimension of education and its highly political significance cannot be refuted.

'L'education peut tout', argues Helvétius several decades before the French Revolution, while Voltaire, one of the most eminent representatives of political liberalism, is fighting to unite all the distinguished philosophers of his time in a struggle against the intellectual and, at the same time, political authority of the Church over the common people. One way or another, therefore, education – both in the Ancient and European Enlightenment – is presented as an effective means not only to interpret the world, but to change men's social and political life as well.[68]

At this point, however, a fine thread of thought, connecting Rousseau's ambivalent relation with Enlightenment and Fichte's philosophical introduction to Romanticism, leads us to further remarks with regard to the philosopher/people relation and the transformative potential of education as such.

To create citizens through public education is, according to Rousseau, the most crucial target of the state:

> If it is good to know how to make use of men as they are, it is better still to make them into what needs them to be; the most absolute authority is that which penetrates a man's inner being and is exerted no less on

---

[67] Hobbes, *Leviathan*, London, Dent, 1973, p.93.
[68] At this point, it is useful to remember once again Peter Gay's vivid description of Voltaire's approach to theory and practice: "Voltaire could have said, as Marx said a hundred years later: 'The philosophers have only interpreted the world in different ways; the point is to change it'." (P. Gay, op. cit., p.25).

his will than on his actions. Certainly, people are, in the long run, what the government makes of them.[69]

Given such a position, it becomes evident that Rousseau believes, without any reservation, in the transformative power of political education. From this point of view, he who rules and/or governs the state, should also have the means to form and adjust citizens to the new social and political environment.[70] As a matter of fact, this is the real aim of the Legislator-founder of the new republic. Moreover, as it has already been noticed, this wise and virtuous Lawgiver has the right to intervene not only in the formation of men's thought and ideas, but in the (re-)shaping of their nature (inner being) as well. Hence, the crucial role of religion, and especially that of political religion.

By all means, the 'blind multitude', according to Rousseau's position, needs an educator who will guide it and transform it into a coherent group of virtuous citizens. Self-education, in the strict sense of the term, especially during the transition from the old to the new society, is impossible according to Rousseau (and Fichte's) philosophical approach; the need for a guide is beyond any doubt. However, Rousseau himself seems very obscure with regard to the crucial question: *who* will be this educational and, in the last analysis, political leader of the masses?

Rousseau's already mentioned description of the Lawgiver enables us to conclude that such a Legislator must be not only wise, but virtuous as well. Knowledge and morality are two components, the most significant perhaps, of his personality. At the same time, the Legislator must be able to make use of the people's language, that is to say the *language of the soul*. Such a description of the Lawgiver's talents, however, as well as Rousseau's specific references to concrete

---

[69] J.J. Rousseau, 'A Discourse on Political Economy' in J.J. Rousseau, *Political Writings*, A. Ritter and J. Conaway Bondamella (eds), New York, Norton Critical Editions, 1988, pp.66–67.

[70] From this point of view, the following quotation from Rousseau's *Confessions*, (Harmondsworth, Penguin Books, 1953), p.377, is revealing: 'I had seen that everything is rooted in politics and that, whatever might be attempted, no people would ever be other than the nature of their government made them. So the great question of the best possible government seemed to me to reduce itself to this: 'what is the nature of the government best fitted to create the most virtuous, the most enlightened, the wisest, and, in fact, the best people, taking the word "best" in its highest sense?'

Legislators, fit a portrait of a demigod. To alter man's deeply alienated nature and way of life is a huge task, the realisation of which demands high or even 'super-human' qualities as regards the Legislator himself. His educational role is not only a matter of knowledge; it is above all a matter of achieving a special kind of internal communication between the wise and virtuous educator, on the one hand, and the people, on the other. In order not to give ground to any sort of religious mysticism, therefore, only one way seems effective: to conceive the Legislator as a *collective entity,* i.e. a kind of an educational and political vanguard. However, it must be admitted, such a collective entity cannot be observed within Rousseau's philosophical works.

At this point, Fichte's analysis of the scholar's vocation proves to be more accurate. Indeed, Fichte faces the 'men of knowledge' as a *gifted group,* wholly devoted to their educational and, ultimately, reforming work. Fichte's 'priests of truth', being the members of a particular social *class,* in which they have freely chosen to participate, are equally united by common features as regards their own way of life. Cultivation of a specific area of science, but above all cultivation of 'the social talents of *receptivity* and the *art of communication*'[71] (Fichte's emphasis) are just a few of the educator's characteristics, as they have been conceived and described by Fichte himself. Besides, this educational vanguard must consist of the 'ethically best men' and 'represent the highest level of ethical cultivation'.[72]

Another equally crucial question, however, which was directly faced this time by both Rousseau and Fichte in regard to the educator/people relation, concerns the way the wise and virtuous educator(s) must act in order to perform his (her) task, in other words the creation of citizens devoted to the public interest and the common welfare.

Starting from Rousseau, it is useful to mention that the way he approaches Emile's relation with his teacher is rather didactic as regards the dynamics of the educational process within the macro-social and macro-political frame of analysis.

In fact, Rousseau, following Plato and Aristotle, is deeply convinced that 'training citizens is not the work of a day, and turning

---

[71] Fichte, op. cit., p.173.
[72] op. cit., p.176.

them into men requires that they be educated as children.'[73] From this point of view, children's education may be conceived as just the first stage of a long-term *political education* (citizen formation), in the broad sense of the term.

Furthermore, contrary to the vagueness of his analysis as regards the person of the educator, Rousseau is very explicit in regard to the *tactics* such an educator must follow in order to perform his task. In fact, Rousseau proceeds to a significant distinction between *governor* and *preceptor* in relation to the science of education:

> I call the master of this science [says Rousseau] *governor* rather than preceptor because his task is less to instruct than to lead. He ought to give *no* precepts at all; he ought to make them be discovered.[74] (Rousseau's emphasis)

The significance of this distinction within the context of a philosophy of education is quite obvious; its repercussion, however, on the field of political theory must be also highlighted. Distinction between *instruction* and *leadership* promotes, indeed, a fertile analysis in connection with the wise magistrate/people relation. It is exactly the wise governor's duty – within the institutional boundaries of elective aristocracy – not to instruct or rule, but lead common citizens, as smoothly as possible, to the general will and the pursuit of public interest.

At the same time, governor and pupil must live a common life and share common experience grounded on the mutuality of their love.[75] At this point, it is worth remembering Plato's *Republic,* where he himself urges his already emancipated philosophers not only to return to the cave but also to join their fellow citizens' life in order to promote their liberation from the darkness of ignorance.

Furthermore, the 'Citizen of Geneva' constructs his well-known model of 'negative education', i.e. education through the removal of obstacles from the path of the pupil, who is discovering reality step by step;[76] on the other hand, the educator must exert his own authority in

---

[73] J.J. Rousseau, *A Discourse on Political Economy,* p.135.
[74] J.J. Rousseau, *Emile,* Penguin Books, Harmondsworth, 1991, p.52.
[75] op. cit., p.53.
[76] In an interesting article George Lapassade, 'Rousseau et les encyclopédistes', (*Arguments,* No 20, 1960, p.19), relates positive education to the process of

such a way that the pupil himself is under the impression that he is acting by his own forces. The effect of such an exercise of authority, on the level of political theory and practice, becomes obvious through Rousseau's analysis itself:

> I prepared [my pupil] to be educated. He is now sufficiently prepared to be docile. He recognises the voice of friendship, and he knows to obey reason. It is true that I *leave him the appearance of independence, but he was never better subjected to me;* for now he is subjected because he wants to be. As long as I was unable to make myself master of his will, I remained master of his person; I was never a step away from him. Now I sometimes leave him to himself, because I govern him always.[77] (our emphasis)

Given this analysis, Rousseau leaves no doubt, as regards his own views on what may be called *self-education* and, in a more general perspective, *self-emancipation*. 'I leave him the appearance of independence, but he was never better subjected to me.' This is indeed a masterpiece of the governor/pupil dialectic! Even if self-determination may be considered the final aim of the educational activity, the way leading to such an end depends totally upon a masterly directed and well-covered subjugation.[78]

Nevertheless, it is exactly this dialectical nature of the educator/pupil relation, which obliges the governor to avoid as much as possible the direct use of his authority. Moreover, such a use of authority, whenever necessary, must be firmly grounded on the pupil's inclinations and plans;[79] the educator must join in his pupil's plans in

---

transmission of knowledge and Rousseau's model of *negative education* to the refusal of such an (external) transmission of knowledge. From this point of view, Rousseau's *governor* is strictly distinguished from Enlightenment's *intellectuals*, whose role was the *external* transmission of knowledge and not the strengthening of the human being's *internal* light and nature. A remark like this, however, should be connected with Rousseau's conception of knowledge (see also note 23 of this introduction).

[77] J.J. Rousseau, *Emile*, 332.

[78] It is worth noting, however, Rousseau's ingenious tactical manoeuvre: 'Show your weaknesses to your pupil if you want to cure his own. Let him see that you undergo the same struggles which he experiences. Let him learn to conquer himself by your example' (J.J. Rousseau, *Emile*, p.334).

[79] op. cit., p.326.

order to guide him successfully. On the other hand, Rousseau warns the future educators about the critical limit, beyond which, a further strengthening of authority leads to its destruction.[80] Finally, Rousseau's wise governor must always take notice of and promote his pupil's instincts, as long as those instincts have not degenerated within man-made institutions. Hence, another significant remark with regard to the relation between philosopher-educators, on the one hand, and common citizens, on the other:

> [Instinct] must not be destroyed, but it must be regulated; and that is perhaps more difficult than annihilating it.[81]

It is exactly at this point that Rousseau and Fichte's positions meet each other. Thus, it is worth remembering, that Fichte himself refers to 'a sense for what is true [which] has to be developed, scrutinised and purified and this is precisely the scholar's task.'[82]

The interesting conclusions derived from this analysis may be effectively extended to the field of political theory and practice as well. As a matter of fact, the transformative power of education cannot be refuted; however, such a power is, one way or another, related to the guiding activity of an individual or collective leader. Thus, without denying the educator/people *interaction,* it is necessary to recognise the *power asymmetry* which at the same time characterises this relation. More specifically, the wise and virtuous leader exerts his intellectual and moral influence on the masses in a way which protects his (her) own guiding role and prepares his (her) fellow citizens to be educated and emancipated. Nevertheless, an educational process like this does not proceed in vacuum and from without; it is based on the cultivation of certain talents both on the side of the educator as well as on this of the pupils. Talking in terms of politics, wise magistrates and educators are supposed to direct the people towards the achievement of their ultimate self-determination. According to Rousseau and Fichte's above discussed analysis of the educator/people relationship, therefore, the road to self-determination passes through a *transitional* stage of intellectual, moral and, ultimately, political leadership, exerted temporarily upon the masses

---

[80] op. cit., p.334.
[81] op. cit., pp.333-334.
[82] Fichte, op. cit., p.174.

by the educators as such.[83] Needless to say, consequently, that an unmediated people's self-emancipation proves to be a pure illusion.

At this point, the most challenging question of this introductory chapter becomes even more acute: to what extent and under which conditions is democracy, in the sense of people's self-determination, compatible with the leading role of philosophers and intellectuals in the field of politics?

In relation to this issue, the well-known example of Athenian Democracy, as this has been described by Thucydides in Pericles's *Funeral Oration,* seems worth noting.

Defining Athenian Democracy, Pericles himself argues as follows:

> Though as to its name, because it is ordered with a view to the many, not a few, our constitution is called 'democracy'; and while as regards the law there is equal treatment for all in our private disputes; yet as regards our claims [to post of honour in the state] each is preferred to public office according to his particular repute – not so much of his class as for excellence: poverty or obscurity will not bar him if he has it in him to give the state good service.[84]

If such a state actually existed, however, as Plato with a sense of irony correctly noted, it might have been called 'democracy' by some, but it should have been called 'aristocracy with the approval of the masses'.[85] Indeed, in a state like this, people may appear as the real agent of political power, but democracy in the sense of people's self-government is really out of question.[86] In other words,

---

[83] From this point of view, what John Hoffman (*State, Power and Democracy,* Sussex, Wheatsheaf Books, 1988, pp.62–63) accurately defines as *Rousseau's paradox* constitutes a constant problem within the field of ancient and modern philosophy; 'a politics to end all politics' is a demand for distinguished philosophers not only after, but before Rousseau as well.

[84] From Thucydides, *History of the Peloponnesian War,* 2.37.1, as quoted in G. Vlastos, *Platonic Studies,* Princeton, Princeton University Press, 1973, pp.196–197.

[85] Plato, *Menexenus,* Loeb Classical Library, 238 CD: 'One man calls it "democracy", another man according to his fancy, gives it some other name; but it is, in very truth, an *"aristocracy" backed by popular approbation.*' (our emphasis).

[86] In relation to this remark, see John Hoffman's analysis of the tension between democracy as a form of the state and democracy as a self-government, restricted

government as such is not exercised by the people themselves but in the best cases, by those wise and virtuous citizens who are accepted by the people to hold public offices. From this point of view, the term *'aristodemocracy'*[87] proves more adequate to describe the real character of this state.

Nevertheless, this hybrid construction of people's power with leadership exerted by the 'aristoi citizens' in favour of the common interest, rests upon very fragile foundations. It is in fact self-evident that the effective function of this aristodemocracy, depends upon the good judgement of the people. However, such a judgement is neither given *a priori,* nor spontaneously attained. Fighting for or the exercise of political power presupposes education and knowledge. As a result, the practical wisdom of the people, on which aristodemocracy should be based, must be conceived as the ultimate outcome of a *long-term* cultivation of the people's social and political talents. Only through such an education common citizens will be able to overcome the particularistic conceptions of their private interests and unfold their practical wisdom in the pursuit of the general interest of their community. Hence, the indisputable importance of the philosopher-educator's intervention in the social and political process of their time.

Here it is worth mentioning Professor Vlastos' interpretation of Plato's critical attack against Athenian Democracy through the lines of his *Menexenus:*

> If [the people], [writes Vlastos] cannot discriminate between the wise men and the one who is merely δημω [people] preferable, if they will not choose the sincere

---

though in Marxist political theory in J. Hoffman, 'The Tension between Democracy as a form of the State and Democracy as a Self-Government.' (unpublished paper).

[87] The term 'aristodemocracy' has been used by Gregory Vlastos in his *'Isonomia Politike',* as included in G. Vlastos, op. cit., p.201, in order to refer to the Athenian democracy in times of Pericles. For our research purposes the term 'aristodemocracy' will be used to denote the fact that the transition to democracy, i.e. people's self-determination and self-government, presupposes a temporary leadership exerted by the *'aristoi'* citizens (aristocratic element) with the approval of the masses (democratic principle). Thus, aristodemocracy is not juxtaposed to democracy in the full sense of the term, but to the parliamentarian image of democracy, as this is conceived within bourgeois society. (For the 'images of democracy' see M. Levin, *Marx, Engels and Liberal Democracy,* London and Basingstoke, The Macmillan Press, 1989, pp.1-14).

> and upright leader in preference to the flatterer, this scheme will not produce αριστοκρατια [aristocracy], but only more δημοκρατια [democracy]. So the intellectual and moral level of the electorate must be raised steeply above that of the present Athenian *demos*. The όχλος [populace] must be transfigured into a junior partner of the αριστοι [aristoi].[88] (Vlastos's emphasis)

The problem highlighted by this comment on Plato's analysis is not a matter of sterile contemplation. Transfiguration of the people to a junior or even to an equal partner of the *aristoi* or the *gnorimoi* is a crucial and long standing, perhaps everlasting, problem of political theory and practice. That is why a critical reference to the way Athenian republic functioned during the years of Pericles leads to a useful insight as regards the 'men of knowledge' – common citizens relationship, we are dealing with.

Actually, the constitution of a political organisation almost unavoidably suffers a severe tension due to the clash of the *principle of majority* with the *principle of knowledge*. The way these two principles are combined *in practice* defines in fact the real tendency of the constitution towards democracy – in the strict sense of the term – or aristocracy, respectively. Besides, it is exactly this tension mentioned above which directly determines the controversial relation of *equality of number* and *equality of value* already noted. Within this context, it would be extremely interesting to examine, for example, the political relation among the elites of ancient Athens on the one hand, and the masses on the other. Though an approach like this lies beyond the specific boundaries of this research, it is worth noting, however, that the intellectual and political elites of this period exerted a significant influence on the formation of people's political judgement.[89] Experts in delivering a political oration, as well as in manipulating psychologically the masses, Athenian orators, demagogues and other politicians played a decisive role in the exercise of political power, *ultimately* attributed to the people themselves.

---

[88] op. cit., p.200.
[89] For a detailed analysis of this problem, see J. Ober, *Mass and Elite in Democratic Athens, Rhetoric, Ideology and the Power of People*, Princeton University Press, 1989, especially pp.84–93, 163–170. In this interesting work, however, Ober insists on the primacy of the people's influence upon the intellectual and political elites of Athenian democracy.

Needless to say, however, rhetoric and rational analysis as particular features of intellectual elites are permanent functions of any kind of democracy both in ancient and modern times as well.

Consequently, either as 'lovers of opinion' [φιλόδοξοι] or as 'lovers of knowledge' [φιλόσοφοι], intellectuals unavoidably tend to intervene, one way or another, in the formation of their fellow citizens' political ideas and decisions. From this point of view, it can be argued that even in states where the people themselves obtain political decisions by majority vote, the crucial role of the, more or less, enlightened intellectual minorities must not be neglected or underestimated. Thus, the central question may be posed as follows: to what extent are people themselves able to react critically upon the influence of such intellectual minorities? This is, of course, a question which cannot be answered in abstract. Concrete historical conditions must always be taken into consideration before giving a reliable answer. It is worth remembering, however, Aristotle's warning, according to which elections always miss the point 'if the masses are too slavish'. Who would dare to insist that a warning like this is out of date?

There is no doubt, therefore, that the transformation of the masses' political *doxa* into a substantial political *knowledge* is *a conditio sine quo non* for an authentic democracy, that is to say for a republic the only rulers of which are the people themselves. On the other hand, the elevation of the people's political consciousness depends upon the highly interventionist role of the 'men of knowledge' in the field of politics.

Besides, even if the people's judgement does not fail to choose the wisest and most virtuous among them to hold public offices, the degeneration of this elected group of governors seems highly possible. Right of resistance, mutual control of one power by the other, revocability and other institutional means, as the history of political practice clearly shows, though necessary, are not sufficient to stop the gradual transformation of an enlightened political and intellectual vanguard into an authoritarian agent of public power. From this point of view, Plato's description of the constitutions' vicious cycle from a genuine philosophers' aristocracy to one man's tyranny,[90] as well as Rousseau's later thoughts expressed in his *Lettres écrites de la*

---

[90] Plato, *The Republic*, Book II.

Montagne,[91] are only two among many representative examples which emit a sense of melancholy as regards the future of the reforming role of wise and virtuous magistrates. It is perhaps human nature as such, as Thucydides points out, which always tends either to dominate or to be dominated, irrespective of the specific type of social and political process.[92] If such a view proves to be correct, however, the action of the philosophers-'lovers of knowledge' in relation to any kind of emancipatory project would directly recall to mind the ancient but always meaningful myth of Sisyphus.

Nevertheless, given this introductory analysis, the time has come to proceed to Marx's own approach to the intellectuals' controversial relation with political power and emancipation. To this end, it seems worth focusing our attention on the hybrid concept of aristodemocracy or, in other words, on the aristocratic leadership (in the strict sense of the term) with the approval of the masses. From such a point of view, the philosophy/emancipation relation, as conceived by the European revolutionary tradition from Marx's times until the October Revolution, may prove to be meaningfully approached and accurately interpreted.

---

[91] J.J. Rousseau, *Lettres écrites de la montagne*: 'What has happened to you, gentlemen, is what happens to every government like yours. In the first place, the legislative power and the executive power which constitute sovereignty are not separate. The sovereign people will for themselves, and by themselves do what they will [...]. Finally, the inactivity of the power that wills makes it subordinate to the power that executes; the latter becomes gradually more independent in its action, and soon in its volition also; and in place of acting for the power that wills, it acts on it [...]. And that, gentlemen, is how all democratic states perish in the end.' (The above extract is quoted by B. de Jouvenel, op. cit., pp.496–497).

[92] Thucydides, op. cit., 4.61.1.

PART I

Philosophers En Route to the Communist League

Chapter 1
A Young Philosopher in the Realm of History

Moments of transition are always crucial as regards an individual's or a nation's life. Such a moment of transition is vividly described by Karl Marx himself in a well-known letter to his father, written in November 1837. In this autobiographical account, the young Marx presents his own *philosophical* transition as follows:

> From the idealism which, by the way, I had compared and nourished with the idealism of Kant and Fichte, I arrived at the point of seeking the idea in reality itself. If previously the gods had dwelt above the earth, now they became its centre.[1]

Through such a *Hegelian* point of view, History becomes the field, within which the Idea, in other words Reason, unfolds and attains self-consciousness.[2] A few years later, however, through *a Young Hegelian* point of view, Karl Marx argues in favour of a link, forged

---

[1] K. Marx, 'Letter to his father, November 10 [-11, 1837]' in K. Marx and F. Engels, *Collected Works*, Moscow, Progress Publishers, 1975, vol. 1, p.18.

[2] Compare Marx's passage, quoted above, with Hegel's notion of *Theodicy*, as exposed in his *Lectures on the Philosophy of World History: Introduction*, Cambridge, Cambridge University Press, 1975, p.42. The connection is very obvious as regards the relation between the idea and history: 'History', writes Hegel, 'is the unfolding of God's nature in a particular, determinate element, so that only a determinate form of knowledge is possible and appropriate to it. *The time has now surely come for us to comprehend even so rich a product of creative reason as world history. The aim at human cognition is to understand that the intentions of eternal wisdom are accomplished not only in the natural world, but also in the realm of the [Spirit] which is actively present in the world. From this point of view, our investigation can be seen as a theodicy, a justification of the ways of God.'* (Hegel's emphasis).

in practice through philosophy, on the one hand, and the external world, on the other. That is to say, philosophy and philosophers must get out of their cave and participate actively in the social and political process of their time.

Following Marx's own words,

> there are moments when philosophy turns its eyes to the external world, and no longer apprehends it, but as a practical person, weaves, as it were, intrigues with the world, emerges from the transparent Kingdom of Amenthes and throws itself on the breast of the worldly Siren. [I]t is essential that the philosophy should then wear character masks. [A]s Prometheus, having stolen fire from heaven, begins to build houses and to settle upon the earth, so philosophy, expanded to be the whole world, turns against the world of appearance.[3]

Is there any doubt that the young philosopher, the young intellectual, while writing those lines, was ready to throw himself 'on the breast of the worldly Siren'? Karl Marx was not, of course, the first who emphasised the practical dimension of philosophy within the world of the German philosophical tradition. From this point of view, it is worth remembering Fichte's activist approach of the philosopher and educator's role in society;[4] it is also worth referring to Cieszkowski and Bruno Bauer's influence on the young Marx's conception of the philosophy/praxis relation.[5]

---

[3] K. Marx, 'Difference between the Democritean and Epicurean Philosophy of Nature in General' in K. Marx and F. Engels, op. cit., vol. 1, p.491 (Preparatory Materials, *Notebooks on Epicurean Philosophy*).

[4] With regard to Fichte's influence on Marx's philosophical thought, see the interesting study of Tom Rockmore, *Fichte, Marx and the German Philosophical Tradition*, Corbondale, Southern Illinois University Press, 1980, especially pp.72-95; according to Rockmore, p.79-80, 'emphasis in the transformation of man's relation to the results of his activity from passive to active form [by both Fichte and Marx], includes stress on three general areas: the practical role of theory in overcoming the difference between concept and social reality, the educational role of theory in effecting social change, and the significance of self-consciousness as a force for change.'

[5] In regard to Bruno Bauer's influence on the young Marx's analysis of the theory/practice relation, see the classical and documented work of David McLellan, *The Young Hegelians and Karl Marx*, London, The Macmillan Press, 1969, pp.69-73.

Actually, it was the Young Hegelian thinker August von Cieszkowski, who suggested and defended without any reservation the *philosophy of praxis* through the lines of his *Prolegomena to Historiosophie* in 1838:

> [S]o must philosophy [argues Cieszkowski] descend from the height of theory to the plane of praxis. To be practical philosophy, or (stated more properly) the philosophy of praxis, whose most concrete effect on life and social relations is the development of truth in concrete activity – this is the future fate of philosophy in general [...]. Formally consciousness now feels entitled to guide true deeds and no longer to merely acknowledge existing reality, but rather to determine it as known and willed.[6]

As regards Bruno Bauer, there is no doubt that the real aim of philosophy is to become 'the critic of the established order'.[7] According to his explicit, though debatable, analysis, '[Hegel's] *theory* is *praxis* and for that very reason most dangerous, far reaching and destructive. It is the revolution itself.'[8] (Bauer's emphasis).

In such an intellectual, highly iconoclastic atmosphere, therefore, the young Marx did not hesitate to point to the 'character mask', which philosophy should wear as it emerges from the 'transparent Kingdom' of the German society just in the beginning of the 1840s. It was the mask of Prometheus, 'the most eminent saint and martyr in the philosophical calendar',[9] the son of Zeus, who openly declared the inner meaning of philosophy:

> 'In simple words, I hate the pack of gods'[10]
> (Aeschylus, *Prometheus Bound)*

---

[6] A. von Cieszkowski, 'Prolegomena to Historiosophie' in L.S. Stepelevich (ed.), *The Young Hegelians, An Anthology*, Cambridge, Cambridge University Press, 1983, pp.77-78.

[7] B. Bauer, 'The Trumpet of the Last Judgement over Hegel' in L.S. Stepelevich (ed.), p.184.

[8] op. cit., p.183.

[9] K. Marx, 'Difference Between the Democritean and Epicurean Philosophy of Nature in General', in K. Marx and F. Engels, op. cit., vol. 1, p.31.

[10] op. cit., vol. 1, p.30.

Prometheus is, therefore, the demigod, the real saviour of the common people and the symbol through which Marx expresses his own decision to intervene in the social and political process of his time. On the other hand, it was Marx's use of the Promethean symbol, which enabled eminent Marxologists of our century to argue at length on the so-called Marx's *Promethean complex,* an argument which undoubtedly demands a critical evaluation, especially in regard to the philosopher/external world relation, which we are here dealing with.

According to Lewis Feuer, one of the most ardent supporters of the argument, 'the Promethean complex determined a philosophy of history; as Prometheus warned Zeus of the 'son more puissant than his sire' who would bring him down 'from the throne of parental sovereignty', so Marx enunciated the warning to all established powers, the all-defiant generalisation – all history is a history of class struggles, and the working class, growing to maturity, would end forever all class exploitation.'[11]

There is no doubt, of course, that the young Marx was inspired by Prometheus' symbolic struggle against any kind of gods; nevertheless, the consequences of such a belief as regards the formation of his thoughts are not as obvious, as Feuer suggests.

Searching for the ultimate source of the Promethean complex, through an interesting, though one-sided, *psychoanalytic* approach, Feuer argues that Marx's attitude is strongly determined by a feeling of rejection on behalf of her mother.

Following Feuer,

> the Promethean complex is basically different from the complex associated with Napoleonic ambition. A Napoleon could venture forth, fortified by his mother's love, with supreme self-confidence. Marx, choosing Promethean revolt, as his life's plan, a perpetual struggle against the gods, was always to re-enact a search of self-confidence, always seeking recognition as a god, always anticipating rejection. His world was always to be one of struggle because he never felt secure

---

[11] L.S. Feuer, 'The Character and Thought of Karl Marx: The Promethean Complex and Historical Materialism', in L.S. Feuer, *Marx and the Intellectuals, A Set of Post-Ideological Essays*, New York, Anchor Books, 1969, p.11.

in love. He took the eternal Empedoclean duality of love and hatred as a motive force in history. It is indeed the rejected son who becomes the Promethean.[12]

Without denying that Feuer's arguments contain a nucleus of truth, it seems, however, impossible to defend this kind of approach on an adequate basis of historical facts. There is no doubt of course that Marx's relationship to his mother was characterised by periods of psychological tension. More concretely, Henriette Marx proved reluctant to accept and, even more, to support her son's way of living and especially the radicalism of his life-plan. On the other hand, however, Marx's love for his future wife Jenny von Westphalen – a fact that Feuer bypasses – is sufficiently documented in such a way that makes it arbitrary to argue that hatred and rejection were the decisive elements as regards the young philosopher's intervention in the realm of praxis.[13]

Besides it is self-evident that Marx was not the only philosopher of his time who revolted against society. A great number of intellectuals, especially those of humanistic education, who were seriously disadvantaged by the nineteenth century capitalist development, expressed a critical approach towards the social and political reality of their time. From this point of view, Alvin Gouldner's *sociological* research proves to be more coherent and better documented than Lewis Feuer's psychoanalytic one.[14]

Finally, in addition to the sociological dimension *cultural* data are also important in order to interpret the young Marx's philosophical

---

[12] op. cit., p.35.

[13] For a documented reference to the young Marx's relations with his parents and his future wife, see:
 a) I. Berlin, *Karl Marx*, Oxford, Oxford University Press, 1978, pp.17–25.
 b) B. Nicolaievsky and O. Maenchen-Helfen, *Karl Marx: Man and Fighter*, Harmondsworth, Penguin Books, 1976, pp.1–45, especially pp.6–7, 23–30.

[14] A.W. Gouldner, *Against Fragmentation, The Origins of Marxism and the Sociology of Intellectuals*, Oxford, Oxford University Press, 1985, especially pp.107–113; according to Karen Lucas, who completed Gouldner's work, p.108, 'it is important to note that industrialisation and modernisation meant that the over-production of educated manpower did not equally affect all intellectuals but centred on those humanistically educated and in certain professions; overcrowding was rather less evident or even non-existent in the newer technological and scientific occupations'. A similar line of analysis has been followed on this issue by Göran Therborn in his *Science, Class and Society*, London, Verso, 1980, pp.317–326.

radicalisation. More concretely, the theoretical movement of the Young Hegelians formed its own *cultural* identity by a direct criticism of the *status quo* of its time based on a conception of a *militant* philosophy;[15] in this context, Marx's attitude of revolt looks rather natural and explicable, without making any use either of psychoanalysis or of the Empedoclean duality of love and hatred, as Feuer himself chose to do. It is rather a modern reformulation of the ancient Platonic desideratum of reshaping the world through philosophy and education, although crucial differences in both content and form render even such a remark highly debatable.

At this point, however, the time has come to make a preliminary comment with regard to the young Marx's conception of the philosopher's relation to the external world, as this was formed during the first years of his intellectual career (1838-1842).

Following Hegel almost word for word,[16] the young Marx faces philosophy and philosophers as children of their time. In his critical attack against the 'Leading Article in No 179 of the *Kölnische Zeitung'*, published in the *Rheinische Zeitung*, Karl Marx argues as follows:

> [P]hilosophers do not spring up like mushrooms out of the ground; they are products of their time whose most subtle, valuable and invisible juices flow in the ideals of philosophy [...].
>
> Since every true philosophy is the intellectual quintessence of its time, the time must come when philosophy not only internally by its content, but also externally through its form, comes into contact and interaction with the real world of its day.[17]

Given a position like the one quoted above, it becomes obvious that the philosopher's relation to the external world presupposes a bipolar theoretical attack against (naturalistic) *objectivism* and (voluntaristic)

---

[15] In regard to the Young Hegelians' cultural milieu of radicalism, see D. McLellan, op. cit., pp.6-33.

[16] According to Hegel's *Philosophy of Right*, p.11: 'to comprehend what is, this is the task of philosophy, because what is, is reason. Whatever happens, every individual is a child of his time; so philosophy too is its own time apprehended in thoughts.' (our emphasis).

[17] K. Marx, 'The Leading Article in No. 179 of the *Kölnische Zeitung*' in K. Marx and F. Engels, *Collected Works*, vol. 1, p.195.

subjectivism as well. This is why the young Marx insists that philosophers are not a kind of natural product; they do not spring up like the flowers in the garden. Though *products* of their time, they should not be regarded as *passive* observers or the mere outcome of social reality. On the other hand, being children of their time, they are also *active* agents of history. Consequently, the 'mask', which a philosopher must wear during his (or her) contact with society, is not a matter of his (or her) own arbitrary and strictly personal choice. From this point of view, Marx's adoption of the Promethean symbol should be conceived as the young philosopher's active *response* to the demands of a concrete historical period and a determinate social reality as well.

Moreover, given the fact that Marx himself points out the need for the philosopher's *active* confrontation with the external world, it becomes obvious that the Hegelian influence is neither the only, nor the most important one, as regards the Marxian analysis of the philosopher/praxis relation. Although Marx himself agrees with Hegel that philosophy and philosophers are children of their time, he openly rejects Hegel's central position concerning the role of philosophy in history. Actually, it is worth repeating that, according to Hegel,

> philosophy in any case always comes on the scene too late to give [instructions as to what the world ought to be]. As the thought of the world, it appears only when actuality is already there cut and dried after the process of formation has been completed [...]. When philosophy paints its grey in grey it cannot be rejuvenated but only understood. The owl of Minerva spreads its wings only with the falling of the dusk.[18]

From such a Hegelian point of view, therefore, philosophers weave their own relation to the external world through interpretation alone. It is just around 1845, however, that Marx and Engels reached finally the following clarification as far as Hegel's position is concerned:

> [T]he philosopher [...] is [according to Hegel] only the organ through which the maker of history, the Absolute Spirit arrives at self-consciousness *retrospectively,* after

---

[18] Hegel, op. cit., pp.12-13.

the movement has ended. The participation of the philosopher in history [argue Marx and Engels] is reduced to this retrospective consciousness, for the real movement is accomplished by the Absolute Spirit *unconsciously*. Hence the philosopher appears on the scene *post festum*.[19] (Marx and Engels' emphasis).

Needless to say, Hegel's argument which Marx and Engels rejected so clearly on the eve of the foundation of their materialist conception of history around 1844–1845, could not be reflected so easily by them in the first years of their philosophical career. Nevertheless, it is worth noting that Marx's conception of the philosopher's role within the realm of praxis is – almost from the beginning of his intellectual itinerary – incompatible with the *one-dimensional* Hegelian approach to philosophers as mere interpreters of the world's history. Action through theory and more concretely social action has always been, according to the young Marx, a creative challenge for the philosophers who appear on the scene neither *ante*, nor *post festum,* but on time – 'products of their time' – in order to intervene in the social process. This is indeed an expression of the 'Fichtean moment' in the young Marx's social and political theory.[20] As a matter of fact, Fichte's belief in the transformative power of (philosophical) education, as well as his faith in *action,* are magnificently expressed in his famous *Lectures on the Scholar's Vocation* and in his equally well-known *The Vocation of Man* and seem to be very close to the Young Hegelian approach to theory as a means to transform social reality.[21] The importance of such an influence, however, especially in regard to the young Marx's

---

[19] K. Marx and F. Engels, 'The Holy Family' in K. Marx and F. Engels, *Collected Works*, vol. 4, pp.85–86.

[20] Fichte's influence on the Young Marx's political philosophy is rejected by T.I. Oizerman, *The Making of the Marxist Philosophy*, Moscow, Progress Publishers, 1981, p.39; *contra*, among others, T. Rockmore, op. cit., especially p.53 ff.

[21] See for example the following quotation from Fichte's, *The Vocation of Man*, Indianapolis, Hackett Publishing Company, 1987, pp.67–68: 'Your vocation is not merely to know, but to act according to your knowledge. This is what I clearly hear in my inmost soul as soon as I collect myself for a moment and pay attention to myself. You do not exist for idle self-observation or to brood over devout sensations. No, you exist for activity. Your activity, and your activity alone, determines your worth.' (Fichte's emphasis).

conception of the philosopher's role in the realm of praxis, can be more accurately observed in his own writings of the years 1843-1844, to which we now turn.

Chapter 2
Philosophers and their 'Discovery' of the Proletarian World

Emerging from the 'transparent Kingdom of Amenthes' the philosopher – Prometheus now turns his action against the 'philistine world', that is '[against] *a political world of animals* [which] centuries of barbarism engendered and shaped it, and now it confronts us as a consistent system, the principle of which is the *dehumanised world.*'[1] (Marx's emphasis).

It was on May 1843, in one of his *Letters from Deutsch-Französische Jahrbücher,* that the young Marx hinted, for the first time, that a kind of an alliance must be constructed among suffering human beings, who think, and thinking human beings, who are oppressed.[2] As a matter of fact, Karl Marx now directly indicates the two main agents of his revolutionary theory: the oppressed philosopher-intellectual, on the one hand, and the suffering people, on the other.[3]

To what extent does he remain faithful, however, to his Young Hegelian origin as regards the primacy of the theory's intervention in the realm of praxis? According to Michael Löwy, Marx's analysis is still moving within the Young Hegelian framework: activity of thought against passivity of matter.[4] Nevertheless, it should be noted that, following Marx's quotation above, thought is no more the privilege of

---

[1] K. Marx, 'Letter to Ruge', May 1843, from his 'Letters from *Deutsch-Französische Jahrbücher*' in K. Marx and F. Engels, op. cit., vol. 3, p.137.
[2] op. cit., p.141.
[3] G. Teeple, *Marx's Critique of Politics*, 1842–1847, Toronto, University of Toronto Press, 1984, p.92 ff.
[4] M Löwy, *La théorie de la révolution chez le jeune Marx*, Paris, François Maspero, 1970, pp.58–59.

intellectuals; there are suffering human beings who think as well. Moreover, it is in the same letter, as Löwy himself admits,[5] that Marx attributes a *practical* role to the masses who suffer. In other words, he is starting to distinguish between the Young Hegelian and his own conception of the philosopher/mass relationship.

> For our part [writes Marx], we must expose the old world to the full light of day and shape the new one in a positive way. The longer the time that events allow to thinking humanity for taking stock of its position, and to suffering mankind for mobilising its forces, the more perfect on entering the world will be the product that the present time bears in its womb.[6]

Marx's departure, however, from the Young Hegelian frame of approach, can be even more clearly illustrated through the lines of his next *Letter from Deutsch-Französische Jahrbücher*, written just several months later, in September 1843.

Although he is still keeping his distance from the dogmatic/utopian communism of his time, as this was represented by Cabet, Dézamy and others, Marx begins to think seriously about the influence he may exert on the dogmatists in order 'to help [them] clarify their positions for themselves'.[7] The young Marx argues that philosophers must stop acting like producers of ready-made dogmatic systems of ideas which the masses are supposed to receive passively. In agreement with Fichte's critical activism, he insists that the philosopher's activity should be directed towards a *'ruthless criticism of all that exists'*[8] (Marx's emphasis). In other words, as has already been mentioned, philosophers must not confine themselves to a *post-festum* interpretative process (Hegel); on the contrary, they should take part in the transformation of all that exists.[9]

---

[5] op. cit., p.59.
[6] K. Marx, 'Letter to Ruge', May 1843, op, cit., p.141.
[7] K. Marx, 'Letter to Ruge', September 1843, op. cit., p.142.
[8] ibid.
[9] ibid. '[I]t is precisely the advantage of the new trend that we do not dogmatically anticipate the world, but only went to find the new world through criticism of the old one. Hitherto philosophers have had the solutions of all riddles lying in their writing-desks, and the stupid, exoteric world had only to open its mouth for the roast pigeons of absolute knowledge to fly into it. Now philosophy has become mundane, and the most striking proof of this is *that philosophical consciousness*

It is, finally, by the end of this same letter that Marx makes a first feeble attempt to settle accounts not only with the Hegelian, but with the whole German idealistic tradition, especially with regard to the philosopher/masses relation. Nevertheless, the extent to which such an effort proved to be successful remains to be examined and evaluated. For the time being, it seems sufficient to take notice of the starting point of this extremely complicated intellectual process, by quoting at length Marx's own words:

> [W]e do not confront the world in a doctrinaire way with a new principle. Here is the truth, kneel down before it! We develop new principles for the world out of the world's own principles. We do not say to the world: Cease your struggles, they are foolish; we will give you the true slogan of struggle. We merely show the world what it is really fighting for, and consciousness is something it has to acquire, even if it does not want to.
>
> The reform of consciousness consists *only* in making the world aware of its consciousness, in awakening it out of its dream about itself, in *explaining* to it the meaning of its actions [...][10] (Marx's emphasis).

It becomes obvious, therefore, from expressions like those quoted above, that Marx's analysis aims at the *minimisation* of the philosopher's role in the formation of people's revolutionary consciousness. More specifically, according to the young Marx, philosophers cannot or, rather, should not create revolutionary ideas (new principles) *ex nihilo*. On the contrary, it is on the basis of the masses' existing practice and consciousness that radical intellectuals should play their reforming role. At this point, it is worth remembering, once again, Fichte's bipolar position:

1. All men have a sense for what is true.

---

itself has been drawn into the torment of the struggle, not only externally but also internally.' (our emphasis).
[10] op. cit., p.144.

2. Such a sense for truth is not sufficient to lead the uneducated masses to a conscious activity; that is why the role of the educator is undoubtedly necessary.[11]

From such a general point of view, Marx himself would hardly disagree with Fichte's theses mentioned above; however, his own positions compared to Fichte's one reveals an interesting difference. Marx's analysis places much more emphasis on the masses' sense of what is true, than on the educator's reforming activity. Without rejecting the importance of the radical intellectual's function within the whole process, he nevertheless minimises their role in favour of the masses' self-direction towards the reform of their own consciousness.

In fact, the young Marx vacillates between *spontaneism,* on the one hand, and *intellectual elitism,* on the other, while trying to avoid both of them. How is such a dialectical contradiction to be finally superseded? It is beyond any doubt that a definite and absolutely convincing answer cannot be given. Besides, it must be mentioned that Marx himself confronted the question not only during the first period of his intellectual career, but during his whole life as a man of theory and practice as well. It is, however, worth noting that Marx's already mentioned *minimalistic tendency,* as regards the philosopher's intervention in the reform of the masses' consciousness, may be creatively linked with preceding *moments* in the history of philosophy.

Note, for example, Heraclitus's fragment, according to which Apollo neither speaks, nor hides anything, but *signifies.*[12] That is indeed a special way of defining the role of the agent of knowledge as regards his (or her) relation to the people who are still far away from the truth. From such a point of view, knowledge of reality is not *transmitted* from the 'educator (demi-)god' to the uneducated masses; it is rather the role of the agent of knowledge to *hint* or to *inspire* in order to – in Marx's own words – awaken the people from its dream and make it 'discover' the truth by its own forces.

It is also worth remembering Socrates' way of educating his fellow citizens in ancient Athens near the end of the fifth century BC It was Socrates himself, the *philosopher-educator,* who insisted that he never became or even tried to become the educator of anyone.[13] This

---

[11] Fichte, *Some Lectures concerning the Scholar's Vocation,* op. cit., p.174.
[12] Heraclitus, *OK Fragment* 93.
[13] Plato, *Apology of Socrates,* 21.

Socratic-ironic negation may be compared with the young Marx's own conception of the radical intellectual's relation to the suffering masses of his time. As has already been mentioned, the activity of the intellectual consists or, rather, should consist, according to Marx, not in transmitting elements of knowledge to the uneducated masses *ex cathedra*, but in convincing suffering human beings to search for the truth, i.e. to find out what is really going on and how reform may take place within their own life and deeds.

Finally, Rousseau's model of *negative education*[14] looks like an authentic source of inspiration with regard to the young Marx's analysis of the problem. Contrary to any kind of *positive 'ought-to-do' education*, the philosopher must devote himself to the fruitful and creative process of removing (negating) any intellectual or institutional obstacle to the exploited masses, i.e. every obstacle which hinders them in the (self-) discovery of the truth and, finally, in the (self-) reform of their own consciousness and practice.

Proceeding now to a further evaluation of the young Marx's conception of the philosopher/masses relation, as expressed in his *Letters from the Deutsch-Französische Jahrbücher*, the following question should be posed: Does the necessity of helping the masses to clarify their ideas cover a deeper need of radical intellectuals, like Marx, to promote their own theoretical plans for changing the world through the instruction or the manipulation of a social movement? In other words, is this minimalistic tendency, we have already mentioned, just the mask which covers Marx's intention to dominate a forthcoming socio-political movement he himself foresees in the near future?

We encounter here one of the most common, although crucial, arguments against Marxism as an ideology and, especially, as an expression of intellectuals' false consciousness.[15] It is of course one of the objects of this study to search for a documented reply to this theoretical and, ultimately, political challenge. For the time being,

---

[14] J.J. Rousseau, *Emile*, p.93 ff.
[15] The most classical formulation of the argument is included in K. Mannheim, *Ideology and Utopia*, New York, Harvest, 1936, p.77.
Among recent reformulations of the same argument see especially:
 a) A.W. Gouldner, *The Future of Intellectuals and the Rise of the New Class*, London, The Macmillan Press, 1979, pp.75–82.
 b) M. Seliger, *The Marxist Conception of Ideology*, Cambridge, Cambridge University Press, 1977, pp.55–57.

however, we will merely argue that Marx's attempt *to minimise* the importance of the philosopher's role, as compared to the masses' (self-) reform of consciousness, represents just the first step towards the formulation of the *self-emancipation principle,* which will be declared by him in a later phase of his work.[16] Anyway, in his 1843 writings he still underlines the need for a *well-balanced alliance* among philosophers and common people,[17] an alliance which can be attained through the simultaneous minimisation of the philosopher's intellectual function and the recognition of the masses' reforming ability as well.

At this point, however, it is Marx's *initial* reference to the proletariat's revolutionary perspective, which must be taken into consideration, since, as Oizerman correctly argues in regard to this specific issue,

> in the open letters in the *Jahrbücher,* Marx says [only] that philosophy has the task of providing ideological equipment for the fighting masses. However great the importance of this idea, which rejects the philosopher's claim to being non-partisan, it does not fully set forth the Marxist conception of partisanship in philosophy and theory generally, because it does not indicate *which class* is in struggle *against which* class. It is only in the 'Contribution of Hegel's Philosophy of Law. Introduction' that Marx first declares that advanced

---

[16] A further step towards the formulation of the proletariat's self-emancipation principle may be noticed in his later work *The Poverty of Philosophy,* where Marx proceeds to the following interesting formulation of the theoretician-proletarian relation, connecting the minimisation of the theoretician's role with the gradual development of the proletariat's consciousness: '[I]n the measure that history moves forward, [argues Marx], and with it the struggle of the proletariat assumes clearer outlines, [the socialist theoreticians] no longer need to seek science in their mind; they have only to take note of what is happening before their eyes and to become its mouthpiece.' (K. Marx, 'The Poverty of Philosophy' in K. Marx and F. Engels, *Collected Works,* p.177 – our emphasis). It becomes obvious, therefore, that by describing the theoreticians as the proletariat's mouthpiece, the way is opened to a declaration of the 'self-emancipation principle'.

[17] Referring to the revolutionary perspectives of mankind, Karl Marx writes to Arnold Ruge in his letter of September 1843: 'This is a work for the world and for us. It can only be the work of united forces.' (K. Marx and F. Engels, op. cit., vol. 3, p.145).

philosophy can and must become the philosophy of the proletariat.[18] (Oizerman's emphasis)

It was indeed near the end of 1843, beginning of 1844 in his 'Contribution to the Critique of Hegel's Philosophy of Law. Introduction', that Marx declared for the first time that the proletariat is the agent of the social revolution, which will lead humanity, through the realisation of philosophy, to its complete emancipation.

[Y]ou cannot supersede philosophy without making it a reality [...]. As philosophy finds its material weapons in the proletariat, so the proletariat finds its spiritual weapons in philosophy. The *head* of emancipation is *philosophy*, its heart is the proletariat. Philosophy cannot be made a reality without the abolition of the proletariat, the proletariat cannot be abolished without philosophy being made a reality.[19] (Marx's emphasis).

It is an open question, of course, whether the *organic* metaphor quoted above, concerning the 'head' and the 'heart', Feuerbachian in its philosophical origin,[20] reveals a kind of hierarchy between intellectuals and workers.[21] There is no doubt, moreover, that the young Marx himself appears as the revolutionary intellectual who is fighting for the realisation of philosophy in the social world of his time. The extent to which, however, philosophers themselves are approached as political leaders of the proletarian movement, remains to be examined in the light of Marx's later works.

---

[18] T.I. Oizerman, op. cit., p.211.
[19] K. Marx, 'Contribution to the Critique of Hegel's Philosophy of Law: Introduction', in K. Marx and F. Engels, op. cit., vol. 3, pp.181-187.
[20] See M. Löwy, op. cit., p.92 in connection with L. Feuerbach, *Principles of the Philosophy of the Future*, Indianapolis, Hackett Publishing Company, 1986, p.71.
[21] See A.W. Gouldner, *Against Fragmentation*, p.14, where Gouldner takes for granted what he should have proved: 'For however such head and heart are mutually defended, there is small doubt, which Marx thought the proper ruler.' At this point, Gouldner mistakes Marx for Plato.
     At the same time, M. Löwy, op. cit., pp.72-75, also seems to bypass the young Marx's minimalistic tendency as regards the philosopher's role; as a result, he insists that there is a kind of hierarchy in Marx's thought between philosopher-head and proletariat-heart of the emancipation. He reaches, therefore, the conclusion that there is an interesting convergence between the young Marx and the young Lenin of *What is to be Done?* as regards the intellectual-proletarian relation.

At this point, it is useful indeed to take note of the young Engels' rather revealing argument, directly connected with Marx's reference to the alliance between philosophers and proletarians.

> Thus, the union between the German philosophers of whom Feuerbach is the most recent representative [writes Engels] and the German working men represented by Weitling, a union which a year ago, had been predicted by Dr. Marx, is all but accomplished. With the philosophers to think, and the working men to fight *for us*, will any earthy power be strong enough to resist our progress?[22] (our emphasis)

It is, of course, beyond any doubt that Engels' celebration of the philosophers' union with the working men, as if it were an already given historical fact, even in March 1845, when the above text was written, seems rather simplistic and premature. It gives us, however, the opportunity to proceed to a brief reference to his early views as regards the philosopher/mass relation,[23] just before referring to Marx's collaboration with Engels and their historical meeting with the proletariat in the streets of Paris, London, Manchester and other European cities as well.

First of all, it must be stressed that, before Marx, Engels has already referred to the socio-political existence of the working class even since the late 1830s, while writing his so-called 'Letters from Wuppertal'.[24] Moreover, his articles concerning the social and

---

[22] F. Engels, 'Rapid Progress of Communism in Germany' in K. Marx and F. Engels, op. cit., vol. 4, p.236.

[23] For an interesting biography and history of Engels's ideas with specific reference to the young Engels's formation of thought, see:
   a) T. Carver, *Friedrich Engels, His Life and Thought*, London, The Macmillan Press, 1989, especially pp.31-132.
   b) J.D. Hunley, *The Life and Thought of Friedrich Engels, A Reinterpretation*, New Haven, Yale University Press, 1991, especially pp.1-22.
   c) S.H. Rigby, *Engels and the formation of Marxism, History, Dialectics and Revolution*, Manchester, Manchester University Press, 1992, especially pp.12-63, where the young Engels's relation with Hegel's philosophy and the Young Hegelians is examined in detail.

[24] Although S.H. Rigby, op. cit., p.18, argues that 'the intellectual development of the young Engels ran along broadly similar lines to that of the young Marx', it must be pointed out that Engels's starting point of analysis lies within the field of political

political question in England, published near the end of the year 1842 in the *Rheinische Zeitung,* reveal his interest in the perspectives of the working class. It is, for example, worth noting the young Engels' following remark, written on December 19, 1842, i.e. around a year before Marx's 'Introduction', mentioned above:

> The working class [writes Engels] is daily becoming more and more imbued with the radical-democratic principles of Chartism and is increasingly coming to recognise them as the expression of its collective consciousness. However, at the present this party is only in process of formation and therefore cannot yet act with full vigour.[25]

As a matter of fact, both his family's milieu – it is well known that Engels was the son of a rather eminent manufacturer – as well as his own professional activity as a manager in his father's firm, gave Engels the opportunity to come in direct contact with the living conditions of the German and English workers. Moreover, his stay in Great Britain proved to be a real source of inspiration, as his famous sociological analysis of *The Condition of the Working Class in England* proves.

Nevertheless, it is worth underlining that, despite the sociological dimension of his work, grounded on and fed by a genuine interest in political economy, the young Engels was still under the strong intellectual influence of the Young Hegelians.[26] From this point of view, his conception of the relation between philosophers, on the one hand, and the (working) masses, on the other, is directly determined by a typical Young Hegelian notion, i.e. the *primary* role of philosophy within the social and political process.

That is why, even though Engels openly supports the union between the German philosophers and the German working men, he nevertheless, faces the workers as if they were the *instruments* – 'the

---

economy and sociological research , while Marx's intellectual career begins with philosophy and arrives at the critique of political economy around 1844–1845.

[25] F. Engels, 'The Position of the Political Parties' in K. Marx and F. Engels, op. cit., vol. 2, pp.374–375.

[26] It must be mentioned that Engels's relation with the Young Hegelian, rather extreme, circle of *The Free*, is the real cause of Marx's frigidity during his first meeting with Engels in Cologne on 16 November 1842. (See T. Carver, op. cit., p.97).

working men to fight *for us'* (our emphasis) – through which the philosopher's theoretical plan would be realised. More concretely, a division of labour and hierarchy between intellectuals and workers is, according to the young Engels, a *conditio sine qua non* for the world's future transformation. It must be stressed, however, once again, that this a kind of *hierarchical* approach which was not suggested by the young Marx, whose 'Introduction to the Contribution to the Critique of Hegel's Philosophy of Law', contrary to the Engels' interpretation, is steadily directed towards a *well-balanced* alliance of philosophers and proletarians.

Nevertheless, it is now time to follow Marx in Paris, where his own collaboration with Engels begins and his contact with the world of the proletarians gradually extends from the philosophical to the social and political level as well.

Chapter 3
Intellectuals and Proletarians: Marx, Engels and the Proletarian Vanguard of the 1840s

There is no doubt that Marx's emigration to Paris in October 1843 played a decisive role in regard to his own theoretical and political orientation towards the proletariat. Even Isaiah Berlin, a thinker who regards Marx 'as a man of unemotional, even frigid nature, upon whom environment produced little effect, and who rather imposed his own unvarying form on any situation in which he found himself', admitted the fact that 'the years 1843–5 are the most decisive in [Marx's] life: in Paris [concludes Berlin] he underwent his final intellectual transformation.'[1]

From this point of view, the timing of Marx's declaration that the proletariat is the agent of a total emancipation is in no way accidental.[2] It was exactly in Paris that Karl Marx completed his 'Contribution to the Hegel's Philosophy of Law. Introduction' and published it in the unique issue of the *Deutsch-Französische Jahrbücher,* supporting the proletariat's revolutionary union with philosophy. More concretely, it can be argued that although, as Michael Löwy's documented research shows, Marx did not come in direct contact with the secret societies in Paris before August 1844,[3] it is beyond any doubt that the proletarian milieu of the German

---

[1] I. Berlin, op. cit., p.63.
[2] It is worth noting that the article 'On the Jewish Question' published in the *Deutsch-Französische Jahrbücher,* written however exclusively in Kreuznach just before the *Contribution to the Hegel's Philosophy of Law, Introduction,* does not mention anything about the proletariat as being the agent of a future social revolution. (See Löwy's comment, in M. Löwy, op, cit., p.68).
[3] M. Löwy, op. cit., p.64.

émigrés, who lived in the French capital, exerted an indirect, though important, influence on his own 'discovery' of the proletariat as a revolutionary class.[4]

At this point, however, it is necessary to proceed to a few historical clarifications concerning the social content of the term 'proletariat' in the early 1840s and the social identity of the secret societies during the same period.

1. It is worth noting that the German émigrés, living in Paris – whose exact number is rather difficult to determine – were mainly artisans and marginalised intellectuals of middle class origin.[5]

2. It must be pointed out that there is an almost unanimous convergence of views among the most eminent modern researchers as regards the social content of the term 'proletariat' as this was used during the early 1840s. More concretely, it is almost unanimously agreed that the vast majority of the proletariat, whom Marx was talking about during the same period, consisted mainly of artisans, severely disadvantaged by capitalist development. Following Gouldner's analysis, for example:

> ...when Karl Marx met those he thought of as real workers, they were actually, for the most part, seething with unrest and bitter about injustice no less than deprivation, artisans who, with their guild traditions, had considerable organisational competence... In short, when the ordinary language of Marx's time spoke of the 'proletariat' and 'proletarianisation', it did not neatly distinguish between uprooted artisans and poor factory

---

[4] It is during his stay in Paris (1844–1845) that Marx studied Lorenz von Stein's work *Der Sozialismus und Communismus des heutigen Frankreichs*, moving thereafter even closer to a kind of a proletarian communism, grounded on the proletariat's capacity for self-emancipation. During the same period Engels studied Flora Tristan's work, *L'Union ouvrière* and started moving in a similar direction. (For historical details, see M. Löwy, op. cit., pp.80-83, 94–96).

[5] According to J. Grandjonc, *Marx et les communistes allemands à Paris*, (François Maspero, Paris 1974), p.12, the German émigrés living in Paris around 1844 amount to 41,700. Contrary to this well-documented study, however, H. Draper, (*Karl Marx's Theory of Revolution: State and Bureaucracy*, Monthly Review Press, New York and London, 1977, vol. I, p.137), talks about a number of 100,000 German émigrés. Finally, B. Nicolaievsky and O. Maenchen-Helfen, op. cit., p.81 refer to 'several tens of thousands'.

workers. As a result, the obvious radicalism of the artisans might metonymically, but mistakenly, be seen as standing for the radicalism of the whole, including the factory workers.[6]

3. The social/professional composition of the secret societies of the 1840s, and especially that of the League of the Just, transformed later to the Communist League, consisted for the most part of artisans and to a lesser degree of propertyless intellectuals.[7] At this point, it is worth noting that Engels himself underlined this historical fact in a way that leaves almost no doubt as to whether he and Marx ignored or even underestimated the concrete social identity of the radicalised proletarians, as Gouldner's analysis mistakenly assumes. According to Engels' *History of the Communist* League, written many years later than the period we are here dealing with,

> the members [of the League of the Just], in so far as they were workers at all, were almost exclusively artisans [...]. The greatest honour is due to them, in that they, who were themselves not yet even full proletarians, but only an appendage of the petty bourgeoisie, one which was being transformed into the modern proletariat, in that these artisans were capable of instinctively anticipating their future development [...].[8]

The significance of such a sociological observation, transferred to the level of political theory, is obvious and will be discussed later on within the historical context of the Communist League and the 1848–1849 revolution. For the time being, however, it is sufficient to note

---

[6] A.W. Gouldner, op. cit., p.105. See also:
  a) D.W. Lovell, *Marx's Proletariat: The Making of a Myth*, Routledge, London, 1988, pp.70–94, and
  b) M. Löwy, op. cit., p.83.
  Finally, Engels himself, talking about the German working class, argues that its vast majority consisted of handicraftsmen. (F. Engels, 'Progress of Social Reform on the Continent' in K. Marx and F. Engels, *Collected Works*, vol. 3, p.401).

[7] For a detailed approach to the communist secret societies in Paris, during the years 1838–1837, see M. Löwy, op. cit., pp.83–84; as regards the history of the League of the Just, see M. Löwy, op. cit., pp.87–91.

[8] F. Engels, 'The History of the Communist League' in K. Marx and F. Engels, *Selected Works*, New York, International Publishers, vol. II, p.10.

the fact that Marx and Engels begin to find not merely a sensitive audience, but an active partner in their effort *qua* intellectuals to transform the social and political reality of their time. But how was this relation among philosophers and proletarians formed? What was the intellectuals' and workers' activity within the secret societies of the 1840s? How did Marx and Engels, revolutionary intellectuals themselves, regard the European proletarians and their organisations?

It is not of course the object of this study to give a historical account of the 1840s proletarian movement. It is, however, through the answers to questions like the above, based especially on Marx and Engels' writings, that a creative analysis of the intellectual/proletarian relation can be promoted aiming at a more general evaluation of the Marxist political theory itself.

From such a point of view, the way Marx and Engels responded to the organised proletarian vanguard during the years 1844-1845 represents a distinguished 'moment' in the whole development of the intellectual/worker relation, the philosophical background of which has already been noted and discussed in the introductory chapter of this research.

It was in the 'Critical Marginal Notes on the Article 'The King of Prussia and Social Reform. By a Prussian'', written within the first days of August 1844 and published in *Vorwärts* – a German newspaper appeared in Paris twice a week during the year 1844[9] – that Karl Marx expressed his faith in the revolutionary capacity of the Silesian workers. This led him in direct and final conflict with his ex-collaborator, the Young Hegelian Arnold Ruge. It is, moreover, at this same article, that the young Marx declared emphatically for the first time his enthusiasm, with regard to the proletarian desire for education and theoretical production as well.[10]

Just a few days later, Marx communicated this enthusiasm to Ludwig Feuerbach, a philosopher who was still exerting an influence on him, with the following revealing words:

---

[9] See Grandjonc's special research, which contains historical data and articles published in Vorwärts (op. cit., especially, pp.9-101).
[10] K. Marx, 'Critical Marginal Notes on the Article "The King of Prussia and Social Reform. By a Prussian."' in K. Marx and F. Engels, *Collected Works*, vol. 3, p.201.

> You would have to attend one of the meetings of the French workers to appreciate the pure freshness, the nobility which burst forth from these toil-worn men [...]. The German artisans in Paris, i.e., the Communists among them, several hundreds, have been having lectures twice a week throughout this summer on your *Wesen des Christenthums* from their secret leaders, and have been remarkably responsive.[11]

Around the same period and through the lines of his 'Economic and Philosophic Manuscripts of 1844', in which Marx starts distinguishing between a crude egalitarian communism and a new type of communism he himself supports 'as the positive transcendence of private property as human self-estrangement',[12] the German philosopher becomes even more eloquent in his own admiration for proletarian progress in the field of education and knowledge.

> When communist *artisans* associate with one another [argues Marx], theory, propaganda, etc., is their first end. But at the same time, as a result of this association, they acquire a new need – the need for society – and what appears as a means becomes an end [...]. Association, society and conversation, which again has association as its end, are enough for men; the brotherhood of man is no mere phrase with them but a fact of life, and the nobility of man shines upon us from their work-hardened bodies.[13] (Marx's emphasis)

At the same time, Engels himself expresses a similar admiration for the socialists' educational activities within the ranks of the English proletarian movement. According to Engels, the English proletarians show a remarkable progress in studying and discussing philosophical

---

[11] K. Marx, 'Letter to Feuerbach', August 11 [1844] in K. Marx and F. Engels, op. cit., vol. 3, pp.355, 357.

[12] K. Marx, 'Economic and Philosophic Manuscripts of 1844' in K. Marx and F. Engels, op. cit., vol. 3, p.295; in regard to Marx's approach to the crude egalitarian communism, see I. Mészáros, *Marx's Theory of Alienation*, London, Merlin Press, 1975, pp.159–161, in which the author argues that 'the crucial Marxian distinction is that between communism as a *political movement* [...] and communism as comprehensive *social practice*.' (Mészáros' emphasis – p.161).

[13] K. Marx and F. Engels, op. cit., vol. 3. p.313.

works such as Rousseau's, *On the Social Contract,* writings of Voltaire, Paine, Shelley, Strauss and Proudhon as well.[14]

At this point, however, this craving for knowledge, which is repeatedly underlined and documented by both Marx and Engels, demands a more detailed consideration with regard to its impact on the way the two thinkers conceive the intellectual/worker relation.

First of all, it must be stressed that not only a thirst for knowledge,[15] but intimate personal relations among the members of educational and/or secret societies as well, helps to explain Marx and Engels' attraction to and admiration for the 'proletarian world'. As a matter of fact, there is no need to regard this kind of attraction, as Lewis Feuer does, as Marx's supposed quest of a 'symbolic mother';[16] a desire for knowledge with a simultaneous transcendence of the bourgeois intellectual's *individualistic* way of life (the most extreme expression of which, in the 1840s' philosophy, may be easily recognised in Max Stirner's ideas) is sufficient motive to attract radical philosophers' interest in the *collectivistic way* communist workers used to live and act,[17] given the fact, however, that neither

---

[14] See Engels's detailed analysis in his 'Letters from London' in K. Marx and F. Engels, op. cit., vol. 3, pp.379-391; Engels, however, seems disappointed by the German proletariat's response to similar activities, which took place in Elberfeld and Barmen around the same period. (See: F. Engels, 'Letter to Marx, 22 February 1845' in K. Marx and F. Engels, op. cit., vol. 38, pp.22-23).

[15] See, for example, K. Marx and F. Engels, 'The Holy Family', op. cit., vol. 4, p.84: 'One must know the studiousness, the craving for knowledge, the moral energy and the unceasing urge for development of the French and English workers to be able to form an idea of the human nobility of this movement.' (Marx's and Engels's emphasis).

[16] L.S. Feuer, op. cit., p.39: 'The rejection of the mother, the internal womb, thus provides the most recurrent thematic imagery for Marx. It is part of the psychology of the Promethean complex, a man engaged in a mother-directed rebellion, even uncertain of his manhood, and looking in the movement of history for a new mother to sustain him. The working class became a symbolic mother, and he hoped for himself, as he said for the Communards, that he would be enshrined forever in the heart of the working class.'

At this point, it is worth noting that a distinguished Marxist Greek philosopher, Dimitrios Glinos, proceeded to a similar *psychoanalytic* approach as regards Plato's own conception of the philosopher/politics relation. (See, Glinos' introduction to Plato's *Sophist*, in the Greek edition Zaharopoulos, Athens, published for the first time in 1940).

[17] From this point of view, it is important to mention the need for a comparative historical approach among the structure, the function and the cultural atmosphere of

Marx nor Engels became members of communist societies until 1847, when they finally entered the League of the Just.[18]

From this point of view, artisans' communities, grounded on a deeper feeling of association and solidarity, represent – in the young Marx and Engels' thought – a kind of embryonic, though still marginal, opposition to the frigid, emotionless and impersonal bourgeois society. At the same time, the communist societies function as the educational institution, within which learning becomes not just a matter of a formal transference of knowledge, but an everlasting process based on and fed by a common sharing of everyday life experience. This is why these proletarian communities were actually approached by both Marx and Engels as an initial response to the alienation created by capitalism itself and diffused throughout bourgeois society.

This kind of multi-functional institution works like a womb, within which a new type of social agent, the *worker-intellectual,* is being formed. As Lewis Feuer correctly argues on this specific issue,

> the 'worker-intellectual' is a workingman with the soul of an intellectual, a workingman becomes articulate, a worker with his hands who has refused to allow his consciousness to atrophy or become the agent of self reproach but who would call the master's social system before an impartial tribune.[19]

In fact, according to Marx and Engels' analysis, these worker-intellectuals form a social group, which incorporates and expresses the objective possibility of transcending the social division of labour.[20] On the other hand, the worker-intellectual represents *in nuce* the portrait of a human being who fights in order to develop symmetrically his capacities in every field of social life; needless to say that such a fight will achieve its real justification in a communist,

---

the *Doctorklub*, to which Marx belonged during his student years in Berlin, on the one hand, and the workers' societies he came across in Paris, on the other.

[18] See the documented analysis of B. Nicolaievsky and O. Maenchen-Helfen, op. cit., p.84 ff.

[19] L.S. Feuer, 'The Alienated Americans and Their Influence on Marx and Engels', in L.S. Feuer, op. cit., p.211.

[20] It is worth mentioning that Weitling and Eccarius correspond to these, whom actually the young Marx and Engels face as worker-intellectuals.

i.e. classless society, within which the social division of labour will be finally overcome.[21]

There is no doubt, therefore, that the activity of worker-intellectuals enhanced Marx and Engels' belief in the proletariat's transformative capacities. Besides that, however, it is exactly within this context that Bruno Bauer's views on the philosopher masses relation provided a provocative opportunity for both Marx and Engels, not only to criticise the Young Hegelian *intellectual elitism*, but to express once more their own approval of the revolutionary perspectives of the proletarian masses.

From such a point of view, Marx and Engels' conflict with Bruno Bauer is significant indeed. In his 'The Genus and the Crowd', an article which appeared in his own journal, the *Algemeine Literaturzeitung*, in September 1844, Bruno Bauer argued as follows:

> [Some people] withdrew the crowd from the critique as they would have liked to withdraw themselves from it. They now make use of the crowd as a remedy against the Spirit. The crowd is now made a cult object, so as to be a new palliative against the old egoism.[22]

There was no doubt, of course, that an argument like this would immediately provoke a critical response on behalf of those who, like Marx and Engels, had already become conscious of the proletarian 'studiousness, craving for knowledge and moral energy'. At this point, Marx's sarcastic irony is worth mentioning indeed:

> On the one side is the Mass as the passive, spiritless, unhistorical *material* element of history. On the other is the Spirit, *Criticism*, Herr Bruno Co. as the active element from which all *historical* action proceeds. The

---

[21] The *locus classicus* of the young Marx's analysis on this issue is his own critique of alienation, as expressed in his *Economic and Philosophic Manuscripts of 1844*. The philosophical similarity, however, of Marx's approach with Fichte's idealism, as regards the fight of the empirical I against the non-I in order to reach the pure I, that is the absolute harmony with itself in a society of equality without government, is worth underlining. (See, especially, the first two of Fichte's *Lectures Concerning the Scholar's Vocation*, Fichte, op. cit. p.145-161).

[22] B. Bauer, 'The Genus and the Crowd' in L.S. Stepelevich (ed.), op. cit., p.198.

act of transforming society is reduced to the *cerebral activity* of Critical Criticism.²³ (Marx's emphasis)

Hence, within the same work, Marx proceeds to a double demarcation, as regards the philosopher/masses relation. On the one hand, as has already been mentioned, he settles accounts with Hegel by rejecting the role of the philosopher-interpreter of history, who is assumed to appear on the scene *post festum*.²⁴ At the same time, however, he openly renounces Bruno Bauer's conception of philosopher or intellectual as the supposed exclusive agent of criticism and the actual creator of the historical process, a conception firmly connected with and nourished by an overall contempt for the masses' capacities.²⁵

As a matter of fact, Marx and Engels continue to remain faithful to Rousseau and Fichte's position as regards the common people's ability to attain knowledge under the influence exerted by the philosopher-educator.²⁶ Moreover, it becomes more and more evident that Marx and Engels during the years 1844-1845 face the social process as a rather effective 'educator' of the working masses themselves. In other words, alienation, massively produced within capitalist society, is characterised by creative dimension despite its

---

[23] K. Marx and F. Engels, 'The Holy Family', op. cit., vol. 4, p.86.

[24] In his *From Hegel to Marx: Studies in the Intellectual Development of Karl Marx*, (Ann Arbor Paperback, 1962), pp.22, 25, Sidney Hook describes Marx's differences with Hegel as follows: 'For Hegel philosophy in the broadest sense is the *denkende Betrachtung der Gegenstände* – "the thinking view of things" (*Encyclopädie*, Sec. 2). Sometimes, even more simply, it is *Nachdenken*. [For Marx] philosophy is not retrospective insight into the past; it is prospective anticipation of the future. It explains why the present is what it is in order to make it different. So often an expression of social quietism, or a means of individual escape, philosophy must now function as an instrument of social liberation.' (Hook's emphasis).

[25] K. Marx and F. Engels, 'The Holy Family', op. cit., vol. 4, p.86: 'Just as the element of Criticism is banished from the Mass, so the element of the mass [argues Marx] is banished from Criticism. Therefore, *Criticism* sees itself incarnate not in a *mass*, but exclusively in a *handful* of chosen men, in Herr Bauer and his disciples.' (Marx's emphasis).

[26] It can be argued that the drives to *communicate* and to *receive*, which Fichte attributes to sensitive/rational human beings, find their true agents in the vanguard proletarian communists, as conceived by Marx and Engels within the Parisian communities of the years 1844-1845. (See Fichte, op. cit., pp.163-164).

disastrous results.[27] It is exactly the 'cunning of the social process', which gives rise to the necessary objective conditions of the proletariat's transformation from a class in itself to a class for itself. Contrary to Bruno Bauer, therefore, whose indisputable contempt for the masses reminds us of Voltaire's position, as revealed especially in his own correspondence with his fellow philosophers during the Enlightenment period, Marx and Engels are consciously trying to link their work with the proletariat, the praxis of which functions as an authentic source of inspiration for their own philosophy.

Whether such a positive approach towards the perspectives of workers causes radical intellectuals to be subjugated to the spontaneous will of the masses, remains however to be examined. At this point, Marx's confrontation with Weitling, as well as his entrance, together with Engels, into the League of the Just, give us the opportunity to discuss the whole matter within a different, though equally interesting historical context.

---

[27] As I. Mészáros, op. cit., p.181 correctly points out, '[i]f one tackles the problem of human self-alienation, one should not start with the self-defeating assumption that alienation is a homogeneous inert totality.'

Chapter 4
Intellectuals and Proletarians in and around the League of the Just

It was on 7 February 1840, that a new educational society, the German Workers' Educational Association, was founded in London.[1] This Association, the leaders of which were the ex-student of forestry Schapper, the shoemaker Bauer and the watchmaker Moll, functioned as a front organisation for the League of the Just, regarding education and propaganda among the proletarians as its main purpose of existence. Around this kind of social and, ultimately, political activity, however, a significant debate took place between the leaders of the Association, on the one hand, and the chief representative of the 1830s–40s egalitarian communism, Weitling, on the other. The theoretical dimension of this debate is vividly described by Nicolaievsky and Maenchen-Helfen as follows:

> Schapper and his friends were patiently seeking a way for themselves along the thorny part of conflicting parties and systems. *Their guide was reason.* Weitling followed his *feelings* only. He took his stand on the Bible, on Love, the Noble and the Good. In his opinion the people were long since ripe for the new social order, and the only remaining task was to free them from their oppressors for which all that was required was the determined initiative of a revolutionary organisation, a small band of resolute brothers.[2] (our emphasis)

---

[1] A vivid presentation of the German Workers' Educational Association is included in B. Nicolaievsky and O. Maenchen-Helfen, op. cit., p.113 ff.
[2] op. cit., pp.119–120.

This means that just several years after the unsuccessful Blanquist insurrection, which took place on 12 May 1839 in Paris, the most crucial dilemma within the field of revolutionary tactics was posed once again: education, propaganda and long-term revolutionary planning or a Blanquist insurrection made by a band of conspirators on behalf of the masses? In the first case, enlightenment is considered as a decisive prerequisite for the revolution; in the second case, a serious scepticism is expressed with regard to the masses' capacity for self-transformation. From this point of view, an apparently paradoxical convergence among Bauer's intellectual and Blanqui's political elitism can be noted.

Nevertheless, Weitling's confrontation with the Association's leaders contains one further interesting philosophical dimension. His own belief in the power of feelings and sentiments, as opposed to the Association's leaders' faith in the guiding role of reason, constitutes a political version of a long-term philosophical debate, the ancient origin of which has already been noted in Plato's political theory, while its modern expression can be easily recognised in the open-ended struggle between the Enlightenment and Romanticism.

The importance of such a conflict, as regards the intellectuals' intervention in the social and political process, becomes even more evident, however, on the ground of Marx's own controversy with Weitling, just a year after the German representative of egalitarian communism lost the battle against Schapper and his fellow proletarians.

Although Marx's participation in a meeting of the organisation cannot be historically documented, there is no doubt that he paid special attention to the Association's activities described above.[3] Moreover, it must be stressed that Engels had met the Association's leaders in 1843 and saw them for a second time, together with Marx, when they were both in London during the summer of 1845.

At this point, Engels' retrospective analysis of the history of the League of the Just is very interesting indeed. Being impressed by Schapper, Moll and Bauer's energy and determination, Marx and Engels almost immediately realised, especially after the members of the organisation rejected Weitling's ideas, that the way was free for them to intervene in this newly born proletarian movement.

---

[3] op. cit., p.121.

> Now, we were by no means of the opinion [argues Engels many years later] that the new scientific results should be confined in large tomes exclusively to the 'Learned' world. Quite the contrary. We were both of us already deeply involved in the political movement [...]. It was our duty to provide a scientific foundation for our view, but it was equally important for us to win over the European and in the first place the German proletariat to our convictions.[4]

The 'scientific foundation', which Engels is talking about, had already been constructed around 1845–1846 through the critique of the *German Ideology,* by which both Marx and Engels present their main positions on the new 'positive science' of society, i.e. historical materialism.[5] Meanwhile – given the fact that the goal of emancipation should not be confronted as 'a question of what this or that proletarian, or even the whole proletariat, at the moment, *regards* as its aim', but as a question 'of *what the proletariat is,* and what, in accordance with this *being,* it will historically be compelled to do'[6] (Marx's emphasis) – it becomes obvious that the radical intellectual's activity cannot be reduced to the *minimal* function of merely showing the workers what they are actually doing. In fact, this claim, so strongly supported by the young Marx, looks rather debatable. So long as scientific knowledge dominates proletarian spontaneity, intellectuals or, in other words, agents of knowledge tend to establish, at least temporarily, their authority over the proletarians.

To what extent did Marx and Engels succeed in reversing this specific tendency? This is a question which is going to be discussed and evaluated in detail a little later. For the time being, however, it is worth pointing to Engels' analysis which refers to Marx's as well as to his own attitude towards the League of the Just during the years 1844–1847.

---

[4] F. Engels, *The History of the Communist League*, op. cit., p.12.
[5] K. Marx and F. Engels, 'The German Ideology' in K. Marx and F. Engels, *Collected Works,* vol. 5, p.37: 'When speculation ends, where real life starts, there consequently begins real, *positive science*, the expounding of the practical activity, of the practical process of development of men. Empty phrases about consciousness end, and real knowledge has to take their place.' (our emphasis).
[6] K. Marx and F. Engels, 'The Holy Family', op. cit., vol. 4., p.37.

> Without worrying ourselves about the internal affairs of the League [argues Engels] we were kept informed, however, of every important happening. On the other hand, *we influenced the theoretical views of the most important members of the League* by word of mouth, by letter and through the press. For this purpose we also made use of various lithographed circulars, which we dispatched to our friends and correspondents through out the world on particular occasions when it was a question of the internal affairs of the Communist Party in process of formation.[7] (our emphasis)

Thus, given the positions presented above, the following conclusions can be reached in regard to Marx and Engels' attitude towards the proletarian vanguard *before* their own entrance in the League of the Just.

1. Both Marx and Engels are highly interested in the activity and perspectives of the workers' organisations, though they still refuse to participate directly in the political process as such.
2. Consequently, they both insist on *theory* and *scientific knowledge* as being the most effective means to intervene in the formation of the proletarians' revolutionary consciousness and practice.
3. On the ground of the above conclusions, it becomes obvious that, at least during this specific period of time (1844-1847), Marx and Engels' views on the intellectual/proletarian relation are actually incompatible with the model of the philosopher-ruler as well as with that of the philosopher-governor.
4. However, their own connection with the proletarian vanguard discloses significant similarities with other models, as far as the philosopher/mass relation is concerned. As a matter of fact, it may be convincingly argued that Marx and Engels acted, at the same time, as *philosopher-advisers and philosopher-educators*.

In fact, Marx and Engels act as philosopher-advisers to the proletarian societies by making *public use of reason*, while still avoiding any direct involvement in the political process *stricto sensu*. From this point of view, both Kant's analysis of the

---

[7] F. Engels, *The History of the Communist League*, p.13.

philosopher/politics relation, as presented in his *Perpetual Peace: A Philosophical Sketch,* and even Voltaire's advisory attitude to the natives of Geneva, may provide fruitful inspiration in regard to Marx and Engels' own relation with the members of the proletarian vanguard.

Both Marx and Engels incarnate, moreover, a special type of philosopher-educator, whose concrete attitude towards the masses reproduces to a certain degree Fichte's conception of the scholar's vocation since, without rejecting the proletarian *spontaneous* drive to truth, they, nevertheless, point out the need for an *active* educational intervention in the social process by the philosopher-agent of knowledge. Note, however, that according to Marx's *Third Thesis on Feuerbach,* the educator must himself be educated through revolutionary practice.

Finally, Engels' already mentioned position, according to which knowledge should not be confined to the limits of the 'Learned world', reminds us of the well-known Platonic position: philosophers must not obtain knowledge for their own interest. They must 'return to the cave' in order to liberate their fellow prisoners from the darkness of ignorance. In other words, knowledge should not be regarded as a matter of privilege, but as a matter of duty. On the other hand, Marx and Engels remain faithful to their initial position: without knowledge the world cannot be transformed. This means that without scientific foundation future proletarian revolution is doomed to fail.

Given, therefore, the positions mentioned above, the Marx/Weitling controversy becomes much more susceptible to a convincing interpretation.

From this point of view, it is not accidental, of course, that it was exactly the need for the scientific foundation of the workers' movement, combined with the necessary education of its members, which was defended by Marx during his well-known meeting with Weitling on March 30 1846 in Brussels. Without referring to the historical details of this particular meeting,[8] it is interesting to take note of the 'battle cry' with which Marx attacked Weitling: 'Ignorance has never helped anybody yet'. Hence, fight against ignorance is openly declared as a vital prerequisite for the social revolution; as a result, this fight for knowledge provides an excellent opportunity for

---

[8] See B. Nicolaievsky and O. Maenchen-Helfen, op. cit., pp.124–128.

the radical intellectuals to act within the leading ranks of the proletarian movement.

Moreover, given the fact that Marx and Weitling represented two different ways of life and thought, it is worth mentioning that a significant number of political theorists of our time have presented the Marx/Weitling controversy as a struggle between an eminent representative of intellectuals and a distinguished proletarian leader.[9] Nevertheless, from our point of view, such an argument cannot be supported.

There is no doubt, of course, that the difference with regard to Marx and Weitling's class origin and social identity should be taken into consideration. Contrary to Marx's bourgeois origin, Weitling's identity can be defined as proletarian.[10] Being himself the son of a French officer and a German maidservant, he worked as a tailor during a period when artisans came face to face with the negative results of capitalistic development.[11] It must be added, however, as Hal Draper correctly points out, that later on he became 'an independent tradesman, and, at the end, a small businessman nearing bankruptcy'.[12]

In fact, Weitling should be regarded as a typical example of a worker-intellectual. Like Bauer, Moll and Eccarius, Weitling was an artisan who developed, actually, a significant intellectual activity, which the young Marx himself was really impressed by.[13] Nevertheless, from our point of view and despite Weitling's class

---

[9] Such a view is supported by:
   a) L.S. Feuer, 'The Alienated Americans and Their Influence on Marx and Engels', in L.S. Feuer, op. cit., p.211.
   b) A.W. Gouldner, op. cit., pp.93–100, where the author analyses the 'Weitling Paradigm', as he calls it, as the 'Critical Episode' of the broader conflict among artisans and intellectuals.
   Against such a symbolic interpretation of the Marx-Weitling controversy, see: H. Draper, *Karl Marx's Theory of Revolution: The Politics of Social Classes*, vol. II, pp.654–659, where the author analyses what he calls the 'Weitling Myth'.

[10] H. Draper, op. cit., p.655, believes that 'Weitling was no proletarian'; nevertheless Draper's view is based on a quite narrow definition of the term 'proletarian', which risks identifying the proletariat with the factory workers.

[11] See C. Wittke. *The Utopian Communist: A Biography of Wilhelm Weitling, Nineteenth-Century Reformer*, Louisiana State University Press, 1950, especially pp.1–10.

[12] H. Draper, op. cit., p.655.

[13] K. Marx, 'Critical Marginal Notes on the Article "The King of Prussia and Social Reform. By a Prussian"', op. cit., vol. 3, p.201.

origin and identity, his own conflict with Marx must not be approached as a symbolic fight among proletarians and intellectuals. It is indeed methodologically wrong to draw general conclusions concerning the way Marx faces the intellectual/proletarian relation simply from the fact that the German philosopher rejected so fiercely Weitling's theory and practice.

On the other hand, the fact that the members of the German Workers' Educational Association, being artisans themselves, had already rejected Weitling's ideas before his crucial meeting with Marx, also leads to the conclusion that Weitling was no longer the distinguished political representative of the proletarian movement. Just the opposite is true; his influence on the proletariat was steadily diminishing by the time he met Marx in Brussels.[14]

At this point, however, it is worth noting that Weitling's theoretical positions prove to be an even more insurmountable obstacle for those thinkers who insist on the symbolic interpretation of the Marx/Weitling controversy.

In fact, Weitling's conception of communist society is totally incompatible with any notion of a self-ruled society. In a way highly reminiscent of Plato's *Republic*, he wrote and fought for a future society based on a strict hierarchy, at the top of which he placed philosophers and scientists.

According to Wittke, Weitling's best known and sympathetic biographer,

> At the apex of the administrative pyramid was the *Trio* or *Dreimannerath*, consisting of the top men in the three branches into which Weitling divided all science: the science of healing, which included the whole spiritual and physical nature of man, for he wanted both philosophers and physicians; physics, by which he meant a study of natural phenomena and the application of the laws of nature to the service of mankind in every field of activity; and mechanics, which included the theory and practice of all manual and machine production. Weitling's Trio [concludes Wittke] suggests Plato's 'philosopher-kings', the elite who were masters of science and 'the rudder of the whole administration'.

---

[14] H. Draper, op, cit., p.655.

Only by such expert leadership, he believed, could harmony be introduced and maintained in the social system.[15] (Wittke's emphasis)

Given such an analysis, Hal Draper is absolutely justified in his view that *'among the protagonists in that discussion there was indeed an advocate of a Dictatorship of the Intellectuals in communist society* – one who had openly set forth his plan in detail. It was Weitling'.[16] (Draper's emphasis). On the contrary, Marx and Engels proved to be very far away from the model of the philosopher-king/ruler. To what extent, however, do they really rid themselves of any idea concerning the intellectuals' dominant position over the proletariat and its movement? The fact that the Marx/Weitling controversy does not provide the necessary documents for such a hypothesis does not render the whole question groundless. Is it not possible to assume that Weitling, by his utopian and sentimentalist way of arguing, reveals what Marx's 'scientific language', being a 'language of mediations', tends to conceal, in special regard to the intellectual's role in the revolutionary transition towards the future classless society?

Actually, the question above may be best confronted within the historical context of Marx and Engels' activity in the Communist League, which will be discussed in the next chapter. For the time being, however, it is worth taking note of the fact that Marx's conflict with Weitling proved to be a significant event from another point of view as well; it provides interesting material for Marx's *psychological* portrait, i.e. an indication of the way the revolutionary intellectual Karl Marx confronts and fights against anyone, intellectual and proletarian alike, whom he thinks of as an obstacle to the future communist revolution.

It was exactly through his participation in the meeting of 30 March 1846, for example, that Annenkov, one of Marx's most faithful followers, was led to use the hybrid term *'democratic dictator'* in order to describe Marx's personality.[17] However, Annenkov's

---

[15] C. Wittke, op. cit., pp.60–61.
[16] H. Draper, op. cit., p.656.
[17] See B. Nicolaievsky and O. Maenchen-Helfen, op. cit., p.125; it is worth noting that Engels himself, while referring to Marx's editorial activity in the *Neue Rheinische Zeitung*, talks about 'Marx's dictatorship [as being] a matter of course, undisputed and willingly recognised by all of us.' (See F. Engels, 'Marx and the *Rheinische Zeitung*' in K. Marx and F. Engels, *Selected Works*, vol. II, p.32).

description of Marx's psychological portrait is not the only one. As Isaiah Berlin correctly notices at this point,

> the portrait of him that emerges from the memoirs of those who were his friends at this time, Ruge, Freiligrath, Heine, Annenkov, is that of a bold and energetic figure, a vehement, eager, contemptuous controversialist, applying to everything his cumbrous Hegelian weapons [...].[18]

Hence, there is hardly any doubt that Marx's particular attitude towards bourgeois or worker-intellectuals vacillates between *paternalism and authoritarianism*.[19]

Nevertheless, it must be underlined, once again, that Marx's philosophical and political analysis and evaluation of the proletariat's revolutionary capacity ought not to be confused with or reduced to a mere psychological observation of his personal relations with specific members of the proletarian vanguard. The philosophical and political meaning of the radical intellectuals' connection with the proletarian class may be effectively pursued and conceived only in the field of *macro*-political theory and practice.

---

[18] I. Berlin, op. cit., p.77.

[19] For Marx's description as a highly authoritarian personality, see, for example, the following first-hand information in:
    a) Schurz's analysis, as included in L.S. Feuer, 'Marxism and the Hegemony of the Intellectual Class', in L.S. Feuer, op. cit., pp.42-43.
    b) Techow's analysis, as included in L. Schwarzschild, *The Red Prussian. The Life and Legend of Karl Marx*, Pickwick, London, 1986, pp.211-212. (In the same work, p.68, see Heinzen's similar evaluation of Marx's personality).
For a more balanced psychological portrait of Marx, see, however, Kamenka's analysis in E. Kamenka (ed.), *Ideas and Ideologies, Intellectuals and Revolution*, (Edward Arnold, London, 1979), p.83: 'Marx's strength as a revolutionary activist was entirely intellectual. His mind was sharper, his thoughts were clearer, his knowledge was greater than that of any other person in the socialist movement, and he backed his capacity for brilliant analysis, cogent general theorising and powerful pamphleteering with total intellectual self-confidence and intransigence. One contemporary after another, in letter and reminiscences, confirms this characterisation of Marx, differing only on the relative importance they ascribe to his arrogance and his abilities.'

Chapter 5
Marx and Engels in the Communist League

Explaining the reason which led him and Marx to enter the League of the Just in February 1847,[1] Engels argues as follows:

> Should we enter, we would be given an opportunity of expounding our critical communism before a congress of the League in a manifesto which would then be published as the Manifesto of the League, and likewise we would be able to contribute our quota towards the replacement of the obsolete League organisation by one in keeping with the new times and aims.[2]

Hence, no doubt remains as regards the reason for Marx and Engels' final decision to enter the League; they sought to diffuse their own theory within the ranks of a proletarian vanguard organisation. The indirect influence, exerted up to that time on the leaders of the League, seemed no longer sufficient. Marx and Engels' direct participation in the organisation's activities proves to be a necessary condition for shaping proletarian theory and practice on the ground of their own 'critical communism'. In other words, intellectual and, ultimately, political leadership cannot be achieved without sharing common organisational experience with the other leading members of the League. This means that the model of the philosopher/intellectual-adviser is no longer effective. Marx and Engels enter the League of the Just not to give advice, but to fight in

---

[1] For Marx and Engels's entrance and participation in the League of the Just, see B. Nicolaievsky and O. Maenchen-Helfen, op. cit., p.129 ff.
[2] F. Engels, *The History of the Communist League*, p.15.

order to make the communists endorse their own views and extend their influence on the great majority of the proletariat.

It was, indeed, in the lines of the 'Manifesto of the Communist Party', i.e. the manifesto of the League of the Just, already reorganised and renamed 'Communist League', that Marx and Engels jointly defend the following thesis;

> The Communists, therefore, are on the one hand, practically the most advanced and resolute sections of the working-class parties of every country, the section which pushes forward all others; on the other hand, theoretically, they have over the great mass of the proletariat the advantage of clearly understanding the line of march, the conditions, and the ultimate general results of the proletarian movement.[3]

From this point of view, the communists, either workers or intellectuals, are confronted as the members of a political vanguard, the revolutionary role of which can no longer be reduced to 'merely showing the world what it is really fighting for'. In this case, however, the following question seems quite natural: where does this theoretical advantage of communists over the great majority of the proletariat come from? What is the ground for this superiority of communists over the great mass of the workers? Marx and Engels' hint seems rather evident; critical communism or the knowledge of the materialist conception of history, as conceived by Marx and Engels themselves, places the communists to this distinguished position within the proletarian movement. Given such an explanation, the theoretical and, ultimately, the political guiding role of radical intellectuals, such as Marx and Engels themselves, within the Communist League is hardly refutable indeed.

At this point, therefore, the time has come to discuss more concretely the hypothesis which we have already formulated as follows: so long as the scientific knowledge dominates over proletarian spontaneity, intellectuals tend to establish, at least temporarily, their own authority over the proletarians. More concretely, it is worth noting whether such a hypothesis is verified or

---

[3] K. Marx and F. Engels, 'Manifesto of the Communist Party' in K. Marx and F. Engels, *Collected Works*, vol. 6, p.497.

contradicted on the basis of the Communist League's historical experience.

Firstly, and in regard to the above hypothesis, a clarification of the specific historical conditions is necessary. In fact, Marx and Engels' decision to enter the League coincided with the beginning of a revolutionary unrest which was rapidly spread all over Europe. As the eminent historian Namier eloquently points out,

> when in 1847-8 a severe ᐯfinancial crisis set in, widespread unemployment ensued both among artisans and workmen [...]. Here was a plenty of inflammable matter in ramshackle buildings.[4]

It was, therefore, almost self-evident for both Marx and Engels that around 1847-1848 the time had come for the proletarians, especially artisans, together with radical intellectuals, to play their social and political role. Nevertheless, the outcome of the 1848 French Revolution as well as the social and political under-development of the German workers led the two German thinkers and their followers to admit that the proletariat was still too immature to transform the middle and petty bourgeois 1848-1849 revolution into a communist-proletarian one. Hence, they drew the conclusion that proletarian revolutionary perspectives must be conceived through *long-term* planning, within the context of which the publication of the *Neue Rheinische Zeitung* as the *Organ of Democracy* played a central role. On such a tactical ground, however, the conflict between radical intellectuals, like Marx and Engels, on the one hand, and the leaders of the artisans, who defended the need for an *immediate* upheaval, on the other, proved unavoidable. As a matter of fact, Marx's and Engels' controversy first with Andreas Gottschalk and, a little later, with the Willich-Schapper group within the Communist League, a controversy which we are going to deal with right now, may be adequately examined only within the historical context described above.

It was just after his arrival at Cologne in the spring of 1848, that Marx decided to publish the *Neue Rheinische Zeitung,* putting the revolutionary process into a long-term perspective. As a result, the

---

[4] L.B. Namier, '1848: The Revolution of the Intellectuals', *Proceedings at the British Academy* (12 July 1944), Vol. xxx, p.5.

classical dilemma, which was already being noted in Weitling's case, was posed again with immense intensity: education, propaganda and long-term revolutionary planning or an immediate Blanquist-type revolt?

Rejecting Marx's tactics, Andreas Gottschalk, a physician, who was also a leader of the Workers' Union in Cologne, an organisation of which Marx himself became president, proceeds to the following characteristic analysis:

> What is the purpose of such a revolution? Why should we men of the proletariat spill our blood for this? Must we really plunge voluntarily into the purgatory of a decrepit capitalist domination to avoid a medieval hell, as you, sir preacher, proclaim to us, in order to attain from there the nebulous heaven of your communist creed?[5]

Marx's own position, however, which Gottschalk openly attacked, was clear:

> We are certainly the last people [writes Marx] to desire the rule [...]. But we say to the workers and the petty bourgeois: it is better to suffer in modern bourgeois society, which by its industry creates the material means for foundation of a new society that will liberate you all, than to revert to a bygone form of society, which, on the pretext of saving your classes, thrusts the entire nation back into medieval barbarism.[6]

As becomes obvious, therefore, a conflict like the above looks similar to the Weitling/Marx controversy. The common denominator of these critical attacks can be observed in the form of a very simplistic argument: people regarding themselves as being *the* political representatives of the proletariat attack Marx as a typical bourgeois

---

[5] Extract from Gottschalk's attack against Marx in his own journal *Freiheit, Brüderlichkeit, Arbeit* on February 25 1849, as it is written down in B. Nicolaievsky and O. Maenchen-Helfen, p.199.
For a sociological approach to the Marx-Gottschalk controversy, see A.W. Gouldner, op. cit., pp.121-126.

[6] K. Marx, 'Montesquieu LVI', *Neue Rheinische Zeitung* in K. Marx and F. Engels, op. cit., vol. 8. p.266.

intellectual, who ignores or underestimates the miserable life conditions of the workers, asking them to postpone their revolution.[7]

Following Gottschalk himself, bourgeois intellectuals like Marx and Engels 'are not in earnest about the salvation of the oppressed. The distress of the workers, the hunger of the poor have only a scientific doctrinaire interest for them. They are not touched by that which stirs the heart of men.'[8]

As far as this argument is concerned however, we would like to make the following comments: there is no doubt that Marx's positions, in regard to the political strategy and tactics of the proletarian movement, were defended not only by intellectuals but by workers as well. From this point of view, any clear-cut class division among intellectuals, on the one hand, and workers, on the other, within the ranks of the political vanguard organisations of the 1840s looks very arbitrary. Moreover, it ought not to be forgotten that the worker-intellectuals, who played a leading role in organisations like the Communist League, think and act in a way which is quite different from that of the vast majority of the proletariat. Consequently, persons as Weitling and, even more, the physician Andreas Gottschalk himself may be characterised 'proletarians' only in the broadest sense of the word.[9]

Given these remarks, it is self-evident that controversies like these should not be confronted as a social-political conflict between

---

[7] A feeling of mistrust against Marx and other bourgeois intellectuals, especially from the side of the League of the Just, is beyond any doubt; see the interesting remarks, which are included in:
   a) I. Berlin, op. cit., p.119.
   b) B. Nicolaievsky and O. Maenchen-Helfen, op. cit., p.143.

[8] A. Gottschalk, op. cit. in B. Nicolaievsky and O. Maenchen-Helfen, op. cit., p.199.

[9] For a historically documented defence of the thesis, according to which the term 'proletariat', as used during the 1840s, refers to artisans and propertyless intellectuals as well, see the classical analysis: P.H. Noyes, *Organization and Revolution, Working-Class Associations in German Revolutions of 1848–1849*, Princeton, Princeton University Press, 1966, p.9 ff.

It is worth mentioning that, according to an anonymous pamphleteer of the 1848–49 period, 'the intelligentsia and the workers: they are one!' Commenting on this declaration, P.H. Noyes, op. cit., p.22, regards it as typical of the time and adds the following interesting remark: '[A]ctors and artists, for example, both thought of themselves as members of the working class – superior ones to be sure – and petitioned the Frankfurt Assembly to be included in the regulations of the workers' guilds.'

intellectuals and proletarians. Such controversies are more adequately interpreted as clashes between the agents of *different ways of life and existence*, which do not unilaterally correspond with class differences. From this point of view it should be admitted that bourgeois intellectuals like Marx and Engels approach proletarians in a way which is remarkably different from the one followed by Weitling and Gottschalk. As a matter of fact, the *rational* analysis of reality, as well as the scientific interpretation of social dynamics, by which Marx and Engels tried to influence the proletarian movement, are directly opposed to the *emotional* approach adopted by a person like Gottschalk who, working and living as a physician, came face to face with poor, ill and even dying proletarians.[10]

It was exactly this difference with regard to the question of thought and lifestyle which set off one more conflict between Marx and his followers, on the one hand, and a group of worker-intellectuals, the Willich-Schapper group, on the other. This conflict, which took place within the Communist League, escalated in September 1850 and led finally to the split and dissolution of the League, as declared by Marx on 17 November 1852.[11]

As Nicolaievsky and Maenchen-Helfen suggest,

> Willich's crude revolutionism was bound to appeal to the hungry, desperate workers [...]. Moreover, Willich was closer to them as a man. While Marx, 'scholar' and 'theorist', lived his own life and only came to the Union to lecture, Willich, who had no family, shared in the joys and sorrows of the exiled proletarians. He had created a co-operative society and lived with the workers, ate with them and addressed them all in the

---

[10] It is worth noting that Marx and Engels themselves make comments of this type, while criticising the bohemian way of life of conspirators and the so called *habits-noirs*, people of a certain culture and education, however. (K. Marx and F. Engels, *'Les conspirateurs de la Hobbe, la naissance de la Republique'* in K. Marx and F. Engels, op. cit., vol. 10, p.31 ff).

[11] As regards the end of the Communist League, see the interesting analysis of B. Nicolaievsky and O. Maenchen-Helfen, op. cit., pp.211–240; it should be mentioned as well that, after the dissolution of the League, Marx did not become a member of a secret society ever again. His participation in the conspiratorial *Société Universelle des Communistes Révolutionnaires* is of marginal importance.

familiar second person singular; Marx was respected but Willich was popular.[12]

At this point, it is worth noting that the difference between Marx and Willich, so vividly described above, invites a reconsideration of the differences between the eighteenth century philosopher-educator and the nineteenth century Russian populist intelligentsia, as far as their respective relation with the common people is concerned. Such a reconsideration, however, especially as regards its impact on the intellectual/masses relation, will be discussed in a later chapter in this study. For the time being, Marx's conflict with Willich, Schapper and their group deserves further analysis indeed.[13]

Having the majority of the central office on his side without controlling, however, either the London branch of the Communist League or the London Workers' Educational Association, Marx proposed to the members of the central office a transfer of the head quarters of the organisation to Cologne. His proposal was accepted, but the minority refused to obey and formed a new central office.

As one may assume, however, the reason for the split was much more serious than the one mentioned above. According to the minutes of the crucial meeting of the central office, which took place on September 15 1850, Schapper and his followers regarded the whole conflict as a controversy between intellectuals and proletarians.[14] As a result, Marx was led to explain how he viewed the proletariat and its movement as well.

In his attack on the *voluntaristic* conception of politics, a conception expressed and defended by the Willich-Schapper group, Marx argued as follows:

> The materialist standpoint of the Manifesto has given way to idealism. The revolution is seen not as the product of realities of the situation but as the result of an effort of will. Whereas we say to the workers: You have 15, 20, 50 years of civil war to go through in order

---

[12] B. Nicolaievsky and O. Maenchen-Helfen, op. cit., p.231.
[13] For an interesting, though one-sided, analysis of the conflict, see H. Draper, op. cit., vol. II, pp.550–554.
[14] According to the documented analysis of M. Löwy, op. cit., pp.153–155, the social composition of the Communist League proved well-balanced among intellectuals of liberal profession, on the one hand, artisans and workers, on the other.

to alter the situation and to train yourselves for the exercise of power, it is said: We must take power at once, or else we may as well take to our beds. Just as the democrats abused the word 'people' so now the word 'proletariat' has been used as mere phrase.[15]

On the basis of this analysis, therefore, the following points become clear:

1. The fact that Marx stresses, once again, the need for the scientific foundation and planning of the revolutionary movement. From such a point of view, revolution is a process which accords with the objective tendencies of social reality, the motion of which can be studied and interpreted, first and foremost, by the men of knowledge and especially by bourgeois intellectuals like Marx and Engels themselves.

2. The abuse of the word 'proletariat' by petty bourgeois and worker-intellectuals; this word is used by and attributed to people who are not always proletarians themselves, but appear so in order to attack intellectuals, whose bourgeois class origin is indisputable. Following this kind of polemics, Schapper accepted the split of the League and concluded: '[I]n that case, *there should be two leagues, one for those who work with the pen and one for those who work in other ways.*'[16] (our emphasis)

3. Although Schapper uses the classical weapon, 'intellectuals against non intellectuals', the real antithesis lies elsewhere. This was not a controversy between intellectuals and proletarians. It was rather a conflict between class renegade bourgeois intellectuals and petty bourgeois or worker-intellectuals, who were fighting to gain influence over the whole proletarian class. Both sides mentioned above contain workers in their ranks; however, the working class

---

[15] From the Minutes of the 'Meeting of the Central Authority, September 15, 1850' in K. Marx and F. Engels, op. cit., vol. 10, p.626.

[16] op. cit., p.628; it is worth mentioning, however, that Schapper himself writes in his leading article for the *Kommunistische Zeitschrift* in September 1847: '[P]roletarians in present-day society are all who cannot live on their capital: the worker as well as the man of learning, the artist as well as the small bourgeois [...]' (quoted in H. Draper, op. cit., vol. II, p.552).

is in no way organically connected with any section of the Communist League.[17]

Given such a remark, it is worth noting, at last, the basis upon which Marx founds his own personal relation with the working class:

> *As for a personal sacrifice, I have given up as much as anyone* [argues Marx]; *but for the class and not for individuals.* And as for enthusiasm, not much enthusiasm is needed to belong to a party when you believe that it is on the point of seizing power. *I have always defied the momentary opinions of the proletariat.*[18] (our emphasis)

It is strange to note, indeed, that Marx, an intellectual who tried so hard to supply the proletarian movement with a scientific theory, is talking about a 'personal sacrifice' for the proletarian cause. Such an appeal to the philosopher's moral duty recalls Kant's portrait of philosopher, as well as Fichte's definition of the scholar as *a priest of truth* devoted to educate humanity despite and against any obstacle he (or she) may find in his (or her) way. On the other hand, Marx and Engels, following Rousseau and Fichte's position on this particular issue, do not understand 'personal sacrifice' as a synonym for the educator's self-subjugation to the masses' instincts. The 'momentary opinions of the proletariat' are never a guide for action; on the contrary, it is the radical intellectual's duty to cultivate the proletariat's social instinct in order to reorientate its practice towards the world's transformation. From this point of view, the philosopher-educators, though sensitive receivers of the masses' spontaneous will, must also be active transformers of the people's will and consciousness as well. That is why science and, more concretely, the materialist conception of history is, according to Marx and Engels,

---

[17] According to Noyes's analysis, 'radical and socialist theories were such discussed, but mainly among the intellectuals, and middle-class, young Hegelians; *working-class understanding of these theories was minimal – class support was marginal.*' (Our emphasis – Noyes, op. cit., p.36). Especially in Germany, as Noyes, op. cit., p.41, argues, Weitling's theories were still more influential among the workers than those of Marx.

[18] From the Minutes of the 'Meeting of the Central Authority. September 15, 1850', op. cit., p.628.

the only efficient means by which revolutionary strategy and tactics can be constructed.

At this point, the *aristodemocratic* role of philosophers becomes evident; aristocratic leadership, in the strict sense of the term, with the approval of the masses proves to be Marx and Engels' choice. The philosophers ought not to confine themselves to the interpretation of the world; they must participate actively in the radical changing of the world. The philosopher-adviser or the philosopher-educator is led to act as a lawgiver or, even more, as an agitator in order to convince the masses to follow the path that scientific analysis suggests for the final conquest of revolution.

In fact, Marx and Engels tried to act as true lawgivers within the Communist League by shaping the political theoretical 'Manifesto' of the organisation. Whether they regretted playing the role of the philosopher-lawgiver remains an open question; nevertheless, the role of the philosopher-agitator, the intellectual origins of which may be easily recognised, for example, in Voltaire and the young Fichte's political theory, proved to be quite unsuitable for both of them. As their own correspondence clearly shows, political agitation within a vanguard organisation like the Communist League was not a task for them. Consequently, their own union with the proletarians – Marx and Engels seem to agree – should not be mediated by 'party' leaders like those they met up to that time.

> At long last we again [writes Engels] have the opportunity [...] to show we need neither popularity, nor the SUPPORT of any party in any country, and that our position is completely independent of such ludicrous trifles. From now on we are only answerable for ourselves and, come the time when these gentry need us, we shall be in a position *to dictate our own terms* [...]. How can people like us, who shun official appointments like the plague, fit into a party?'[19] (our emphasis)

---

[19] F. Engels, 'Letter to Marx', 13 February 1851 in K. Marx and F. Engels, *Collected Works*, vol. 38, p.289, in response to Marx's 'Letter to Engels', 12 February 1851, op. cit., p.286, in which Marx argues as follows: '[I] am greatly pleased by the public authentic isolation in which we two, you and I, now find ourselves. It is wholly in accord with our attitude and our principles. The system of mutual concessions, half measures tolerated for decency's sake, and the

Is this a declaration of withdrawal from the 'dirty field' of politics? Not at all. It is just a brief interval or rather a change of direction. From the moment they agreed that the crux of the matter is not just the interpretation, but the transformation of the world, intellectuals like Marx and Engels could but remain deeply involved in political activity. They could only change their 'masks', i.e. their roles, when they were ready to 'dictate their own terms' to the 'party' leaders of the proletariat.

At this point, however, a methodological reassessment of the way Marx and Engels faced the intellectual/proletarian relation from the first steps of their career up to the dissolution of the Communist League is necessary, since it will give us the opportunity to reach some significant conclusions which will be crucial for the next part of this study.

---

obligation to beat one's share of public ridicule in the party along with all these jackasses, all this is now over.'

Chapter 6
Proletarian Self-Emancipation or Intellectual Elitism? A Critical Reconsideration

It was the confrontation of the intellectual/proletarian relation within the context of the nineteenth century working class' movement, which has led a significant number of political theorists, such as Feuer, Avineri and Gouldner to suggest, that Marxism is actually a bourgeois intellectuals' ideology, which tends to conceal the intellectuals' domination of the proletariat itself.

To give just an example of the way this argument reads, Alvin Gouldner's remarks seem eloquent indeed:

> The Communists have nothing to hide said *Communist Manifesto*. Nothing but the fact that they were bourgeois intellectuals.[1]

And he continues by raising the crucial question:

> [H]ow can the working class submit itself to the tutelage of theory without at the same time submitting itself to the authority of theorists and intellectuals, which is dissonant with Marxism's claim that its socialism involves the *self emancipation* of the working-class?[2] (Gouldner's emphasis)

The philosophical and political implications of the argument, so explicitly pointed out by Gouldner, were not of course unknown either to Marx or to Engels. Besides, it is worth noting that the charge of

---

[1] A.W. Gouldner, op. cit., p.7.
[2] op. cit., p.12.

creating a new [political] religion was, more or less, emphatically levelled against the 1840s' communists and especially against Marx himself by thinkers like Stirner, Proudhon and Bakunin. From this point of view, Proudhon's refusal to participate in the Communist Correspondence Committee, organised by Marx in Brussels around the beginning of 1846 requires a special reference. Actually, the French anarchist was still afraid that a new religion may be created in the name of Reason, as a result of Marx's own attempt to form an international communist vanguard.[3] Unfortunately, however, neither Marx, nor Engels seem to take such an argument into serious consideration.

It was by taking advantage of this undoubted underestimation of the whole issue by both Marx and Engels, that Lewis Feuer suggests, therefore, an interesting, though one-sided reformulation of the intellectual question within the frame of Marxist political theory:

> It is a remarkable fact [says Feuer] that Marx and Engels provided no theory of the intellectual class. Why do intellectuals join the socialist movement? To this question Marx and Engels had a parenthetical reply in a brief sentence in *the Communist Manifesto* [...]. As far as intellectuals are concerned, in other words, it affirms that existence does not determine consciousness, but that rather theoretical consciousness determines existence. The revolutionary intellectual evidently then stands with Promethean exceptionalism against the whole materialist conception [...]. This was the dilemma that the intellectual class posed for Marx's sociology: either historical materialism was false or the advent of a new class society was likely. Marx and Engels met this dilemma by choosing not to discuss it.[4]

---

[3] For Marx's correspondence with Proudhon, as regards this particular issue, see B. Nicolaievsky and O. Maenchen-Helfen, op. cit., pp.122–123. Proudhon's answer to Marx is included in P. Ansart (ed.), *Proudhon, textes et débats*, Librairie Générale Française, 1984, pp.56–60.

[4] L.S. Feuer, 'Marxism and the Hegemony of the Intellectual Class', in L.S. Feuer, op. cit., pp.53–54.

Consequently, the main argument, raised against Marx and Engels by thinkers like Feuer, Gouldner and others, may be formulated as follows:

Marxism, being itself constructed by bourgeois intellectuals, provides no answer as regards the intellectuals' role in the socialist movement. Actually, the revolutionary class-renegade intellectuals express and promote their own social interests and not the class interests of the proletariat. As a result, Marx's theory is merely an ideology – in the negative sense of the term – which functioned as an effective means of establishing intellectual domination over the proletarians themselves. From such a point of view, proletarian self-emancipation – conclude the supporters of the argument – proved to be just a motto, which masked the intellectuals' elitist intentions. The time has, however, come to reassess the crux of the whole matter, as clearly expressed in the positions noted above.

First of all, there is no doubt that the materialist conception of history was constructed by bourgeois intellectuals; it is a self-evident historical fact that Marx, as well as the members of his cultural milieu, under the influence of which he created his own social and political theory, may be characterised – up to a certain degree – as bourgeois. Nevertheless, one ought not to underestimate the fact that the foundation of 'critical communism', following Engels' terminology, became possible not through a mere theoretical contemplation, but only after Marx and Engels came in contact with the proletarians living in Paris, London and elsewhere.

It is also beyond doubt that Marx and Engels did not work out a cohesive theoretical approach to the intellectuals' relation with the proletarian movement. As a matter of fact, it may be argued that the lack of such an approach was the indirect outcome of the fact that both of them, at least in the beginning of their career, tried to *minimise* their own role in the formation of revolutionary ideas. Moreover, it is worth remembering that this [already mentioned and discussed] minimalistic tendency was a reaction against the Young Hegelian elitism and the utopian 'ready-made' systems as well.[5]

---

[5] From this point of view, it is worth pointing out Engels' following remark: 'The people, once thinking for themselves, freed from the old socialist tradition, will soon find socialist and revolutionary formulas which shall express their wants and interests for more clearly than anything invented *for them* by authors of systems and by declaiming leaders. And then, arrived thus at maturity, the people will

On the other hand, it seems quite arbitrary to argue that Marx and Engels hide the fact that Communists are bourgeois intellectuals. Firstly, such an argument, openly declared by Gouldner, does not fully correspond to historical reality, since the communist political vanguard itself was not exclusively composed of bourgeois intellectuals; as it has been shown, artisans, and especially worker-intellectuals, represent a significant number among the members of the communist organisations. Furthermore, even these scanty references to the issue, made by Marx and Engels, may prove to be an adequate introductory approach to the problem.

At this point, it is useful to refer, for example, to Marx and Engels' position on the bourgeois intellectuals' social role, which Feuer hastened to characterise as a 'parenthetical reply'.

> Finally [argue Marx and Engels], in times when the class struggle nears the decisive hour, the process of dissolution going on within the ruling class, in fact within the whole range of the society, assumes such a violent, glaring character, that a small section of the ruling class cuts itself adrift and joins the revolutionary class, the class that holds the future in its hands. Just as, therefore, at an earlier period, a section of the nobility went over to the bourgeoisie, so now a portion of the bourgeoisie goes over the proletariat, and in particular, a portion of the bourgeois ideologists, who have raised themselves to the level of comprehending theoretically the historical movement as a whole.[6]

The clarity of this formulation leaves no doubt that Marx and Engels recognised themselves as members of this small section of the bourgeois ideologists who went over the proletarian movement.[7]

---

again be enabled to avail themselves of whatever talent and courage may be found among the old leaders, without becoming the tail of any of them.' (Engels' emphasis – F. Engels, 'Letters from France' in K. Marx and F. Engels, *Collected Works*, vol. 10, p.35).

[6] K. Marx and F. Engels, 'Manifesto of the Communist Party', op. cit., p.494; this social phenomenon, however, has been described for the first time in K. Marx and F. Engels, 'The German Ideology', op. cit., p.52.

[7] In his remarkable article 'The Formation of the Marxian Revolutionary Idea', *The Review of Politics*, July 1950, vol. 12, No. 3, p.298, Eric Voegelin reaches the following conclusion: 'Thus, we have finally arrived at Marx and Engels

Nevertheless, they continue to minimise the importance of the intellectuals' social and, ultimately, political activity.[8] More specifically, Marx and Engels underestimate the significance of the class-renegade intellectuals' participation within the communist vanguard organisation. Undoubtedly, they are both bypassing the fact that the proletariat becomes conscious of its role not only due to the impact of its life conditions, but through the concrete analysis of the capitalist society as well, an analysis which is initially provided by bourgeois intellectuals like Marx and Engels.

It is exactly at this point that the crucial methodological question arises, as regards the compatibility of Marx and Engels' approach to class renegade intellectuals with their own theory of ideology.

According to Gouldner,

> this is one of the major reasons for Marxism's silence and confusion about the role of the revolutionary intellectual. It cannot deal with the question of their middle-class origins without contradicting itself: the revolutionary intellectual is either (1) just another interest-pursuing egoist, and his revolutionary commitment and theory are therefore a disguise for that interest or (2) he is truly an idealist who can transcend his interest. In the first case, revolutionary theory and Marxism itself become another 'false consciousness' that can make no superior claim to truth or loyalty; in the second case, the facts acknowledged contradict the materialism premised by Marxist theory.[9]

---

themselves, the bourgeois ideologists who can tell the proletarians what the historical process is all about and provide *intellectual* leadership in their capacity as organisers of the Communism Party,' (our emphasis); nevertheless, Voegelin, supporting a quite 'orthodox' approach to Marx's position, avoids mentioning and discussing the transformation of the bourgeois ideologists' *intellectual* leadership to a political one.

[8] Contrary to Marx and Engels, Auguste Blanqui explicitly declares and defends the leading role of bourgeois class-renegade intellectuals over the proletarians themselves during the transitional phase of the revolution. (See A. Blanqui, 'Letter to Maillard', June 6 1852 in A. Blanqui, *Textes choisis*, V.P. Volguine (ed.), Paris, Editions Sociales, p.127–140.).

[9] A.W. Gouldner, op. cit., p.33.

As it becomes obvious, therefore, Gouldner's position as well as Feuer's reference, a few decades earlier, to the *Promethean exceptionalism* of the revolutionary intellectual, invites a direct reconsideration of the following question: are these class-renegade intellectuals really exempt from the historical materialist thesis, according to which 'it is not the consciousness of men that determines their being, but, on the contrary, their social being that determines their consciousness!'?[10]

First of all, it must be mentioned that, as regards this crucial question, Marx does not remain as silent as Gouldner seems to believe. Taking advantage of the historical example of the French Revolution, Marx himself argues as follows:

> It is perfectly 'possible' that what individual persons do is not 'always' determined by the class to which they belong, although this is no more crucial to the class struggle than an aristocrat going over the tiers-état was crucial to the French Revolution. And then these aristocrats at least joined a specific class, the revolutionary class, the bourgeoisie.[11]

Consequently, Marx is fully conscious of the social and, ultimately, political phenomenon, which we are dealing with here.[12] Nevertheless, he still insists that such a phenomenon is of marginal importance for the evolution and the final outcome of the class struggle. As a result, he sees no problem with regard to the macro-social validity of the 'being-consciousness' relation, as this is conceived and defended by him and Engels within the materialist analysis of history.

At this point, however, it is necessary to draw the following preliminary conclusion: Instead of confronting the sociological origin and the political repercussion of their own participation in the proletarian movement, Marx and Engels chose to undervalue the role of class-renegade intellectuals in the revolutionary process as such.

---

[10] K. Marx, 'Preface to A Contribution to the Critique of Political Economy' in K. Marx and F. Engels, *Selected Works*, vol. I, p.356.

[11] K. Marx, 'Moralising Criticism and Critical Morality' in K. Marx and F. Engels, *Collected Works*, vol. 6, p.330.

[12] See Draper's presentation of the issue under the title 'The exceptional cases' in H. Draper, op. cit., vol. II, pp.507–510.

Hence, contrary to what Feuer, Gouldner and other political theorists say, Marxism should not be criticised as an ideology which promotes bourgeois intellectuals' social interests, but as a social and political theory which avoids dealing directly with those interests, and even more with their articulation within the proletarian movement.

It is, of course, beyond any doubt that the recognition of such a crucial gap within the corpus of Marxist political theory does not mean that Marxism itself cannot deal with it. On the other hand, it should be mentioned that efforts to fill this gap by deriving arguments from other theoretical currents, such as Mannheim's sociology of knowledge and his own conception of the 'free-floating intelligentsia', have proved to be incompatible with the methodological content of Marxist political theory and its theory of ideology as well.

From such a point of view, it is worth referring, for example, to Avineri's theoretical attempt; according to the well-known Marxologist,

> Marx never maintained that a person's economic situation alone determines his consciousness, as some of the more vulgar interpretations of Marx's ideas seem to imply [...]. The intellectuals are a social group determined as such by society to possess the individual power of choice [...]. There is no *a priori* determination, as in the case of the capitalist or the worker. Choice is the very embodiment of the intellectual's determined 'social being'.[13]

Without underestimating, however, Avineri's effort to distinguish between crude economism and Marx's theoretical position on this specific issue, it is self-evident that this extremely loose interpretation, grounded on the subjective concept of 'choice', turns out to be incompatible with the materialist conception of history and is much

---

[13] S. Avineri, 'Marx and the intellectuals', *Journal of the History of Ideas*, April–June 1967, vol. XXVIII, pp.276–277; see also a similar, though much more recent, analysis in B. Parekh, *Marx's Theory of Ideology* (London, Croom Helm, 1982), within which Parekh argues as follows: 'Marx could not simply take over and theoretically justify the opinions of the proletariat, for these are all derived from the ideologically constituted social world, and necessarily "vulgar" [...]. One must therefore criticise them and decide which of them are socialist. This presupposes a standard which cannot itself be derived from them.' (op. cit., p.174). Within such an analysis, Marx is viewed as a 'free-floating' intellectual.

more like Mannheim's theory of ideology. Nevertheless, from our point of view, the question whether or not Marx's social and political theory is able to deal with the intellectual issue *by its own theoretical resources alone* still remains open.

A fruitful research as regards the question above should start with the Marxist conception of the social division of labour.[14] Hence, according to Marx and Engels, intellectual and material activity being promoted by different social agents, 'the only possibility of their not coming into contradiction lies in negating in its turn the division of labour.'[15] Such a perspective, however, may be fulfilled only within the classless (communist) society; in a class society the division of labour remains determinant and produces interesting results even within the social classes themselves.[16]

In relation to this point, it is important to note that, following Marx and Engels' analysis, the ruling class is divided among its thinkers-ideologists, on the one hand, and the rest of its members, on the other. It is this group of ideologists composed by individuals belonging to the ruling class, which 'make[s] the formation of the illusions of the class about itself [its] chief source of livelihood'.[17] In the case of the revolutionary class, however, such a division is silently bypassed by both Marx and Engels. Although they believe that 'the existence of revolutionary ideas in a particular period presupposes the existence of a revolutionary class',[18] they avoid arguing that the revolutionary class or, rather, a group within it creates the revolutionary ideas through its own activities. This means that there is a crucial *asymmetry* in the way Marx and Engels approach the social and, ultimately, the political effects of the division of labour within the ruling and the revolutionary class respectively.[19]

The recognition of this asymmetry verifies, once again, Marx and Engels' constant tendency to undervalue the social and political role of class-renegade intellectuals. One more example of such a meaningful

---

[14] For a critical approach to the question, grounded on Marx's theory of ideology, see the interesting analysis of D.W. Lovell, op. cit., pp.131-147.
[15] K. Marx and F. Engels, 'The German Ideology', op. cit., p.45.
[16] op. cit., pp.59-60.
[17] op. cit., p.60.
[18] ibid.
[19] *Contra* Löwy, op. cit., pp.132-133.

omission may be noticed in Marx's well-known *Eleventh Thesis on Feuerbach:*

> The philosophers have only interpreted the world in various ways; the point is to *change* it.[20] (Marx's emphasis)

It is exactly the impersonal character of the second part of this thesis which binders an overall answer to the question of the revolutionary subject of the world's transformation. Actually, Marx and Engels' belief in the proletariat's self-transformative capacities does not mean of course that philosophers are excluded from or marginalised within the revolutionary process. Nevertheless, their role still remains indeterminate.

Even Marx's remark, according to which the political and literary representatives of a class do not go beyond the limits which the class itself confronts in life,[21] does not seem appropriate enough to give a convincing answer to the bourgeois intellectual's relation with the proletarians. On the contrary, revolutionary intellectuals, according to Marx's personal example, not only have the possibility, but they ought to surpass those limits set by the proletariat's 'momentary opinions'.

Thus, it can be argued that the intellectual/proletarian relation should be approached according to the following methodological principles, which are compatible, in the last analysis, with the materialist conception of history, though not systematically worked out by Marx and Engels themselves.

1. Although class-renegade intellectuals may be relatively autonomous as regards the formation of their personal consciousness and practice, they, nevertheless, conceive the revolutionary ideas as such not *ex nihilo,* but within concrete social/historical conditions. That is why Marx and Engels argued that the revolutionary ideas presuppose the existence of a revolutionary class.

2. From such a point of view, and especially with regard to the revolutionary class, a methodological distinction should be made between the *historical creators* of the revolutionary ideas, on the one hand, and the *social agents* of those ideas in revolutionary

---

[20] According to Marx's original version.
[21] See K. Marx, 'The Eighteenth Brumaire of Louis Bonaparte' in K. Marx and F. Engels, *Collected Works*, vol. 11, pp.130–131.

practice itself, on the other. As regards the proletariat, such a distinction is not a matter of *internal* division of labour, but it is actually a problem of an *organic unity between bourgeois intellectuals and proletarians*.

3. This organic unity of revolutionary (class-renegade) intellectuals and proletarians should not be seen as an *a priori* fact, but as a goal, the achievement of which depends upon a fruitful combination of objective and subjective conditions.

4. Within the framework of a classical Marxist methodology, the notion of organic unity [explicitly illustrated, for example, in the highly debatable 'base-superstructure' model] denotes two specific functions: *interaction and determination.* From such a point of view, the organic unity of revolutionary intellectuals and proletarians indicates not only the interaction among the two poles of the relation, but also the fact that one of them is finally determinant.

Consequently, if it is argued that, according to Marx, revolutionary intellectuals play the determinant role, the way seems open for those who argue that the German philosopher was thinking and acting as an *intellectual elitist.* If it is argued, however, that, according to Marx, proletarians ultimately determine the revolutionary process, the way is open for those who believe that Marx's theoretical and practical confrontation of the intellectual/proletarian relation is a defence of the working class' *self*-emancipation.

From our own point of view – given the fragmentary formulation of these methodological principles within the field of the Marxist political theory – such a complicated problem as the intellectual/proletarian relation cannot be adequately conceived and discussed on the basis of an *either/or* logic. The classical dilemma, proletarian self-emancipation or intellectual elitism, proves quite inadequate in the long run to give a definite answer to the question of Marx and Engels' relationship *qua* philosopher-intellectuals with the proletarian movement of their time.

The complex character of the whole issue – actually inconceivable on the ground of the *either/or* logic – becomes even more evident, when we consider the fact that both Marx and Engels, though arguing in favour of the self-emancipatory capacities of the proletariat, enjoy at the same time a feeling of indisputable intellectual superiority over the political leaders of proletarian organisations. It is just this feeling of intellectual superiority [so vividly expressed for example in Marx's controversy with Weitling] that is explicitly pointed out in Engels' letters as well, either to the Communist Correspondence Committee or to Marx personally.[22]

Nevertheless, such a superiority, founded on and fed by the privilege of knowledge, which was often attributed to Marx and Engels even by leading members of the communist organisations, should not be confused with elitism; the feeling of contempt, whenever expressed by both German intellectuals is constantly levelled against concrete proletarians and not against the proletarian class as a whole.[23] There is no doubt, of course, that such a distinction is not so simple to make in practice, as it may appear in theory; furthermore, it must be admitted that intellectual superiority which Marx and Engels enjoyed over the proletarians of their time was not always so easy to keep under control.

From this point of view, a brief extract from a letter of Engels to Marx seems rather telling. Referring to the process of approval of the draft programme of the Communist League by its local communities, Engels argues as follows:

> *Strictly between ourselves,* I've played an infernal trick on Mosi [Moses Hess]. He had actually put through a delightfully amended confession of faith. Last Friday at the district I dealt with this, point by point, and was not yet half way through when the lads declared themselves *satisfaits. Completely unopposed,* I got them to entrust me with the task of drafting a new one which will be discussed next Friday by the district and will be sent to London *behind the backs of the communities.* Naturally

---

[22] See for example:
    a) F. Engels, 'Letter to the Communist Correspondence Committee', 16 September 1846 in K. Marx and F. Engels, *Collected Works*, vol. 38, pp.61–67.
    b) F. Engels, 'Letter to the Communist Correspondence Committee', 23 October 1846, op. cit., pp.81–86.
    c) F. Engels, 'Letter to Marx', Middle of November–December 1846, op. cit., pp.89–94.
    d) F. Engels, 'Letter to Marx', 13 March 1852, op. cit., vol. 39, pp.66–69.

[23] Such a confusion is self-evident in S. Avineri, op. cit., p.257.

not a soul must know about this, otherwise we shall all be unseated and there'll be the deuce of a row.[24] (Engels' emphasis)

As it becomes obvious, therefore, from this characteristic extract, Marx and Engels, being directly involved in the life of a political organisation like the Communist League, were often led to endorse a highly *instrumentalist* and *manipulative* practice with regard to the organisation and its leaders. For both, the League seems to represent, in fact, a promising instrument, through the use of which they might exert a more effective influence on the working class of their time. Nevertheless, it is worth insisting that it is arbitrary, indeed, to reach a conclusion concerning Marx and Engels' approach to the working class by deriving arguments exclusively from the way they confronted proletarian leaders like Weitling, Schapper, Willich and others. In any case, taking note of Marx and Engels' activity in the proletarian movement of the 1840s, the following argument can be supported: since the choice between proletarian self-emancipation and intellectual elitism does not constitute an answer to the complicated and multiform problem we are here dealing with, it is preferable to direct this research towards the investigation of the *aristodemocratic* version of the intellectual/people relation, as has already been noted and defined in the introductory chapter of this study. It is exactly the aristodemocratic type of leadership, in contrast to the elitist/quasi-dictatorial and the ultra-libertarian models of governing, which best links the intellectual vanguard's activity with proletarian instinct, preparing in this way the ground for the working class' self-emancipation.

Within such a framework of analysis, therefore, the following conclusions may be reached as far as Marx and Engels' aristodemocratic relation with the proletarian movement of the 1840s is concerned.

From the early 1840s indeed until the dissolution of the Communist League, Marx and Engels acted as philosopher-interpreters. As has already been mentioned, however, contrary to Hegel's *retrospective* approach to the role of philosophy in world history, Marx and Engels never accepted that (radical) philosophers come on the scene too late. According to them, the

---

[24] F. Engels, 'Letter to Marx', 25-26 October 1847, op. cit., vol. 38, pp.138-139.

philosophical interpretation of past and present social reality is not an end-in-itself, but a guide for action. As a matter of fact, Marx and Engels, while acting as philosopher-interpreters, refused to confine themselves to the critique of what has been done already; they extended their theoretical activity to the analysis of the way social process unfolds in order to play a crucial role in the revolutionary transformation of the world.

It was exactly the need to transmit the outcome of their social and political critique to the masses, and especially to the workers, which caused intellectuals like Marx and Engels to appear on the scene of history as philosopher-educators. At this point, it is worth noting that despite the variety of roles, which undoubtedly characterises Marx and Engels' participation in the proletarian movement, their bilateral interpretative-educational activity constantly accounts for their commitment to the revolutionary cause.

On the other hand, it is worth remembering that Marx's conception of education is quite different from any kind of elitist approach to the educational process, given the fact that as he himself suggests by his *Third Thesis on Feuerbach*, 'the educator must himself be educated'. In other words, following Istvan Mészáros' interesting comment,

> education [according to Marx] is an inherently personal, internal matter: nobody can educate us without our own active participation in the process. The good educator is one who *inspires self educating*.[25] (Mészáros emphasis)

The fact, however, that Marx and Engels definitely reject any authoritarian and elitist conception of education does not necessarily lead to the conclusion that the proletariat can be educated by its own forces alone. At this point, the social and, ultimately, the political asymmetry produced by the class diffusion of knowledge turns out to be decisive for the intellectual/proletarian relation. As a matter of fact, interaction between philosophers and proletarians should be conceived in relationship to the concept of *determination* as defined by the Marxist political methodology. In other words, the

---

[25] I. Mészáros, op. cit., p.184; a similar argument can be noticed in the following works:
  a) H. Draper, 'The Principle of Self-Emancipation in Marx and Engels', *The Socialist Register 1971*, pp.95–96.
  b) M. Löwy. op. cit., pp.122–123.

philosopher-educator, though in continuous interaction with the proletariat, does not stop acting in the last analysis as the *leading* agent of the whole process.

At this point it is worth mentioning Rubel's inspiring remark, referring to the role of the bourgeois class-renegade intellectuals:

> They join the proletariat [argues Rubel] adopt its needs and its interests as their own, and assume the role of Socratic educators who teach the working men to think for themselves.[26]

Was actually Marx himself a Socratic educator, as Rubel suggests? Even from this point of view, it seems true that the philosopher-educator functions, at least temporarily, as the real guide of his (her) students. Even Socrates, who did not want to be a teacher himself, acted as a teacher coming in direct contact with his fellow citizens, while never missing the opportunity to make them know how to liberate themselves. Thus, while in constant interaction with the Athenian citizens, the ancient Greek philosopher played a guiding role within the educational process itself. For his own part, Marx does not represent an exception to the rule. For him and for Engels self-emancipation cannot be spontaneously achieved; a certain kind of intellectual guidance is, at least transitionally, necessary. The aristodemocratic way, however, by which this intellectual guidance should be promoted in order not to degenerate to any sort of intellectual elitism or vulgar workerism, remains a real challenge for the philosopher-educator.

In conclusion, it can be argued that, given their standard theoretical activities of interpretation and education, class renegade intellectuals often tended to vacillate over whether to cross the Rubicon of political practice or not. Actually, Marx and Engels took this decision, when entering the League of the Just in 1847. It was in this particular organisation that they both acted as philosopher-lawgivers and philosopher-governors through their leading participation in the central authority of the League, which we have already discussed. Did, however, Marx and Engels succumb to the temptation of forming a new political religion as Jean-Jacques

---

[26] M. Rubel, 'Socialism and Ethics' in *Rubel on Karl Marx, Five Essays*, J. O'Malley and K. Algozin (eds and trans.), Cambridge, Cambridge University Press, 1981, p.68; see also, M. Rubel, op. cit., pp.30–33.

Rousseau suggested that his Lawgiver should do? Did they even try to do so, as Pierre Joseph Proudhon suspected? It is beyond any doubt that the Communist League period proved too short to provide us with definite answers to these questions. Moreover, it must be noted that, just after the dissolution of the League, both Marx and Engels chose to withdraw from any sort of political organisation and to confine themselves to their theoretical activity *qua* philosopher-interpreters and philosopher-educators. It was about twelve years later that they came back to the field of political praxis by taking part in the International Working Men's Association. Hence, they were led to confront once again, though under different circumstances, the challenging question of their own relation as intellectuals with the proletarian movement itself.

PART II

Intellectuals and Proletarians in the International Working Men's Association

Chapter 7
Marx, Engels and the International – Motives and Tactics

It was in September 1864 that Marx and Engels' 'sleepless night of exile' – as Nicolaievsky and Maenchen-Helfen magnificently described it[1] – was actually over. After more than ten years of abstention from any kind of political activity, they both decided to take part once again in the proletarian movement of their time. The role of the philosopher-interpreter, as well as the role of the philosopher-educator, who confines himself (or herself) to the narrow limits of his (or her) scientific duties proved to be quite inadequate for radical intellectuals like Marx and Engels themselves.

> A certain Le Lubez [Marx writes to Engels] was sent to ask me if I would participate pour les ouvriers allemands, and, in particular, whether I was willing to provide a German worker to speak on the meeting. I provided them with Eccarius, who put on a splendid performance, and I was also present myself in a non-speaking capacity on the PLATFORM. I knew that on this occasion people 'who really count' were appearing, both from London and from Paris and I therefore decided to waive my usual standing rule to DECLINE ANY SUCH INVITATIONS.[2] (Marx's emphasis)

As it becomes obvious, therefore, the participation of 'people who really count' in the founding process of the International Working Men's Association exerted a special influence on Marx and Engels'

---

[1] B. Nicolaievsky and O. Maenchen-Helfen, op. cit., p.276 ff.
[2] K. Marx, 'Letter to Engels', 4 November 1864 in K. Marx and F. Engels, op. cit., vol. 42, pp.15–16.

final decision to change their mind. According to Engels, there are people, *'who at least represent their class,* which is what really matters ultimately'.³ (our emphasis)

Needless to say, of course, that the concept of 'representation' as such, being highly problematic, deserves a separate analysis. For the time being, however, it is worth noting that the so-called First International was, in the main, an organisation of radical artisans, more or less seriously affected by the capitalist development.⁴ Besides, it should be stated that the committee, which assumed the responsibility for the programme and the statutes of the International, though politically heterogeneous, was quite homogeneous as regards the social origin of its members, since most of them were artisans, i.e. workers in the broadest sense of the term.⁵ As a result, Marx – a member of the committee himself – was led to act, once again, as a lonely intellectual among proletarians, who aimed at the defence and exclusive promotion of their own social and political interests.⁶

At this point, therefore, we should proceed to a critical presentation and evaluation of the deeper motive which pushed, Marx (and Engels) to yield again to the 'wordly Siren' of politics, especially during the founding period of the International.

It was on 18 October 1864, during the first meeting of the leading committee, that Marx took note, once more, of the gap which divided

---

[3] F. Engels, 'Letter to Marx', 7 November 1864 in K. Marx and F. Engels, op. cit., vol. 42, p.20.

[4] According to Paul Thomas, (*Karl Marx and the Anarchists*, London, Routledge and Kegan Paul, 1980, p.256), the International was a working-class organisation, although 'in mining, engineering and heavy industry generally, its strength was small or non-existent.'

In a similar way Gouldner in *Against Fragmentation*, p.143, argues as follows: 'In short, while the I.W.A. spoke to and on behalf of the working class and proletariat, it was, once again, another organisation largely created by artisans.'

Finally, David W. Lovell in his *Marx's Proletariat: The Making of a Myth*, op. cit., pp.170–171, draws his arguments from Collins and Abramsky's classic analysis of the British labour movement and suggests that: 'those trade unions which were represented in the International, and which were protected by it, did not truly represent the industrial working class.'

[5] B. Nicolaievsky and O. Maenchen-Helfen, op. cit., p.281.

[6] It is worth noting how Marx describes his own relation with the other members of the leading committee in letter to Engels, 14 November 1864 in K. Marx and F. Engels, op. cit., vol. 42, p.22: 'You will receive the "ADDRESS" along with the "Provisional Rules" [Marx wrote to Engels], in a few days. The thing was not quite so difficult as you think, because we are dealing with "workers" all the time'.

his own conception of the working class from the ideas of its actual representatives. That is how he himself describes his shocking experience to Engels:

> I went along and was really shocked when I heard the worthy Le Lubez read out a fearfully cliché-ridden, badly written and totally unpolished preamble PRETENDING TO BE A DÉCLARATION OF PRINCIPLES [...]. I was absolutely determined that NOT ONE SINGLE LINE of the stuff should be allowed to stand if I could help it [...]. I altered the whole preamble, threw out the déclaration des principes and finally replaced the 40 RULES by 10 [...]. It was very difficult to frame the thing so that our view should appear ACCEPTABLE to the present outlook of the workers' movement [...]. We must be *fortiter in re, suaviter in modo*.'[7] (Marx's emphasis)

In other words, the aristodemocrat philosopher-lawgiver of the political vanguard organisation tried to express his positions in the *language* of the common people, without proceeding, however, to any compromise as regards the content of his ideas. From this point of view, it can be argued indeed that the International's intellectual-legislator benefits, up to a certain degree, from Rousseau's instructions to his Lawgiver, as presented in Chapter 7 of Book II of the *Social Contract*: on the other hand, Marx still insists that such a legislator, while making good use of the proletarian class instinct, should never succumb to spontaneity of the masses.

In fact, the International offers the opportunity to both Marx and Engels to 'educate the masses [and] bring them the awareness and theoretical comprehension of that which [they] must do and of the experiences through which [they] must pass'.[8] This is the duty of the philosopher-educator, for whom theory does not mean contemplation, but a special way of acting in order to change the world.

Under such circumstances, therefore, Marx and Engels' motive as regards their own participation in the International becomes evident; as Cole argues, their true motive was:

---

[7] K. Marx, 'Letter to Engels', 4 November 1864 in K. Marx and F. Engels, op. cit., vol. 42, pp.17-18.
[8] B. Nicolaievsky and O. Maenchen-Helfen, op. cit., pp.283-284.

to take the workers' movement as it was and to build up its strength in the day-to-day struggle, in the belief that it could thus be led into the right courses and develop under ideological leadership, a revolutionary outlook arising out of the experience of the struggle of partial reforms, economic and political.[9]

For his part, Marx himself leaves no doubt as regards the real reason, which led him to join the International. Writing to Weydemeyer on 29 November 1664, he proceeds to the following explanation:

> Although I have been systematically refusing to participate in any way whatsoever in all the 'organisations' etc. for years now, I accepted *this time* because it concerns a matter by means of which it is possible to have a significant influence.[10] (Marx's emphasis)

From this point of view, it becomes obvious that, according to Marx's openly declared expectation, the International may function as an effective means – a 'mighty engine' as he himself calls it[11] – for revolutionary intellectuals in their effort to influence the proletarian movement. Given, therefore, this *utilitarian* and *instrumentalist* approach, Marx did not hesitate not only to enter the International, but to play the leading role within its ranks.

Fully convinced of his leading position in the proletarian movement, Marx argues as follows several years after the foundation of the organisation and just a little before Bakunin appeared on its stage:

---

[9] G.D.H. Cole, *A History of Socialist Thought, Marxism and Anarchism, 1850–1890*, London, The Macmillan Press, 1954, vol. II, p.92.

[10] K. Marx, 'Letter to Weydemeyer', 29 November 1864 in K. Marx and F. Engels, *Collected Works*, vol. 42, p.44.

[11] K. Marx, 'Letter to Engels', 11 September 1867 in K. Marx and F. Engels, *Collected Works*, vol. 42, p.424: '*Les choses marchent*. And when the revolution comes, and that will perhaps be sooner than might appear, we (i.e., you and I) will have this mighty ENGINE *at our disposal.*' (Marx's emphasis).

See also Richard Hunt's unsuccessful effort to interpret Marx's use of the expression 'mighty ENGINE *at our disposal*' as follows: 'Although Engels had joined the I.W.A. as an individual member in Manchester, he remained for some time lukewarm and sceptical about its prospects, so that Marx needed to impress his partner with the importance of the organisation.' (R.N. Hunt, *The Political Ideas of Marx and Engels*, London, The Macmillan Press, vol. II, p.272).

Apart from the fact, were I to move away from here at this critical period, the whole working-class movement, which I influence *behind the scenes,* would fall into very bad hands and leave the right track.[12] (our emphasis)

Obviously, the attempt to influence a social movement 'behind the scenes' or to 'work on the masses', according to Engels' own words[13] is not a question for philosophers who confine themselves to the role of advisers. Voltaire's relation with the common people of Geneva, for example, which has been pointed to in the introductory chapter of this analysis, cannot be taken as a model to interpret Marx and Engels' way of dealing with the workers of the International. The organisational track is moving, the 'mighty engine' functions; hence, Marx himself must hold the reins of the movement through the intellectual and, ultimately, political influence he may exert on the organisation itself. Consequently, the question, perhaps the most difficult to be answered, is as follows: *how should this influence be exerted so as to prepare the ground for proletarian self-emancipation?* Furthermore, to what extent has the International's experience freed us from the arid dilemma: intellectual elitism or proletarian self-emancipation?

Before dealing, however, with these questions at length, it is important to note that Marx's decisive influence on the intellectual and, ultimately, the political activity of the working class becomes apparent from the beginning of his participation in the leading committee, later called 'General Council', of the International. The fact that, as Hunt correctly mentions, Marx wrote down the rules and the address of the organisation 'within a perfectly democratic organisational process'[14] should not conceal, the *aristocratic* side of the historical reality, which the same political theorist also points to, when referring to the Marx/Eccarius relation:

---

[12] K. Marx, 'Letter to Kugelmann', 17 March 1868 in K. Marx and F. Engels, op. cit., vol. 42, p.552.
[13] F. Engels, 'Letter to Bebel', 20 June 1873 in K. Marx and F. Engels op. cit., vol. 44, p.511.
[14] R.N. Hunt, op. cit., p.270.

Marx enjoyed a strong intellectual influence over the general council and a personal influence over its general secretary Eccarius.[15]

At this point, a further issue arises in relation to Marx's leading role in the organisation: Why did he choose to exert his indisputable influence on the proletarian movement from 'behind the scenes'? As far as this question is concerned, it seems beyond doubt that a member of a working men's association, while not a worker himself, he was led to this tactical choice in order to avoid the repetition of the Communist League's deplorable experience. As a matter of fact, Marx's precautions proved to be justified and useful as well.

It was in the Geneva congress of the International (1866), that 'non-manual' workers became the target of a severe attack, especially on behalf of the Proudhonists, who – following their leader Tolain – proposed the exclusion of the intellectuals from the organisation as a threat to proletarian self-emancipation.[16] The proposal was rejected by votes 25 to 20, but even when the English delegates proposed Marx for president of the General Council, he preferred to remain faithful to his 'sotto voce' tactics by refusing the proposal.[17] Action 'behind the scenes' seemed to be a safer and more effective method of leading the proletarian movement, especially when this leadership is exerted by a

---

[15] op. cit., p.274; nevertheless, Hunt, op. cit., p.272, insists that 'Marx threw in his lot with an organisation he did not control, nor did he make any concerted effort at direct control before the Bakunin conflict changed the stakes of the game in 1869.'
As B. Nicolaievsky and O. Maenchen-Helfen, op. cit., p.285, suggest, 'in the General Council, as the committee elected at the inaugural meeting soon came to be called, *Marx was the acknowledged leader.*' (our emphasis)

[16] See Draper's interesting analysis in H. Draper, *Karl Marx's Theory of Revolution*, Monthly Review Press, New York and London, 1978, vol. II, p.555 ff.

[17] This is how Marx himself presented the whole affair in a 'Letter to Engels', 26 September 1866 in K. Marx and F. Engels, op. cit., vol. 42, p.318: 'By way of demonstration against the French monsieurs – who wanted to exclude everyone except *'travailleurs manuels'* in the first instance from membership of the INTERNATIONAL ASSOCIATION, or at least from eligibility for election as delegate to the congress – the English yesterday proposed *me as President of the Central Council*. I declared that under no circumstances could I accept such a thing and I proposed *Odger*, who was then in fact re-elected, although some people voted for me despite my declaration.' (Marx's emphasis)

bourgeois intellectual surrounded by several workerist groups, more or less suspicious of his intentions.[18]

Under these circumstances, Marx's attitude towards the various groups of workers within the organisational frame of the International was constructed on two levels; on the *manifest* one, where the philosopher-lawgiver appeared as the impartial referee between the conflicting groups,[19] and on the *deeper* level, on which the philosopher-leader tried to take advantage of his intellectual superiority in order to pull the whole movement towards his own theoretical and political positions.[20] From this point of view, he was not interested in the question of the official presidency of the General Council.[21] His main interest – at least during the first period of the International's life, i.e. before Bakunin's entrance in the organisation – consisted in creating an association which should have been as broad as possible, since he was convinced that the time of sectarian groups was definitely over. In his opinion, the coexistence of diverse ideological and political trends within the International, especially during its founding period, was not a negative feature in itself; what actually mattered at this point was the creation of an open type of organisation, within which his own theory might influence the greatest

---

[18] It is important to note that, even after Bakunin's entrance to the organisation, Marx still believed that he 'actually [did] exercise a decisive intellectual influence upon the General Council.' (K. Marx, 'Letter to Bolte', 23 November 1871 in K. Marx and F. Engels, op. cit., vol. 44, p.256).

Marx's own belief that he is actually the 'head' of the International is also explicitly expressed in the following letters:
a) K. Marx, 'Letter to Engels', 13 March 1865 in K. Marx and F. Engels, op. cit., vol. 42, p.130.
b) K. Marx, 'Letter to Engels', 26 December 1865 in K. Marx and F. Engels, op. cit., vol. 42, pp.206-207.

[19] 'As far as I am concerned – I mean as MEMBER of the GENERAL COUNCIL – I must conduct myself impartially between the various organised groups of workers [writes Marx to Engels]. It is their business and not mine whom they have as leader.' (Marx's emphasis – 'Letter to Engels', 29 July 1868 in K. Marx and F. Engels, op. cit., vol. 43, pp.75-76).

[20] See, for example, Marx's detailed instructions to Eccarius and Lessner on the way they should act during the Brussels Congress of the International. (K. Marx, 'Letter to Eccarius and Lessner', 10 September 1868 in K. Marx and F. Engels, op. cit., vol. 43, pp.93-94).

[21] As a matter of fact, Marx viewed the issue of presidency through a strictly *tactical* prism. (See R.N. Hunt, op. cit., p.273).

number of workers.[22] According to Marx and Engels, it was exactly this kind of organisation which would give them the opportunity to work on the masses, while not being trapped in the logic of intellectual and political sectarianism.

At this point it is worth noting indeed how Marx himself presented his own activity in the International during its first period of existence. In a letter to Schweitzer, written on 13 October 1868, Marx argues as follows, referring especially to the German proletariat:

> I declare that my role must necessarily be confined to that of 'impartial referee' at a duel [...]. You yourself know the difference between a sect movement and a class movement from personal experience [...] I shall merely remark that a centralist organisation, suitable as it is for secret societies and sect movements, contradicts the nature of the TRADE UNIONS [...]. Here [in Germany] where the worker is regulated bureaucratically from childhood onwards, where he believes in authority, in those set over him, the main thing is *to teach him to walk by himself.*[23] (Marx's emphasis)

Given such an analysis, therefore, Marx's main positions in terms of strategy and tactics during the first phase of the International may be recapitulated as follows:

1. Total rejection of sectarianism and further construction of a vanguard organisation as broad as possible and open to the various ideological and political trends of the proletarian movement;

2. Intellectual and political action on a manifest and latent level as the impartial referee and the actual leader respectively;

---

[22] According to Cole, op. cit., pp.265–266, 'Marx had indeed insisted, in the earlier years of the First International, on the need for building an actual movement rather than constructing a dogma into which movements were required to fit. But when the actual movement took forms which he disliked [...] he was apt to forget his own precepts and to become the grand inquisitor into heretical misdeeds.'

[23] K. Marx, 'Letter to Schweitzer', 13 October 1868 in K. Marx and F. Engels, op. cit., vol. 43, pp.132–134.

3. Education of the workers in order to make them able to walk by themselves; needless to say, such an education may vary in form according to specific historical and social conditions, though its constant goal should consist in the working class' self-emancipation.

In fact the philosopher-lawgiver who decided to play a crucial role in the founding process of a political vanguard organisation must not stop acting as an educator. According to Marx himself, 'to teach [the worker] to walk by himself' is the most drastic antidote against bureaucracy and blind faith in authority. Teaching, however, is actually inconceivable without a certain kind of authority. It is exactly at this point, as has already been mentioned, that Marx's analysis of the intellectual/proletarian relation may be connected with Rousseau's theory of education as expressed in his well-known *Emile*. From this point of view, Rousseau's model of *negative education,* his own distinction between *preceptor* and *governor,* as well as the creative way Rousseau himself approaches his student's *instinct* in order to make him achieve *self*-determination, are just a few points of convergence between Marx and Rousseau's conceptions of education. Finally, the *power asymmetry* itself, which undoubtedly characterises Rousseau's view on the teacher/student relation, is definitely recognisable in Marx's own contact with the workers of the First International. Within such a framework of analysis, however, Marx's explicit declaration of proletarian self-emancipation in the first lines of the International's Provisional Rules brings my research even closer to the central question which we have already discussed with regard to the Communist League: Is there any way out of the simplistic dilemma 'intellectual elitism or proletarian self-emancipation'?

Chapter 8
Intellectual Leadership and Proletarian Self-Emancipation: the Aristodemocracy Question

'The emancipation of the working class must be conquered by the working classes themselves'[1] Marx wrote in the 'Provisional Rules of the International Working Men's Association'. That is to say the proletarians should fight by their own forces in order to achieve their social and political liberation.[2] In such a case, however, what would be the role of radical intellectuals within the leading ranks of the proletarian movement? Is there not an immanent contradiction between the concept of proletarian self-emancipation, on the one hand, and the leading role of intellectuals, on the other?

To this question, the Inaugural Address of the International, written by Marx as well, makes a meaningful allusion:

> One element of success [the working classes] possess—numbers; but numbers weigh only in the balance, if

---

[1] K. Marx, 'Provisional Rules of the Association' in K. Marx and F. Engels, op. cit., vol. 20, p.14.

[2] According to Marx, 'what was new in the International was that it was established by the working men themselves and for themselves. Before the foundation of the International all the different organisations had been societies founded by some radicals among the ruling classes for the working classes, but the International was established by the working men for themselves.' ('Record of Marx's Speech on the Seventh Anniversary of the International' in K. Marx and F. Engels, op. cit., vol. 22, pp.633–634). Contrary to Marx's insistence on this minimalistic approach as regards the radical intellectuals' role in the proletarian movement, however, it is self-evident that neither the ideological nor the institutional formation of the International would have been reached without his own leading engagement in the proletarian cause.

united by combination and led *by knowledge*.³ (our emphasis)

In other words, according to Marx, the fulfilment of proletarian self-emancipation, and especially the proletariat's 'great duty', i.e. the conquest of political power,⁴ presupposes the combined action of numbers and knowledge. From here, Marx proceeds even further by suggesting that knowledge should play the *leading* role with respect to numbers.⁵

It is exactly from this point of view that Marx's conception of democracy, as this can be defined through the founding documents of the International, proves compatible with a certain element of intellectual and moral *aristocracy,* in the etymological sense of the word; the 'best men' in terms of knowledge and ethos should be the real leaders of the vanguard organisation. As a matter of fact, therefore, Marx's position concerning the intellectual/proletarian relation within the International, as regards the question of leadership, reveals a spiritual affinity to Aristotle's *polity* and Rousseau's *elective aristocracy.* Although Marx did not elaborate on the relations of authority within a working class organisation, it can be argued, that he hinted at a mixture of democratic elements (principle of majority, *de jure* equality of numbers) and aristocratic equivalents (principle of knowledge, *de facto* equality of value). This kind of *aristodemocracy* expresses the organic unity of the power of numbers with that of knowledge. More concretely, decisions of the majority provide the political legitimisation to the virtuous agents of knowledge who, for their part, share their intellectual insights with the rank and file of the political body.

In case, however, majority decisions come in conflict with conclusions which have been based upon superior knowledge, one way seems to remain open for the intellectual-leader, i.e. a *temporary* retreat to his (or her) strictly educational role. Drawing his (or her)

---

[3] K. Marx, 'Inaugural Address of the Working Men's International Association' in K. Marx and F. Engels, op. cit., vol. 20, p.12; as Maximilien Rubel correctly points out, however, 'led by knowledge' does not mean led 'by professional "know-it-alls" or revolutionaries' (M. Rubel, op. cit., p.73).

[4] K. Marx, 'Inaugural Address of the Working Men's International Association' in K, Marx and F. Engels, op. cit., vol. 20, p.12.

[5] Once again, Marx's concept of knowledge should be definitely distinguished from any kind of *ex cathedra* transmission of truth to the uneducated masses.

attention to philosophical/scientific research, the aristodemocrat intellectual may temporarily act as well as the adviser of the social movement, without being directly involved in everyday politics. This was exactly the course followed by Marx and Engels themselves after the dissolution of the Communist League until the foundation of the International. Thus, the philosopher-leader who fails to convince the common people to endorse his (or her) positions should not insist upon imposing these views on the masses against their own will. The intellectual mentor of a movement should be ready at any moment to concentrate on *long-term* educational activity in order to prepare the ground for the proletariat's transformation from a class in itself to a class for itself. As a matter of fact, the aristodemocrat intellectuals should neither obey passively, nor disregard the people's will.

What are the specific conditions, however, under which intellectual leadership may prove an effective means to proletarian self-emancipation? At this point, Marx's own activity during the early years of the International is suggestive indeed. According to his own proposal, the intellectual-lawgiver should try, first of all, to guarantee the proletarian character of the vanguard organisation.[6] From this point of view, the power of numbers appears to be necessary in order to counterbalance – in favour of the workers – qualitative parameters such as the power of knowledge, which cannot be exerted by the workers themselves, at least during the founding period of the revolutionary organisation. On the other hand, the intellectual leaders should prepare the ground for proletarian self-emancipation through a *gradual* transcendence of the social division of labour within the vanguard organisation. Nevertheless, during the first period of the organisation's life, as Marx and Engels' activity in the International proves, the division of labour between intellectuals and workers

---

[6] According to the International's Provisional Rules, as written by Marx, 'the Central Council shall consist by working men' (K. Marx and F. Engels, op. cit., vol. 20, p.15). Moreover, some years later, due to the negative experience of the North American section of the International, Marx legislated as follows: '[I]n order to guarantee the proletarian character of the Association, no less than two thirds of the members of each branch must consist of wage-workers.' (K. Marx, *Amendments to the General Rules and Administrative Regulations of the International Working Men's Association Adopted by the General Council in the Summer of 1872* in K. Marx and F. Engels, op. cit., vol. 23, p.201). A similar position may be noticed in K. Marx, 'Letter to Lafargue', 21 March 1872 in K. Marx and F. Engels, op. cit., vol. 44, p.346.

neither could, nor should have been overcome *at once*. As a matter of fact, a *transitional* aristodemocratic stage is required, within the framework of which the best people in terms of intellectual and moral virtue, being supported by the rank and file of the proletarian movement, would be able to act as the true lawgivers and educators, preparing the ground for the proletarian self-emancipation.

To this end, both intellectuals and workers should try to transcend their mutual mistrust, of which Marx himself was fully conscious.[7] Radical intellectuals, through creatively building upon the insight of Rousseau, Fichte and other eminent theorists' philosophical work, must seek not to annihilate but to regulate the people's 'instinct' towards truth and revolution; at the same time, workers ought to admit in fact that knowledge is a *conditio sine qua non* for their attempt to change the world. From this point of view, therefore, proletarian self-emancipation does not mean that revolutionary strategy and tactics have been conceived and elaborated by the proletarian themselves. Especially in regard to the planning of the revolution, it can be argued that the role of radical intellectuals may prove determinant, without being in conflict with the working class' self-emancipation, given the fact that political decisions depend finally upon the workers' own approval.

Hence, the apparent contradiction between intellectual leadership and proletarian self-emancipation can be overcome, if both intellectuals and proletarians succeed in walking together within the limits being set by the fragile dialectic of aristodemocracy which connects (political) education with (political) authority. In regard to this specific hypothesis, however, the second period of the International, as determined by the Marx/Bakunin controversy, seems very revealing indeed.

---

[7] K. Marx, 'Letter to Engels', 25 February 1865 in K. Marx and F. Engels, op. cit., vol. 42, p.109: '[T]he workers, [argues Marx], seem to take things to the point of excluding any LITERARY MAN, etc., which is absurd, as they need them in the press, but is pardonable in view of the repeated treachery of the LITERARY MEN. Conversely, the latter are suspicious of any workers' movement, which displays hostility towards them.' (Marx's emphasis).

Chapter 9
Bakunin and the International – Motives and Tactics

As it is well known, Michael Bakunin joined the International in 1869, having accepted the official dissolution of his own organisation, named L'Alliance Internationale de la Democratie Sociale. Nevertheless, this was not the only organisation founded by the Russian Anarchist, a man of energy and passions,[1] among which, as he himself admitted, the passion of destruction possessed an eminent position.[2] Several years before, and more concretely in November 1864, Bakunin founded a secret conspiratorial society, the so-called International Brotherhood. Moreover, in autumn 1867, he took part in the first congress of a pacifist democratic organisation, named the League of Peace and Freedom, becoming a member of its central committee as well. In 1868, however, after their failure to draw the League towards their own ideas, Bakunin and his supporters left the organisation.[3] It was after this unsuccessful attempt that he took the decision to found L'Alliance Internationale de la Democratie Sociale.

---

[1] For a vivid description of Bakunin's personality see:
    a) A. Kelly, *Mikhail Bakunin, A Study in the Psychology and Politics of Utopianism*, New Haven, Yale University Press, 1987, p.158 ff. and especially pp.161–162.
    b) G. Woodcock, *Anarchism, A History of Libertarian Ideas and Movements*, Harmondsworth, Penguin Books, 1986, pp.121–123.

[2] According to Bakunin's well-known dictum, 'the passion of destruction is a creative passion, too!' (M. Bakunin, 'The Reaction in Germany' in S. Dolgoff (ed.), *Bakunin on Anarchism*, Montreal, Black Rose Books, 1980, p.57).

[3] As B. Nicolaievsky and O. Maenchen-Helfen, op. cit., p.304, argue, '[Bakunin] did all he could to make the League accept a revolutionary programme and bring it into line with the International. His undoubted aim was to bring the two organisations together and, by means of his secret organisation, to become the unseen leader of both. In this he failed.'

In fact, Bakunin's decision to found an organisation such as the Alliance represents just one side of a broader, tactical plan, which is described by Carr as follows:

> The Alliance would be recruited from the members most sincerely devoted to the cause and the principles of the International [...]; and its object was to train propagandists, apostles, and finally, organisers! In short, the Alliance was to provide the aristocracy, or the general staff of the workers' movement.[4]

To the extent that this historical analysis is accurate, serious questions arise, however, as regards the intellectual/political vanguard's relation with the mass movement itself. Nevertheless, before proceeding to the discussion of these questions it is worth defining, as clearly as possible, Bakunin's own tactics.

According to Nicolaievsky and Maenchen-Helfen,

> [the] open association, L'Alliance Internationale de la Democratie Sociale, was founded to exist side by side with the secret society. The Alliance was intended to include members outside the secret society [...]. There was to be a three-storey pyramid, with the International on the base, the Alliance on top of it and on top of the Alliance the secret society, with Bakunin the 'invisible dictator' at the pinnacle.[5]

In other words, Bakunin aimed to control the First International through the action of the Alliance, which at the same time would have been directed by a very small, secret and conspiratorial society. That

---

[4] E.H. Carr, *Mikhail Bakunin*, London, The Macmillan Press, 1937, p.345; as a matter of fact, Carr's analysis converges with Nettlau's, one of Bakunin's most eminent followers: 'Bakunin [argues Nettlau] felt compelled to assemble and educate a group of clear-thinking revolutionists freed from the fetters of religion and religious philosophy, and opposed to the idea of the State, and to establish among them close contacts which would facilitate international activities.' (See Nettlau's biographical sketch of Bakunin in G.P. Maximoff (ed.), *The Political Philosophy of Bakunin Scientific Anarchism*, The Free Press, Glencoe, Illinois, 1953, p.44).

[5] B. Nicolaievsky and O. Maenchen-Helfen, op. cit., pp.304–305.

is why he tried, though unsuccessfully, to incorporate the Alliance within the organisational structure of the International.[6]

At this point, it is worth recalling Marx and Engels' tactics during the early years of the International. As has already been mentioned, they both aimed at the formation of an open and broad vanguard organisation, within which various theoretical and political trends could be represented. That is why, Bakunin and his followers were finally admitted into the International, after having accepted the anti-sectarian character of the Association and its rules and statutes.

Despite the formal dissolution of Bakunin's alliance, however, Marx himself proved fully aware of the Russian anarchist's inner motive and plan:

> We answered [writes Marx to Lafargue] that the General Council was not the Pope, that we allowed every section to have its own theoretical views of the real movement, always supposed that nothing directly opposite to our Rules put forward [...]. Thus the Alliance was nominally dissolved. In fact, it continued to form an imperium in imperio [...]. It acted under Bakunin's dictatorship.[7]

Nevertheless, Marx's assertion that 'the General Council was not the Pope' does not mean that the International functioned without any kind of leadership;[8] as a matter of fact, the specific type of this leadership should be carefully analysed, since it represents one of the most important aspects of the Marx/Bakunin controversy, a controversy

---

[6] For Marx's reaction to Bakunin's attempt to incorporate the Alliance within the organisational framework of the International, see: K. Marx, 'The General Council of the International Working Men's Association to the Central Bureau of the International Alliance of Socialist Democracy' in K. Marx and F. Engels, op. cit. vol. 21, pp.45-46.

[7] K. Marx, 'Letter to Lafargue', 19 April 1870 in K. Marx and F. Engels, op. cit., vol. 43, pp.491-492; on the same issue, see as well:
 a) K. Marx, 'Letter to Engels', 27 July 1869, pp.332-333.
 b) F. Engels, 'Letter to Marx', 30 July 1869, pp.335-336.

[8] As regards the leadership question, see K. Marx and F. Engels, 'Fictitious Splits in the International' in K. Marx and F. Engels, op. cit. vol. 23, pp.79-123, especially p.102 ff.

connected with the way in which intellectuals and workers came in contact with this vanguard organisation.[9]

According to Bakunin's own words, the International was to be an organisation open to all proletarian groups and trends:

> [W]hat political or philosophical program [asks Bakunin] can rally to its banners all these millions? Only a program which is very general hence vague and indefinite, for every theoretical definition necessarily involves elimination and in practice exclusion from membership.[10]

At this point, however, the similarity between Bakunin's quoted position and Marx's own activity during the first period of the International proves quite surprising. It is worth noting, for example, how Marx himself argued, while referring to the programme written by him for the London delegates of the International's Geneva Congress.

> I deliberately confined [the programme] to points which allow direct agreement and combination of efforts by the workers and give direct sustenance and impetus to the requirements of the class struggle and the organisation of the workers into class.[11]

Hence, Bakunin and Marx seem to agree on the antisectarian character of the International. Nevertheless, they could still accuse each other of acting as the would-be dictators of the proletarian movement. According to Bakunin, Marx and his followers should be regarded like 'the midwives rather than the parents'[12] of the International, while Marx himself behaves as a 'new Moses'[13] who provides a new decalogue for the proletarians.[14] As a result, Bakunin

---

[9] A critical presentation of the main points of the Marx/Bakunin controversy is included in G.D.H. Cole, op. cit., pp.116–118.
[10] M. Bakunin in *The International and Karl Marx* in S. Dolgoff (ed.), p.293.
[11] K. Marx, 'Letter to Kugelmann', 13 October 1866 in K. Marx and F. Engels, op. cit. vol. 42, pp.326–327.
[12] M. Bakunin in, *The International and Karl Marx*, p.298.
[13] op. cit., p.299.
[14] It is worth noting, however, that the word 'proletariat' in Bakunin's own terminology also refers to the social stratum which Marx characterised as

argues that 'like all theorists Marx is an inveterate and incorrigible dreamer when it comes to practical activity. He proves it in his hapless campaign to establish his dictatorship in the International, and through the International over the entire revolutionary movement of the proletariat of Europe and America [...]. By education and by nature he is a Jacobin, and his favourite dream is of a political dictatorship.'[15] In other words, from Bakunin's point of view, Marx incarnates the model of the philosopher-dictator and more concretely the model of the Rousseauist lawgiver, who dominates the people by totally subjugating them to his own ideological and political views.[16] For our part, however, it is Bakunin's own political activity as a revolutionary agitator that seems much more compatible with the psychological portrait of the Rousseauist lawgiver. From this point of view, Isaiah Berlin's description of the way Bakunin came in contact with the proletarians is revealing indeed:

> To dominate individuals and to sway assemblies was his *métier:* he belonged to that odd, fortunately not very numerous class of persons who contrive to hypnotise others into throwing themselves into causes.[17] (Berlin's emphasis)

In any case, remarks, such as those expressed above, deserve a further consideration within the broader context of the intellectuals' relation with political power and emancipation. For the time being, however, it is worth insisting on Bakunin's own position as regards the International's theoretical and political identity.

According to Bakunin's argument, therefore,

'lumpen-proletariat'. For Bakunin's definition of proletariat, see M. Bakunin, *The International and Karl Marx*, p.294.

[15] M. Bakunin, *Statism and Anarchy*, Cambridge, Cambridge University Press, 1990, p.182.

[16] M. Bakunin, *The International and Karl Marx*, p.299 ff.

[17] Quoted from P. Thomas, op. cit., p.287. It is worth comparing, indeed, Berlin's description of Bakunin's way of acting with Rousseau's presentation of the Lawgiver's activity: '[...] employ neither force, nor argument, he must have recourse to an authority of another order, one which can compel without violence and persuade without convincing, [...]. The lawgiver's great soul is the true miracle which must vindicate its mission.' (J.J. Rousseau, *The Social Contract*, p.87).

> to save [the International's] integrity and assure its progress, there is only one procedure: to follow and preserve the original policy and *keep the political question out of the official and obligatory program and statutes of the International Working Men's Association [...] and absolutely refuse to let it be used by anyone as a political instrument.* Those who would [capture the International] and commit it to a positive political policy in the struggle between the rival political parties will be immediately demoralised.[18] (Bakunin's emphasis)

In our opinion, however, Bakunin actually misses the point of the intellectual/politics relation. Was it really possible to keep the political and the philosophical question out of the International's programme and statutes?[19] Is it possible for a social movement to proceed towards its own strategic goal without a 'positive political policy'? It is beyond doubt that the radical intellectuals' participation in the proletarian movement is *ab initio* connected with the creation of the movement's theoretical and political platform. From this point of view, it is worth pointing out that Marx and Engels' struggle against sectarianism,[20] based on the International's broad programme of action, is not identical with the negation of politics in general. For Marx and his followers, such an antisectarian fight was not an end in itself; it was just the first stage of their tactical plan, which aimed at drawing the 'mighty engine' of the International to their own

---

[18] M. Bakunin, *The International and Karl Marx*, pp.300-301.

[19] According to Bakunin, op. cit., p.302, 'on the one hand the political and philosophical questions oust be excluded from the program of the International. On the other, they must necessarily be discussed. How can this seeming contradiction be resolved? This problem will solve itself by liberty. No political or philosophical theory should be considered a fundamental principle, or be introduced into the official program of the International. [...] But it does not follow from this that free discussion of all political and philosophical theories cannot occur in the International.'

[20] In regard to Marx and Engels' critique against Bakunin's policy as being sectarian, see, for example:
a) K. Marx, 'Confidential Communication' in K. Marx and F. Engels op. cit., vol. 21, p.113.
b) F. Engels, 'Declaration sent by the General Council to the Editors of Italian Newspapers concerning Mazzini's articles about the International' in K. Marx and F. Engels, op. cit., vol. 23, p.61.

theoretical and political views.[21] At the same time, Bakunin's tactics – despite his *apparent* disapproval of any *positive* political identity – proved no exception to the rule. Although the content of his political theory is quite different from Marx's one, Bakunin himself tried to take advantage of the greatest possible recruitment of workers within the ranks of the International in order to direct the whole proletarian movement towards his *self*-appointed strategic goal of the anarchist society.

Consequently, one may doubt whether Bakunin was sincere when writing that 'the proletariat can itself *spontaneously* find and develop true philosophical principles and political policies'[22] (our emphasis). In such a case, what would have been the need for intellectual and political leaders like Bakunin himself?

Finally, it is worth adding that the Russian anarchist does not always confine himself to minimising the importance of the philosopher-educator or the philosopher-lawgiver's role; sometimes, he gives the illusory impression that he even rejects such roles completely and it is on the basis of this questionable rejection that he launches his own attack on Marx and his followers.[23] For his part, Bakunin insists, quite often indeed, that the role of the vanguard organisation should have been that of the night-keeper who guarantees the *spontaneous* development of the revolutionary consciousness by constantly negating the intellectual's demoralising influence on the proletarian movement itself.

Nevertheless, questions like these mentioned above will be further discussed a little later; for the time being, it should be stressed that

---

[21] The achievement of a common theoretical program was actually one of Marx's tactical ends: 'The community of action [argued Marx] called into life by the Intern. W. Ass., the exchange of ideas facilitated by the public organs of the different national sections, and the direct debates at Geneva Congresses, are sure by and by to engender a common theoretical program.' (K. Marx, *The General Council of the International Working Men's Association to the Central Bureau of the International Alliance of Socialist Democracy*, op. cit., p.45).

[22] M. Bakunin, *The International and Karl Marx*, pp.302-303.

[23] On the other hand, it is worth mentioning that it is the underestimation of education and the intellectual's role, which lies among other reasons behind Marx's criticism of secret societies: 'This type of organisation [argues Marx] is opposed to the development of the proletarian movement because, instead of instructing the workers, these societies subject them to authoritarian, mystical laws which cramp their independence and distort their powers of reason.' ('Record at Marx's Speech on Secret Societies' in K. Marx and F. Engels, op. cit., vol. 22, p.261).

Bakunin's insistence on the 'negative political position' proves interesting in another context. The formation of an 'official truth',[24] which may be imposed upon the rank and file of a social movement by professional revolutionaries, is not of course a fictitious, but a real danger to the people's self-emancipation. At this point, Bakunin's critique against Marx and his followers seems to reach the heart of the relation between intellectuals and politics by overtly posing the crucial question: is the power of knowledge compatible with the proletarian self-emancipation? As a matter of fact, this was exactly the challenging question – which we have already confronted in relation to the Communist League, as well as during the early years of the International – which brought the Marx/Bakunin controversy to its climax.

---

[24] According to Bakunin, *The International and Karl Marx*, p.302, 'it is precisely the very existence of an official theory that will kill such discussion [of all political and philosophical theories] by rendering it absolutely useless instead of living and vital, and by inhibiting the expression and development of the workers' own feelings and ideas.'

Chapter 10
The Marx/Bakunin Controversy: Knowledge, Organisation and Authority

There is no doubt that discussion over the 'self-emancipation principle' holds a central position in the way radical intellectuals confront the revolutionary perspectives of the working class. As a matter of fact, this was one of the main points, where Marx and Bakunin's political theories met, since not only Marx, but the Russian anarchist as well defended the workers' capacity for emancipating themselves by their own forces.

> The preamble of the statutes of the International [argues Bakunin] states: 'The emancipation of the workers is the task of the workers themselves.' It is absolutely right. This is the fundamental principle of our great association.[1]

Nevertheless, Bakunin seems fully aware of the fact that the proletarian self-emancipation cannot be achieved at once, since workers 'lack two things [...] organisation and knowledge';[2] thus, self emancipation presupposes a *transitional* stage, during which the proletariat would learn to act in full autonomy. From this point of view, however, Bakunin's analysis gives rise to two crucial questions:

1. How can knowledge be transmitted to or obtained by the proletarians in order to become conscious of their revolutionary capacity and execute their mission to change the world?

---

[1] M. Bakunin, 'The Policy of the International' in S. Dolgoff (ed.), op. cit., p.167.
[2] M. Bakunin, 'The Program of the Alliance' in op. cit., p.255.

2. Which type of organisation promotes the cause of proletarian self-emancipation?

Needless to say, attempts to answer both questions depend upon the intellectuals' position and activity in the proletarian movement itself.

In regard to the knowledge question, there is no doubt that Bakunin's views reveal a certain similarity to the young Marx's approach to the same issue. In agreement with the latter's theory of alienation, the Russian revolutionary believes, in fact, that the vast majority of the working class is deeply oppressed by the conditions of its everyday life; at the same time, however, these material conditions constitute the framework within which a truly revolutionary consciousness may arise and develop.

> The great mass of the workers, exhausted by daily drudgery, are miserable and ignorant. Yet this mass, despite its political and social prejudices, is socialistic without *knowing* it. Because of its social position, it is more truly socialist than all the scientific and bourgeois socialists combined [...] What the workers lack is not a sense of reality or socialist aspirations, but only socialist thought.[3] (Bakunin's emphasis)

In this context of analysis, however, the role of a socialist vanguard, which is determined to act as the collective educator of the masses, becomes unavoidable. In fact, the workers' spontaneous inclination towards socialism, though valuable indeed, is not a sufficient means to change the world radically. A socialist vanguard is required to make the proletarians discover within themselves and through their own *practical action*[4] true knowledge, i.e. knowledge of

---

[3] M. Bakunin, 'The Policy of the International', op. cit., p.166; See also M. Bakunin, 'Federalism, Socialism, Anti-Theologism' in op. cit., p.113, where he argues in a way highly reminiscent of Rousseau: 'Being miserable themselves, [the representatives of manual labour] keenly sympathise with the misery of others; their common sense has not been corrupted by the sophism of a doctrinaire science or by the mendacity of politics and since they have not abused life, or even used it, they have faith in life.'

[4] M. Bakunin, 'The Policy of the International', op. cit., p.167: 'The only way for the workers to learn theory is through practice: emancipation through practical action.' (Bakunin's emphasis).

the exploitative character of the social and political system, and furthermore the way to abolish it.

> The socialist aim is to make the worker fully conscious of what he wants, *to awaken in him an intelligence,* which will correspond to his inner yearnings. Once the intelligence of the workers is raised to the level of what they instinctively feel, their will is bound to be concentrated and their power irresistible.[5] (our emphasis)

From this point of view, therefore, despite his rather fragmentary and contradictory theoretical discourse, Bakunin subscribes to Rousseau and Fichte's way of dealing with the cultivation of the people's social instinct in favour of the emancipatory cause.[6] On the other hand, Bakunin insists that 'propaganda and education are excellent but insufficient means'.[7] As a matter of fact, the Russian thinker does not explicitly reject the role of the intellectual-educator within the proletarian movement; on the contrary, Bakunin seems to admit the social and political significance of knowledge and education as such.[8] Thus, intellectuals, at least a portion of them, should play some role in the revolutionary process.[9] Nevertheless, their educational/ instructional activity derives power from a specific organisational structure, without which knowledge and education

---

[5] op. cit., pp.166–167.

[6] In the 'Program of the Alliance', (op. cit., pp.254–255), Mikhail Bakunin, argues as follows: 'Social Science as a moral doctrine is the development and the formulation of those instincts [of equality, liberty and social solidarity]. Between these instincts and science there is a gap which must be bridged. For if instinct alone had been sufficient for the liberation of peoples, they would have long since freed themselves.'

[7] M. Bakunin, 'The Policy of the International', op. cit., p.167.

[8] M. Bakunin, 'Science and the Urgent Revolutionary Task' in G.P. Maximoff (ed.), op. cit., p.355: 'Knowledge is power, ignorance is the cause of social impotence [...]. What is education, if not mental capital, the sum of mental labor of all past generations? How can an ignorant mind, vigorous though it may be by nature, hold out in a struggle against collective mental power produced by centuries of development?'

[9] See M. Bakunin, 'The Policy of the International', in op. cit., p.161, where the Russian thinker argues that not only workers, but people of different class origin as well may become members of the International, if they really embrace the workers' cause.

would never generate their revolutionary social and political consequences:

> [N]either the writers, nor the philosophers, nor their books are enough to build a living, powerful, socialist movement. Such a movement can be made a reality only by the awakened revolutionary consciousness, the collective will, and the organisation of the working masses themselves. Without this, the best books in the world are nothing but theories spun in empty space, impotent dreams.[10]

It is time, therefore, to confront the organisational question, as conceived by Bakunin, in specific relation to the intellectuals' involvement in the proletarian movement.

As a matter of fact, Bakunin's analysis of the organisational question is basically determined by two crucial concepts, *social division of labour* and *authority*, without which it is impossible to shed light on his controversial views on the issues we are dealing with here.

For Bakunin, as with Marx, the transcendence of the social division of labour should be the founding stone of the future classless society:

> The artificial separation between manual and intellectual labor must give way to a new social synthesis. When the man of science performs manual labor, and the man of work performs intellectual labor, free intelligent work will become the glory of mankind, the source of its dignity and right.[11]

Contrary to Marx, however, Bakunin seems to push his analysis even further by arguing that the revolutionary organisation must promote the *immediate* abolition of the social division of labour within its own ranks:

---

[10] M. Bakunin, 'Letters to a Frenchman on the Present Crisis' in S. Dolgoff (ed.), op. cit., p.212.

[11] M. Bakunin, 'National Catechism' in op. cit., p.92; for the negative consequences of the social division of labour, see M. Bakunin, 'Federalism, Socialism, Anti-Theologism' in op. cit., pp.112-113.

> The International Working Men's Association [argues Bakunin] can become an instrument of the emancipation of humanity only when it has emancipated itself first, and that will happen only when it has ceased dividing into two groups – the majority as blind tools and the minority of learned savants who do all the directing – and when every member of the Association has become permeated with science, philosophy and politics of Socialism.[12]

At this point, it is worth distinguishing between two levels of Bakunin's analysis; a *manifest* one, in which Bakunin does not hesitate to defend an *ultra-libertarian* and *anti-authoritarian* type of organisation, and a *latent* one, where he supports a kind of *invisible collective dictatorship* that will open the way to the post-revolutionary classless and stateless society. As a matter of fact, both versions of the Bakuninist analysis provoked the fierce critique of Marx, Engels and their followers. From this point of view, therefore, the direct conflict over the [political] authority issue gives us an excellent opportunity to juxtapose Bakunin's with Marx and Engels' views on the intellectuals' role within the revolutionary movement.

Bakunin's position on the *manifest* level of his analysis can best be illustrated by the following question, as this is included in the documents of the Bakuninist congress, which took place at Sonvillier on 12 November 1871.

> How could one expect an egalitarian and free society to grow out of an authoritarian organisation? That is impossible. The International embryo of the future human society, must henceforth be the faithful image of our principles of liberty and federation.[13]

Leaving apart for the moment the fact that Bakunin himself did not follow the direction described above, as far as his alliance and the International Brotherhood are concerned,[14] it is worth mentioning

---

[12] M. Bakunin, 'Protestation at the Alliance' in G.P. Maximoff (ed.), op. cit., pp.320–321.
[13] Quoted by Marx and Engels in K. Marx and F. Engels, 'Fictitious Splits in the International', as included in K. Marx and F. Engels, op, cit., vol. 23, p.115.
[14] See Engels' critique against Bakunin's authoritarian practice, as expressed in the following letters:

Marx's ironical comment on this libertarian egalitarian approach of the International:

> In other words, just as the medieval convents presented an image of celestial life, so the International must be the image of the new Jerusalem, whose 'embryo' the Alliance bears in its womb.[15]

Consequently, according to Marx (and Engels), the crucial question regarding the International's structure and perspective should not take the form of an 'authoritarianism versus self-liberation' dilemma. The real question must be posed as follows: which kind of authority is the most suitable to prepare the ground for proletarian self-emancipation? From this *realistic* point of view, 'wherever there is an organisation, some autonomy is sacrificed for the sake of unity of action'[16] and 'whoever mentions combined action speaks of organisation; now is it possible to have organisation without authority?'[17]

In fact, Engels' arguments strike at the heart of Bakunin's anti-authoritarian ideology. It is worth mentioning as well that, while fighting against the anarchist conception of political authority, he did not hesitate to characterise the revolution as 'the most authoritarian thing there is.'[18] It is in connection with this remark that he also makes an ironic use of the captain-sailors analogy, often mentioned by Plato, when Plato was himself dealing with the controversial philosopher/political power relation: 'Just try abolishing 'all authority even by consent' among sailors on board a ship! [Engels mocks at the Anarchists]'.[19] The analogy is appropriate indeed. Who should be the captain and who should be the sailors on board the *International* however? Who would be the leader – even a collective one – who would educate the workers to walk by themselves, i.e. to be self-emancipated? Clearly it would be the true agents of knowledge,

---

  a) F. Engels, 'Letter to Bert', 7 June 1872, op. cit., vol. 44, p.392.
  b) F. Engels, 'Letter to Cafiero', 14 June 1872, op. cit., p.397.
  c) F. Engels, 'Letter to Guno', 5 July 1872, op. cit., p.408.
[15] K. Marx and F. Engels, 'Fictitious Splits in the International', op. cit., p.115.
[16] F. Engels, 'Letters from London', op. cit., vol. 23, p.283.
[17] F. Engels, 'On Authority', op. cit. vol. 23, p.423.
[18] op. cit., p.425.
[19] F. Engels, 'Letter to Lafargue', 30 December 1871, op. cit., vol. 44. p.286.

who are in a position to plan – at least during the initial period – the revolutionary strategy and tactics.

Looking, moreover, behind the screen of Bakunin's manifest approach to the proletarian self-emancipation, it becomes obvious that like Marx and Engels, he himself acknowledges the need for a transitional/preparatory stage, during which political leadership, as exerted within the ranks of the revolutionary movement, can hardly belong to the proletarians. Nevertheless, before reaching Bakunin's latent level of analysis, let us follow once again Marx and Engels' broad hint about the aristodemocratic stage of transition, which we have already noted in their theory and practice during the early years of the International.

It was indeed en route to the 1872 Hague Congress of the International that the Marx/Bakunin controversy reached its climax. This conflict provided Marx with the opportunity to attack Bakunin's apparent anti-authoritarianism by commenting on the kind of authority which should be exerted by the General Council over the whole organisation.

> Has [the General Council] a bureaucracy and an armed police to ensure that it is obeyed? *Is not its authority solely moral*, and does it not submit its decisions to the Federations which have to carry them out? In these conditions, kings with no army, no police, no magistracy, and reduced to maintain their power by moral influence and authority [argues Marx] would be feeble obstacles to the progress of the revolution.[20] (our emphasis)

According to this comment, it becomes obvious that while talking about authority within the International, Marx actually refers to a kind of moral and intellectual power, which always depends upon the political judgement of the organisation's participants. Hence, regardless the fact that the International did not survive and enjoy such an aristodemocratic leadership, our preliminary conclusion can be reaffirmed: for both Marx and Engels, a revolutionary transition to a socialist society is unthinkable without the action of a vanguard, which

---

[20] K. Marx, 'On the Hague Congress', op. cit., vol. 23, p.255.

derives its power from the intellectual status and moral virtue of its (leading) members.

Contrary to Marx and Engels' analysis, however, Bakunin *appears* to believe that authority of any kind, and especially intellectual authority that is 'always represented by minorities',[21] constitutes a real threat to the revolutionary movement as such. Hence, imprisoned by his own apparent anti-authoritarian ideology, he seems to contradict his own practice, since he questions every kind of transitional power by arguing that 'nothing is as dangerous for man's personal morality as the habit of commanding. The best of men, the most intelligent, unselfish, generous and pure, will *always* and *inevitably* be corrupted in this pursuit.'[22] (our emphasis). In other words, any version of aristocracy or aristodemocracy, in the strictest sense of the term, is – following to Bakunin's argument – a mere fiction, doomed to become a cruel oligarchic state of power.[23]

Nevertheless, within such an approach, Bakunin proves unable to confront the central question posed by Engels: 'Is it possible to have organisation without authority?' Moreover, is it possible to make a revolution without using any kind of authority? Thus, facing the blind alley into which he led his analysis, Bakunin proposes the following solution as regards the authority problem during the revolutionary period:

> At the moment of action, in the midst of a struggle, the roles are naturally distributed in accordance with everyone's attitudes evaluated and judged by the whole collective; some direct and command, while others execute commands. But no function remains fixed and petrified, nothing is irrevocably attached to one person. Hierarchic order and advancement do not exist, so that

---

[21] See M. Bakunin, 'Federalism, Socialism, Anti-Theologism' in S. Dolgoff (ed.), op. cit., p.142.

[22] op. cit., p.145.

[23] According to Bakunin, Marx and his followers' practice would inevitably lead to the creation of a new state and, consequently, to the formation of a ruling aristocracy, that is, an entire class of persons who have nothing in common with the masses. And, of course, this class would exploit and subject the masses, under the pretext of serving the common welfare or saving the State.' (M. Bakunin, 'The Paris Commune and the Idea of the State' in op. cit., p.270).

the executive of yesterday may become the subordinate of today.[24]

Contrary to what Bakunin seems to believe, however, it is 'at the moment of action' that hierarchical order proves to be necessary. It is exactly 'in the midst of a struggle', Engels would have argued, that the sailors need their captain. From this point of view, it is worth mentioning that even Bakunin himself, in one of his self-defeating formulations, admits that 'actual self-government of the masses, despite the pretence that the people had all the power, remains a fiction most of the time. It is always, in fact, minorities that do the governing [...]'[25]

The time has come, therefore, to tackle Bakunin's *latent* level of analysis on the authority issue. In fact, Bakunin is trapped in an apparently contradictory situation; on the one hand, he tries to make his criticism of Marx and Engels as attractive as possible to the proletarians. That is why he constantly argues in favour of proletarian self-emancipation in an ultra-libertarian way. On the other hand, he is fighting to win the International's leadership, an end which could be attained only by strictly organised and hierarchical action. In reality, however, Bakunin's anti-authoritarian ideology and authoritarian practice, which appear to be contradictory, complement each other. From this point of view, his manifest defence of an International Working Men's Association without central authority functions like a screen for Bakunin's 'invisible power, the only dictatorship [however he] will accept, because it alone is compatible with the aspirations of the people and the full dynamic thrust of the revolutionary movement'.[26] But how can the action of those 'invisible pilots guiding the Revolution, not by any kind of overt power but by the collective dictatorship of all [their] allies'[27] be compatible with proletarian

---

[24] M. Bakunin, 'The Knouto-Germanique Empire and the Social Revolution' in G.P. Maximoff, op. cit., pp.259-260. In relation to Bakunin's conception of the revolutionary organisation, see A. Lehning, 'Bakunin's conceptions of Revolutionary Organisations and their Role; A Study of his Secret Societies', as included in C. Abramsky (ed.), *Essays in Honour of E.H. Carr*, London, The Macmillan Press, 1974, pp.57-81.
[25] M. Bakunin, 'Federalism, Socialism, Anti-Theologism' in S. Dolgoff (ed.), op. cit., p.143.
[26] M. Bakunin, 'Letter to Albert Richard' in op. cit., p.178.
[27] op. cit., pp.180-181.

self-emancipation? It is indeed strange to note how Bakunin, while arguing in favour of a 'small party',[28] which should act like the invisible leading group of the revolution, at the same time accused Marx and his followers of being the dictators of the International and the proletarian movement as well.

As Professor Venturi correctly points out,

> when descended to the level of programmes, Bakunin thought in terms of revolutionary dictatorship. He eventually accepted the methods of the French Revolution and of Babeuf which he developed along lines parallel to those of Blanqui.[29]

In other words, the dialectics of political discourse and practice definitely confirm the two-dimensional character of Bakunin's relation with the proletarians; the anti-authoritarian discourse of the intellectual-agitator is strongly connected with the authoritarian practice of the intellectual-ruler, who tries to exert his invisible power over the proletarian movement.

At this point, it is worth noting that, as far as the latent level of his analysis is concerned, Bakunin agrees in fact with Marx and Engels' realistic position, according to which a certain kind of authority is a *conditio sine qua non* for the revolutionary transition from the old to the new society. Nevertheless, while Marx and Engels conceive such a transition through an aristodemocratic stage – without any further elaboration however – Bakunin passes directly from his anti-authoritarian verbiage to a *quasi* dictatorial conception of this transition.

The significance of this conclusion with regard to the intellectual's role in the revolutionary movement is self-evident. As has already been mentioned, the radical intellectual, according to Marx and Engels, while acting as interpreter of social processes and educator of the masses, may also function as the true lawgiver and actual leader of the proletarian vanguard organisation. Moreover, for Marx and Engels, such an intellectual leader can and should avoid any kind of

---

[28] M. Bakunin, 'Letter to a Frenchman on the Present Crisis', op. cit., pp.195-196.

[29] F. Venturi, *Roots of Revolution, A History of the Populist and Socialist Movements in Nineteenth Century Russia*, Chicago, The University of Chicago, 1983, pp.61-62. A similar view is expressed by Aileen Kelly, p.237; *contra*, Dolgoff in S. Dolgoff (ed.), op. cit., pp.181-182.

contempt for the masses, while promoting at the same time their active participation in the political process as such.[30] From Bakunin's point of view, however, intellectual leaders are always suspect and finally guilty of taking advantage of the proletarian cause for their own authoritarian purposes. That is why intellectuals should by no means act, not even transitionally, as the leading agents of the revolutionary change. Intellectual and moral leadership, as exerted by class, renegade intellectuals, are, according to Bakunin, doomed to degenerate in an oligarchic power.[31] The only exception to this 'iron law', Bakunin seems to suggest, is the small party of the 'invisible pilots guiding the Revolution' – pilots who are guided by him.

---

[30] From this point of view it is worth noting the General Council's political authority and social composition, as discussed in 'Fictitious Splits in the International', K. Marx and F. Engels ,op. cit. pp.108–109, where Marx and Engels explicitly argue in favour of the workers' decisive participation in the leading committee of the International.

[31] At this point, Bakunin's position foreshadows Michels' analysis of the oligarchic tendencies of 'Modern Democracy' in the early 1910s. Special attention should be paid, however, to the fact that Michels, as well as Bakunin, sometimes substitutes the term 'aristocracy' for the term 'oligarchy'. Moreover, it is worth noting that he approaches aristocracy by focusing on the class-content of the word. Thus, his reference to 'Democratic Aristocracy and Aristocratic Democracy' has nothing to do with the concept of aristodemocracy as defined and elaborated in the present study. (See R. Michels, *Political Parties, A Sociological Study of the Oligarchical Tendencies of Modern Democracy*, New York, The Free Press, 1962, especially pp.43–51).

Chapter 11
Marx and Bakunin: Philosophy and Emancipation – a Critical Summary

Although Bakunin's views on the intellectual/proletarian relation demand a special consideration within the context of the intelligentsia question (to be discussed in the next part of this work), we can reach a general conclusion: as the historical experience of the First International shows, Marx and Bakunin followed two distinct ways of dealing with the intellectuals' political engagement in the proletarian movement.[1]

According to Marx, a revolutionary movement is actually inconceivable without the action of a leading group, the members of which should take advantage of their own intellectual and moral virtue in order to prepare the proletariat for its self-emancipation. Such a leadership derives its political power not from the field of violence, but through the respect which the masses express towards their leaders. For their part, these distinguished leading personalities should exert their intellectual and moral authority not for their own benefit but for the proletarian cause as such. Hence, according to Marx (and Engels') analysis, the workers become conscious of their self-emancipatory capacities not by themselves, but by taking advantage of a transitional aristodemocratic leadership, as mentioned above.

Contrary to this approach, Bakunin's analysis proceeds on two apparently contradictory and actually complementary levels. He

---

[1] For a general comparison of Marx and Bakunin's theories of social transformation, see: J. Clark, 'Marx, Bakunin and the problem of social transformation', *Telos*, 42, Winter 1979–80, pp.80–97.

argues overtly in favour of an ultra-libertarian concept of revolution, which is incompatible with any kind of leading activity on behalf of the 'men of knowledge'. On the latent level of his analysis, however, Bakunin points to the need for an organised leading group, which confronts and directs the proletarian masses as their invisible collective 'dictator'. Moreover, Bakunin's political discourse – especially in its manifest libertarian version – proves quite anti-intellectualist.[2] From this point of view, it can be argued as well that Bakunin's anti-intellectualism goes hand in hand with his anti-Marxian politics. He recognises in Marx an intellectual-leader of a future ruling 'aristocracy of learning', which would dominate the proletarian class. According to Bakunin, Marx and his fellow 'learned intellectuals' constitute the embryo of a new domination over and against the masses.[3] From a similar point of view, Bakunin also rejects the so-called 'People's State', the actual ruler of which would not be the people itself, but an intellectual pseudo-aristocracy.

> The pseudo-popular state [says Bakunin] will be nothing but the highly despotic government of the masses by a new and very small aristocracy of real or pretended scholars. The people are not learned, so they will be liberated in entirety in the governed herd. A fine liberation![4]

As a matter of fact, Bakunin's negative stance towards the 'men of knowledge' cannot be explained in *political* terms alone. It is impossible indeed to follow Bakunin's critique against scholars or scientists without taking into consideration the *philosophical* context of his political views, especially in regard to the intellectual question. From this point of view, it is worth noting that two of Bakunin's major works, *The Knouto-Germanic Empire and the Social Revolution*

---

[2] In his *Statism and Anarchy*, p.134, Bakunin argues as follows: 'By his very nature a scholar is disposed to intellectual and moral depravity of every kind, but his principal vice is to exalt his own knowledge and intellect and scorn all the ignorant. Let him govern, and he will become the most unbearable tyrant, for scholarly pride is repulsive, offensive, and more oppressive than any other.'

[3] See Marx's reaction to Bakunin's views in his rather superficial 'Notes on Bakunin's Book *Statehood and Anarchy*', in K. Marx and F. Engels, op. cit., vol. 24, pp.518–520.

[4] M. Bakunin, *Statism and Anarchy*, pp.178–179; on the same issue, see M. Bakunin, *The International and Karl Marx*, p.319.

(especially its part under the title *God and the State*) and *Statism and Anarchy* are strongly characterised by a *quasi* romantic and vitalist critique of science.[5] According to Bakunin, science proceeds from abstraction to abstraction, negates the concrete and, therefore, rejects life itself. In a way foreshadowing Nietzsche's approach to the same issue, the Russian thinker calls for the revolt of life against science or, in other words, the revolt of the concrete against the abstract.

> What I preach then is, to a certain extent, the *revolt of life against science,* or rather against the *government of science,* not to destroy science – that would be high treason to humanity – but to remand it to its place so that it can never leave it again.[6] (Bakunin's emphasis)

Consequently, by putting science to its place, i.e. away from government, Bakunin affirms that scientists should be kept apart from governmental duties: 'an aristocracy of learning! From the practical point of view the most haughty and insulting – such would be the power established in the name of science.'[7]

In fact, Bakunin, for whom science 'is accessible only to a very insignificant minority',[8] believes that 'better an absence of light than a false and feeble light, kindled only to mislead those who follow it [...]. The practical summary of [people's] painful experience constitutes a sort of traditional science, which in certain respects is worth as much as theoretical science.'[9]

A further examination of Bakunin's concept of science lies of course beyond the boundaries of this work. Nevertheless, as far as the object of this research is concerned, it is worth noting that behind his critique of the social and political role of the 'aristocracy of learning' there is an indisputable scepticism towards science as a coherent theoretical attempt to confront and give shape to life.[10]

---

[5] See Bakunin's analysis on science in M. Bakunin, *God and the State*, New York, Dover Publications, 1970, p.56 ff; see also M. Bakunin, *Statism and Anarchy*, p.133 ff.
[6] M. Bakunin, *God and the State*, p.59.
[7] op. cit., p.63.
[8] op. cit., pp.133–134.
[9] op. cit., p.64.
[10] According to Bakunin, op. cit., p.135: 'Woe to mankind if thought ever become the source and sole guide of life, if science and learning began to govern society. Life would dry up, and human society would be turned into a dumb and servile herd.

Moreover, it must be admitted that Bakunin's analysis is actually trapped in a peculiar fetishism of terms and concepts. Science is identified with a closed system of *a priori* given ideas, applied in the observation and further reconstruction of reality in 'cold blood'. On the other hand, life is described as a dynamic process which overturns every systematic research of social reality.

In other words, identifying science with positivism, Bakunin fails just at the point where Marx's analysis gains in terms of coherence and inspiration. Blocked by his polemics against science and intellectuals, he proves unable to distinguish between ideology, in the negative sense of the term, and its revolutionary critique, the main agents of which are class renegade intellectuals. This is exactly, however, the ground, on which Marx and Engels constructed a new conception of science,[11] as a radical critique of the existing state of things.[12] While rejecting the 'Comtist recipes for the cook shops of the future',[13] Marx – contrary to Bakunin – argues in favour of a further elaboration of a 'real positive science'. Whether Marx succeeded or not in developing a critical notion of science is an open and extremely complicated question, which lies beyond the scope of this work.[14] There is no doubt, however, that Bakunin's approach to science was very different. Based on his undifferentiated use of the concepts of 'science' and 'scholar', Bakunin was unavoidably led to a crude attack on the 'aristocracy of learning' as a whole. From this point of view, even Plato's well-known distinction between 'lovers of knowledge' and 'lovers of opinion' seems of no use for Bakunin's one-sided analysis of the intellectual question.

At this point, it is worth remembering (as has already been mentioned in the introductory pages of this work) that the tension between knowledge and its agents, on the one hand, and people's self-emancipation, on the other, runs through almost every phase of the

---

The government of life by science would have no other result than to turn all mankind into fools.'

[11] On Marx's conception of science, and especially on Marx's defence of positive science, as it is basically expressed in K. Marx and F. Engels, *The German Ideology*, see I. Mészáros, *Ideology and Social Science*, Sussex, Wheatsheaf Books, 1986, pp.112-124.

[12] K. Marx and F. Engels, *The German Ideology*, vol. 5, p.37.

[13] K. Marx, *Capital*, London, Lawrence and Wishart, 1954, vol. I, p.26.

[14] On this issue, see the interesting analysis of Paul Thomas, 'Marx and Science', *Political Studies*, vol. XXIV, No 1 (1976), pp.1-23.

history of ancient and modern philosophy as well. With regard to Bakunin's one-dimensional confrontation with the issue, however, it can be argued that his analysis converges with Rousseau's overall attack on science and intellectuals in eighteenth century Europe. At the same time – despite the significant convergence of Rousseau and Bakunin's views on the question of intellectuals within the context of a (pre)romantic ideology – it can be also noted that Bakunin was influenced by the liberal trend within the European Enlightenment as well. Here, Paul Thomas' comment proves interesting indeed:

> Enlightenment speculation about politics is not all of a piece. The aspect it turns towards anarchism that of negative liberty and of certain disdain for power [...] is not the only face it has to present. There is also a very different approach epitomised by Rousseau, whose view of liberty was not negative, but positive and whose desire was not to minimise power [...]. There is a divide [concludes Thomas], a watershed in Enlightenment thinking about power, authority and politics. Marx is on one side of it, the anarchists on the other.[15]

It is however difficult to agree with such a clear-cut demarcation line. As far as Marx and Bakunin are concerned, the divide of a Rousseauist versus a liberal type of politics does not work. Marx, though constantly refusing to adopt the liberal theory of politics, argues in favour of the ultimate annihilation of the state. On the other hand, though it is possible to admit that Bakunin's manifest version of political discourse reveals a certain connection with the Enlightenment's concept of negative liberty, his latent version of the vanguard/masses relation remains very authoritarian.

From a different point of view, it is worth noting that Aileen Kelly – stressing the romantic element of the Bakunin's thought – reaches a

---

[15] P. Thomas, *Karl Marx and the Anarchists*, pp.10-11; for Thomas's more detailed approach to the Bakunin-Enlightenment relation, see op. cit., p.7 ff. On the same issue see G. Crowder, *Classical Anarchism, The Political Thought of Godwin, Proudhon, Bakunin and Kropotkin*, Oxford, Clarendon Press, 1991, pp.6-38, where Crowder places Bakunin in the so-called perfectionist tradition which starts from Plato and through Spinoza, Rousseau, Kant and Hegel, reaches classical anarchism.

conclusion which accurately describes Bakunin's political intervention in the proletarian movement:

> [T]he relations between the intellectuals and the masses, centred on the romantic cult of spontaneity [argues Kelly] were an ingenious transposition onto the historical plane of the dialectical relationship of the Idealist with its Absolute.[16]

Is it, however, legitimate to attach the above portrait of the romantic intellectual to Marx and Engels as well, whose relation with the Enlightenment is quite different from Bakunin's? In other words, is it possible to observe 'a romantic cult of spontaneity' in Marx and Engels' theory and practice *qua* intellectuals and leaders of the proletarian movement during the years of the International? Contrary to Bakunin's political romanticism, both Marx and Engels attempted to construct their own relation with proletarians in a way which was *positively* influenced by the philosophical tradition of the Enlightenment, as far as the intellect/people relation is concerned. The radical intellectual, being himself (or herself) the vanguard agent of knowledge, transforms spontaneity into (revolutionary) consciousness. To this end, science, and more concretely knowledge grounded on the materialist conception of history, is the necessary means, without which socialist revolution is doomed to fail.[17] Thus, contrary to what Bakunin apparently suggests, practical or traditional science – as expressed by people's common experience – should not be made equal to theoretical or 'real positive science'. This means that the vanguard role of the revolutionary intellectual must not be annulled in the name of the people's spontaneous drive to truth, as long as the masses themselves are still devoid of knowledge.

From this point of view, and contrary to what has been often suggested, Marx and Engels never struck at the essence of the vanguard idea.[18] In elaborating even further the Enlightenment's

---

[16] A. Kelly, op. cit., p.139.

[17] As David W. Lovell correctly argues, however, 'Marx himself was ambivalent about the status of his theoretical project [...]. The relationship between his project and the working-class movement was neither formulated nor resolved.' (D.W. Lovell, *From Marx to Lenin, An Evaluation of Marx's Responsibility for Soviet Authoritarianism*, Cambridge, Cambridge University Press, 1984, pp.29-30).

[18] See for example Richard Hunt's analysis in his *The Political Ideas of Marx and Engels*, vol. II, p.316 ff, and especially p.323.

concept of an intellectual vanguard, both tried to prove that the transformative action of such a vanguard may be compatible with proletarian self-emancipation. The fact that Marx and Engels were against a Blanquist or a Bakuninist type of elite organisation does not mean that they were also against any kind of intellectual and political leadership. Their own activity in the International explicitly illustrates their belief in the necessity of the working class' vanguard organisation.[19] In fact, Marx and Engels' participation in this institution definitely confirms the conclusion already reached through the study of the Communist League's history. The intellectual-educator should not be dogmatically confined to the role of a 'disinterested adviser' of the workers.[20]

At this point, it is worth remembering once again that, according to our earlier interpretation of Marx and Engels' approach to the intellectual/proletarian relation, the two thinkers definitely opposed both the (ultra) libertarian and the *(quasi)* dictatorial versions of this relation, as these were expressed and defended by Bakunin in the manifest and latent level of his political discourse. The transitional aristodemocratic type of the intellectual/proletarian relation, which Marx and Engels merely hinted at, seems to be their own embryonic solution with regard to the problem of successfully linking of the intellectual leadership with proletarian self-emancipation.[21]

Nevertheless, a global evaluation of these particular approaches to the intellectuals' political engagement in the proletarian movement must not be limited to the International's historic experience. Thus, we now turn to the discussion of the Russian populism and Marxism

---

[19] As Professor Venturi, op. cit., p.444, correctly argues, 'the International had given the working classes a fuller degree of awareness. Yet it had to be admitted that internationally minded were still a minority and constituted the aristocracy of the intelligentsia in the world of the working classes.'

[20] For the opposite view, see D. Guérin, 'Marxism and Anarchism' in D. Goodway (ed.), *For Anarchism, History, Theory and Practice*, London, Routledge, 1989, p.122.

[21] On the contrary, Gouldner does not believe that such a linking can be achieved within the framework of the Marxist political theory and concludes as follows: '[Marx and Engels] enmeshed in a contest with competing intellectuals against whom they developed their own exclusionary tactics, in the name of the 'self-emancipation of the proletariat'' (A.W. Gouldner, op. cit., p.144). Clearly Gouldner juxtaposes in a mechanistic way the *ultimate* goal of proletarian self-emancipation for the *transitional/preparatory* phase of intellectual leadership.

during the second half of the nineteenth and the first years of the twentieth century.

PART III
Intellectuals, Intelligentsia and Proletarian Self-Emancipation – a Debate within the European Proletarian Movement

Chapter 12
Intellectuals and Proletarians: from the Paris Commune to the International's Dissolution

Having already discussed the intellectual/proletarian relation within the First International, it is now time to extend this analysis to the 1871 Paris Commune, which Marx himself identified as the political form of the liberation of labour, while Engels did not hesitate to characterise it as an example of the dictatorship of the proletariat.[1]

> The great social measure of the Commune [writes Marx] was *its own working existence*. Its special measures could but betoken the tendency of *a government of the people by the* people.[2] (our emphasis)

From Marx's point of view, therefore, it seems quite obvious that the Paris Commune should be considered as the first stage of the proletarian self-emancipatory process. 'The insurrection in Paris [Marx insists] was made by the workmen of Paris. The ablest of the

---

[1] See Engels' introduction to Marx's, 'The Civil War in France' in K. Marx and F. Engels, *Selected Works*, vol. 2, p.460: 'Of late, the Social Democratic philistine has once more been filled with wholesome terror at the words: Dictatorship of the Proletariat. Well and good, gentlemen, do you want to know what this dictatorship looks like? Look at the Paris Commune. That was the Dictatorship of the Proletariat.'

[2] K. Marx, 'The Civil War in France' in K. Marx and F. Engels, *Collected Works*, vol. 22, p.339. Marx's approach to the Paris Commune as the institutional expression of the workers' self-emancipation is also recognisable in op. cit., pp.335, 336, 338; see, however, Marx's quite different views on this issue as expressed in his first draft of 'The Civil War in France' in op. cit., pp.490–491.

For an overall assessment of Marx and Engels's position, see M. Levin, op. cit., pp.113–132.

workmen must necessarily have been its leaders and administrators [...].'[3]

Nevertheless, such a position does not actually correspond to historical reality. The Paris Commune is by no means the expression of the working class' self-emancipation in the realm of history. As far as its social composition is concerned, it is beyond doubt that intellectuals and not workers constituted its majority. Even the worker-participants of the Commune should be considered – at least with regard to their leading figures – as worker-intellectuals.[4]

Following Cole's highly documented analysis,

> there were more intellectuals than workers, among them many journalists of varying views; and there were quite a number of tradesmen and other members of the lower middle-classes.[5]

As regards the political composition of the Commune, it is worth noting that there was just one follower of Marx – Leo Frankel – among the ninety-two elected representatives.[6] Blanquists, Jacobins and Federalists – and Proudhonists as well – were the most important political/ideological groups within the ranks of the Paris insurrection.[7] Thus, due to this plurality of political and ideological groups, there was no common theory of revolution among the Communards and, as Cole points out, '[they] were, during the few months of the Commune's existence, much too busy to make one'.[8]

On the basis of these historical facts, therefore, certain conclusions may be reached, with regard to the intellectual/proletarian relation during the Paris Commune.

---

[3] 'Record of Marx's Interview with The World Correspondent' in K. Marx and F. Engels, *Collected Works*, vol. 22, p.601.

[4] C. Rihs, *La Commune de Paris, 1871, sa structure et ses doctrines*, Paris, Editions de Seuil, 1973, p.109.

[5] G.D.H. Cole, op. cit.
The same conclusion is reached by C. Rihs, op. cit., p.120, and M. Levin, op. cit., p.115.

[6] C. Rihs, op. cit., p.91.

[7] See:
  a) G.D.H. Cole, op. cit., pp.134–148.
  b) C. Rihs, op. cit., pp.87–108.

[8] G.D.H. Cole. op. cit., p.172.

Intellectuals played, in fact, a leading role in the Commune, though not as theory producers, but as political representatives and instructors of the Parisian proletarian masses.

Intellectual-educators like Marx and Engels themselves did not exert any particular theoretical or political influence on the Commune's fate. This is why Kolakowski rightly argues that 'the Commune was not the child of the International, still less of the Marxists'.[9] Besides, it is worth mentioning that Marx himself openly rejected any *direct* involvement of the International in the Commune's action.[10]

The historical existence of the Commune, and especially the tragic end of the Communards' revolutionary attempt, proved that the necessary unity among intellectuals and workers on the solid ground of a common theory of revolution had not yet been achieved. In particular, Marx's social and political theory, despite the International's activity, did not have an impact on the workers themselves.[11]

On the other hand, the Commune's fate exerted a serious influence on the International's life and Marx's political and intellectual conception of the proletarian movement. From our point of view, it was the International's inability to connect with and direct a massive

---

[9] L. Kolakowski, *Main Currents of Marxism*, Oxford, Oxford University Press, 1981, vol. 1, p.256.

[10] See: 'Record of Marx's Interview with The World Correspondent' in K. Marx and F. Engels, op. cit., vol. 22, p.601: 'The ablest of the workmen must necessarily have been its leaders and administrators; but the ablest workmen happen also to be members of the International Association. Yet the association as such may be in no way responsible for their action.'

See also G.D.H. Cole, op. cit., p.171: '22 at least [of the Commune elected members] are known to have been members of the International, and 24 Blanquists or near-Blanquists. Half a dozen were members of the Central Committee of the National Guard about whose political views nothing definite is known. The majority of the remainder were left-wing Radicals, of varying types and colours, with no known International or Blanquist connections [...]'.

[11] C. Rihs, op. cit., pp.90–94; Marx himself, ten years after the Paris Insurrection, proceeds to a similar conclusion: '[A]part from the fact that [the Paris Commune] was merely the rising of a city under exceptional conditions, *the majority of the Commune was by no means socialist, nor could it be*. (Our emphasis – K. Marx, 'Letter to Ferdinand Domela-Nieuwenhuis' 22 February 1881 in K. Marx and F. Engels, *Selected Correspondence*, Moscow, Progress Publishers, 1955, p.318).

revolutionary movement – an inability definitely proved during the 1871 Paris insurrection – which led to its own dissolution.[12]

As Molyneux correctly mentions,

> this very looseness which was the International's strength in that it enabled Marx to hold together its various factions, while at the same time providing a general guidance, was also its weakness.[13]

Moreover, it is worth noting that even after their pyrrhic victory in the International's internal affairs, Marx and Engels did not succeed in bringing under their own intellectual control either the International or the European proletarian movement.[14] At last, the Commune's collapse seems to stabilise Marx and Engels' views on the organisational question. In fact, a centralised political leadership, capable of counterbalancing the reactionary state-machine, proves to be a matter of vital necessity for the further unfolding of the revolutionary process.[15]

As a result, about a year after the Paris insurrection, the International's Congress, which took place at the Hague, leading to Bakunin's exclusion from the Association's ranks, voted for a further increase of the General Council's powers and declared the transformation of its own organisation into a political party to be urgent duty of the working class.[16]

---

[12] The International's dissolution took place at Philadelphia on July 15, 1876.
[13] J. Molyneux, *Marxism and the Party*, London, Bookmarks, 1978, p.27.
[14] See Fernbach's 'Introduction' to D. Fernbach (ed.), *Karl Marx: The First International and After*, Harmondsworth, Penguin Books, 1974, p.49: 'By the time the Hague Congress met, however, it was already obvious to Marx that, despite formal majorities, he had failed to win sufficient support to make his envisaged transformation of the International possible, or even to guarantee that Bakunin would not take over the International at a future date.'
  Boris Nicolaievsky and Otto Maenchen-Helfen, op. cit., pp.390–391, adopt a similar line of analysis.
[15] According to M. Johnstone, 'Marx and Engels and the Concept of the Party', *The Socialist Register*, 1967, p.135, 'in the aftermath of the Paris Commune, faced with persecution from the reactionary forces of Europe and disruption from the Bakuninists, Marx and Engels had no alternative but to fight, to give the International an effective centralised leadership. Yet, in so doing, they precipitated its end.'
[16] See articles 2, 6 and 7a in 'Resolutions of the General Congress held at The Hague from the 2nd to the 7th September, 1872' in K. Marx and F. Engels, *Collected Works*, vol. 23, pp.243–244.

At this point, it is worth mentioning as well that after the Hague Congress Marx and Engels came face to face with a new political milieu. As Molyneux points out, 'from 1872 onwards Marx and Engels were never again directly involved in, or members of, any organisation or party, but they nonetheless regarded themselves as having 'special status as representatives of *international* socialism', and in that capacity dispensed advice to socialists throughout the world.'[17] (Molyneux's emphasis)

From this point of view, it may be argued that Marx and Engels finally withdrew to the intellectual-adviser position, in a way reminiscent of Voltaire's advisory attitude towards the native artisans of Geneva. Nevertheless, times have changed; the philosophers of the European Enlightenment seemed to have given their leading place to the European proletariat. The movement of the working class looked mature enough to proceed to the next stage of its development. Political sects and conspiratorial groups, as far as Western Europe is concerned, belong to the past.[18] The formation of workers' parties is just a matter of time. Hence, both Marx and Engels were led to reorientate their own fragile relations with proletarians by taking into consideration the foundation of workers' parties and by making, therefore, subtle use of their own intellectual and moral authority over the European movement itself.

Under these circumstances, however, Marx and Engels' attitude towards German social democracy and other social democratic parties as well deserves a more detailed evaluation with regard to the intellectual question we are dealing with.

---

[17] See J. Molyneux, op. cit., p.31 in connection with F. Engels, 'Letter to Bernstein', 27 February – 1 March 1883 in K. Marx and F. Engels, *Selected Correspondence*, p.337.
[18] See the 'Record of Marx's Speech on Secret Societies' in K. Marx and F. Engels, *Collected Works*, vol. 22, p.621.

Chapter 13
Marx, Engels and European Social Democracy: Intellectuals and Workers' Parties

According to the research hypothesis, which has been examined up to this point, Marx and Engels' status within the ranks of the proletarian movement was determined by the moral and intellectual superiority they both enjoyed over the cadres and the common members of the movement all over Europe.

As Terell Carver, Engels' well-known biographer, comments, for example,

> [Engels] was not an officer in a national party or other such organisation in which decisions were taken and binding commitments to action enforced. His advice was sought, considered and amended in contexts where he himself did not function directly and his views had the prestige that they did because he had made himself well-known as a theorist [...].[1]

In fact, Engels himself seems to have no doubt about Marx's and his own relation with the representatives of national workers' parties and movements.

> It is therefore [writes Engels] not a case of Marx forcing his opinion, and still less his will on people but of the people themselves coming to him. And it is upon this that Marx's specific influence, so extremely important for the movement, reposes [...].

---

[1] T. Carver, *Friedrich Engels, His Life and Thought*, London, The Macmillan Press, 1989, p.243.

Marx and in the second place I have adopted the same attitude towards the French as towards the other national movements. We maintain constant contacts with them in so far it is worth our while and there is the opportunity to do so. But any attempt to influence these people against their will would only do harm; it would destroy the old confidence dating back to the time of the International. We really have had too much experience of revolutionary matters for that...[2]

Given the above position, it is, therefore, beyond doubt that Marx and Engels confront the newly born institution of the national workers' party from the point of view of an intellectual-adviser. They both avoid becoming the rulers of such a party and confine themselves to giving advice to the political leaders of these vanguard organisations.[3] At the same time, however, it is worth mentioning that through their advisory activity Marx and Engels were often led to become *de facto* legislators, deriving their power not from political authority as such, but from the intellectual and moral superiority they themselves enjoyed over the proletarian masses and the workers' parties.

Nevertheless, at this point a crucial question arises: which of these parties can be regarded as a real workers' party?

According to a *quantitative* criterion, the class character of a party depends upon the *class identity* of the majority of its members. In such a case, however, additional data should be taken into account: the type of the decision making process and the degree to which the party leaders genuinely *represent* its rank and file, as well as the degree to which the party itself actually *represents* the working class as a whole.

On the other hand, according to a *qualitative* criterion, the class character of a party depends upon the *theoretical identity* of its members. From this point of view, a party may be considered

---

[2] F. Engels, 'Letter to Bernstein', 25 October 1881 in K. Marx and F. Engels, *Selected Correspondence*, pp.324-325.

[3] See, for example, Engels' 'Letter to Bebel', 18-28 March 1875 in K. Marx and F. Engels, *Collected Works*, vol. 45, p.65, in which Engels describes Marx's and his own relation with the German Social Democracy as follows: 'People imagine that we run the whole show from here, where you know as well as I do that we have hardly ever interfered in the least with internal party affairs, and then only in an attempt to make good, as far as possible, what we considered to have been blunders – and *only theoretical* blunders at that.' (Engels's emphasis).

proletarian, if its members interpret social reality and fight for its transformation by adopting what is methodologically defined as a *proletarian outlook*. It is well known, however, that within the vast domain of the history of ideas, from the second half of the nineteenth to the first decades of the twentieth century, not only Marx and Engels, but other intellectuals as well argued that their own political theory had been formed on the basis of proletarian interests. Under such circumstances, the theoretical and, ultimately, the political conflict among various intellectual and political currents becomes unavoidable. Such was the case with the ideological struggle within the framework of the First International and this was also the case with the European political movement of the working class during the last decades of the nineteenth century.

In regard to this problem, it also worth underlining that, although – according to Engels – 'scientific socialism' is the 'theoretical expression of the proletarian movement',[4] neither he nor Marx surrendered to the siren of spontaneism, even when workers' parties were being founded, one after the other, all over Europe. From Marx and Engels' point of view, the workers' party should avoid being either a mere mouthpiece of the working class or a Blanquist organisation which substitutes itself for the proletarian movement. Revolutions, Marx and Engels continue to believe, are not made by a small minority according to a plan worked out in advance and behind the backs of the people.[5] Revolutions are the historical outcome of mass movements, and they require for their success the effective leadership of an intellectual and political vanguard.[6]

---

[4] F. Engels, 'Socialism: Utopian and Scientific' in K. Marx and F. Engels op. cit., vol. 24, p.325.

[5] See Engels' critique of Blanqui and his followers as expressed in F. Engels, 'Refugee Literature, II. Programme of Blanquist Commune Refugees' in K. Marx and F. Engels, op. cit. vol. 24, especially pp.13–14.

[6] To this end, it is worth distinguishing the elite from the vanguard. In our opinion, the elite group substitutes itself for the class, while the vanguard organisation, as conceived by Marx and Engels, directs the class movement, which, at the same time, reacts upon the vanguard organisation itself. Contrary to this view, George Lichtheim in *From Marx to Hegel*, (New York, The Seabury Press, 1974, p.78) seems to confuse the concept of elite with that of vanguard, reaching therefore the wrong conclusion that the vanguard thesis is actually a defence of elitism and substitutionism: 'This development [concludes Lichtheim] signifies the dissolution of the Marxian "union of theory and practice", a union originally built upon the

> The first great step of importance for every country newly entering into the movement [writes Engels] is always the constitution of the workers as an *independent* political party, no matter how, so long as it is a *distinct* workers' party [...][7] (our emphasis)

What Engels actually hints at, however, is that there is no contradiction between the need for a political vanguard organisation, on the one hand, and the self-emancipation principle, on the other, as long as such an organisation is in fact a working-class' party.

Nevertheless, the tension between the concept of the vanguard and that of self-emancipation cannot so easily be overcome in practice as it may appear in theory, since – as has already been mentioned – the proletarian character of a party cannot be guaranteed, even if the vast majority of its members are workers themselves.

From this point of view, Marx and Engels' critical stance towards German social democracy becomes even more challenging. More specifically, taking advantage of the so-called 'Höchberg case',[8] Marx and Engels address the following instructions to the most distinguished leaders of the German social democratic movement.

> It is an inevitable manifestation, and one rooted in the process of development, that people from what have hitherto been the ruling class also join the militant proletariat and supply it with educative elements. We have already said so clearly in the *Manifesto*. But in this context there are two observations to be made:
>
> *Firstly,* if these people are to be of use to the proletarian movement, they must introduce genuinely educative elements.
>
> *Secondly,* when people of this kind, from different classes, join the proletarian movement, the first

---

faith that the working class can and will emancipate itself [...].' (*contra* R. Miliband, *Marxism and Politics*, Oxford University Press, Oxford, 1977, p.128).

[7] F. Engels, 'Letter to Sorge', 29 November 1886 in K. Marx and F. Engels, *Selected Correspondence*, p.374; it is worth noting as well that Karl Marx himself, while dictating to Guesde the *Preamble to the French Workers' Party*, declares once again the need for organising the proletariat into an 'independent political party' (K. Marx and F. Engels, *Collected Works*, vol. 24, p.340).

[8] For a detailed presentation of the 'Höchberg case', see H. Draper, op. cit., vol. II, pp.515–518, 569–572.

requirement is that they should not bring with them the least remnant of bourgeois etc., prejudices, but should unreservedly adopt the proletarian outlook [...].

[H]ence, we cannot simply co-operate with men who seek to eliminate [...] class struggle from the movement. At the founding of the International we expressly formulated the battle cry: The emancipation of the working class must be achieved by the working class itself. Hence we cannot co-operate with men who say openly that the workers are too uneducated to emancipate themselves and must first be emancipated from above by philanthropic members of the upper and lower middle classes.[9]

There is no doubt, therefore, that, according to Marx and Engels, the working class' self-emancipation is compatible indeed with the existence and action of a vanguard party, given the fact that this party is actually a proletarian organisation.[10] Nevertheless, since they believe that the proletarian character of the party is not just a matter of numbers, Marx and Engels pay special attention to the party's theoretical identity as well. Not only must the vast majority of its members be workers, but its guiding theory must be proletarian, i.e. it must express and serve the proletarian struggle for the radical transformation of capitalism to a socialist and, ultimately, a communist/classless society.

Within such a context, Marx and Engels' position on the intellectual question is formed as follows: the bourgeois and petty bourgeois intellectuals may join the working class' movement and party. Nevertheless, these class renegade intellectuals should be admitted within the ranks of the workers' party, if they really supply

---

[9] K. Marx and F. Engels, 'Circular Letter to Bebel, Liebknecht, Bracke and others', 17–18 September 1879 in K. Marx and F. Engels, op. cit., vol. 45, pp.407–408.

[10] See, for example, Engels' argument on this concrete issue as expressed in F. Engels, 'A Working Men's Party' in K. Marx and F. Engels, op. cit., vol. 24, pp.405–406: 'Enlightened men of other classes (where they are not so plentiful as people would make us believe) might join that party and even represent it in Parliament after having given pledges of their sincerity [...]. But no democratic party in England, as well as elsewhere, will be effectively successful unless it has a distinct working-class character. Abandon that, and you have nothing but sects and shams.'

the proletarians with 'genuinely educative elements', freeing themselves from any residues of bourgeois or petty bourgeois ideology. Consequently, any kind of political theory, which leads the workers in intellectual and political tutelage, must be kept out of the party.[11]

It is exactly at this point that a further question arises, however: who judges which are the 'genuinely educative elements' and what really constitutes a bourgeois or a petty bourgeois ideological prejudice? Unless the party is mature enough to play the role of a *self*-directed collective legislator and educator of the proletarian masses, class renegade intellectuals of a high theoretical and moral status must not be ignored. Nevertheless, even in this case, according to our interpretation of Marx and Engels' views, the relation of such distinguished intellectuals with the proletarian party should be constructed not upon a dictatorial or a messianic basis, but upon an aristodemocratic one. This means that vanguard intellectuals must neither dictate their terms to, nor obey passively the party and its leaders; they should rather exert theoretical and moral influence through their own critical discourse, as this will be addressed to the cadres and the rank and file of the revolutionary organisation. On the other hand, such an organisation must always seek the enlightened views of eminent intellectuals in order to play its own educational and political role even more effectively.

From such an aristodemocratic point of view, the party itself is in the last analysis, the collective legislator/referee which selects the

---

[11] A classical example of a severe critique against the working class's tutelage by bourgeois or petty bourgeois intellectuals can be observed in Engels' attack on the Fabian Society and its members. See, especially,
a) F. Engels, 'Letter to Kautsky', 4 September 1892
b) F. Engels, 'Letter to Sorge', 18 January 1893
c) F. Engels, 'Letter to Sorge', 11 November 1893

From the same point of view, Marx himself criticises the German Social Democracy as follows: 'In Germany, a corrupt spirit is asserting itself in our party, not so much among the masses as among the leaders (upper class and 'workers'). [...] The workers themselves, when like Mr. Most and Co. they give up working and become *literati* by *profession*, invariably wreak 'theoretical' havoc and are always ready to consort with addle-heads of the supposedly 'learned' caste.' (K. Marx, 'Letter to Sorge', 19 October 1877 in K. Marx and F. Engels, op. cit., vol. 45, p.283 (Marx's emphasis).

In the same direction: F. Engels, 'Letter to Becker', 8 September 1879 in op. cit., vol. 45, p.384.

'genuinely educative elements', suitable to be admitted in its ranks. It does this having taken into consideration the critical judgement of the agents of knowledge who, even standing outside of the party, exert *de facto* a decisive influence on the formation of party's strategy and tactics.

At this point, however, Marx and Engels' approach to the intellectual question brings us again to the classical philosophical problem: to what extent and under what conditions can the intellectual-educator's activity be compatible with the self-formation and, furthermore, the self-emancipation of the revolutionary subject?

As with their previous political experience, Marx and Engels' relation with the European workers' parties reaffirms the hypothesis that, despite their belief in the proletariat's education through its own mistakes and within the ranks of its own movement,[12] they never endorse the self-education principle. Such a declaration would have drawn them directly to the ideological impasse of spontaneism. Rejecting spontaneism, however, they were unavoidably led to the recognition of the need for a revolutionary educator, distinct from, though influenced by the mass movement itself.[13]

From this concrete point of view, Marx and Engels may be seen, therefore, as philosophical heirs of the Enlightenment's theory of education. By adhering to and at the same time extending the limits of this philosophical tradition, they constantly support the thesis that the political education of the masses is a dialectically *mediated* process, opposed both to self-education and to educational tutelage as well. It is at this point that European liberalism and Marx's political philosophy seem to meet on the ground of an *educational aristodemocratism,* which must be clearly distinguished from

---

[12] 'The masses [argues Engels foreshadowing Luxemburg's analysis] must have time and opportunity to develop, and they have the opportunity only when they have a movement of their own – no matter in what form so long as it is their own movement – in which they are driven further by their own mistakes and learn from their experience.' (F. Engels, 'Letter to Sorge', 29 November 1886 in K. Marx and F. Engels, *Selected Correspondence*, p.374 – Engels's emphasis).

[13] Contrary to this opinion, Herbert Marcuse in his *Soviet Marxism: A Critical Analysis*, (New York, Vintage Books, 1961, p.12), refers to the *natural* growth of the proletarian party on the basis of the modern proletariat's activity: '[According to Marx and Engels], the class organises itself into a 'party' [argues Marcuse] but this party develops *naturwüchsig* out of the 'soil of modern society itself': it is the *self-organisation* of the proletariat.' (Marcuse's emphasis).

intellectual elitism, on the one hand, and *proletarian spontaneism*, on the other.

With regard, however, to Marx and Engels' position, a final comment should be made; they both see the foundation of German social democracy and other workers' parties all over Europe – to the extent that these parties were proletarian at all – as a further step towards the working class' self-emancipation. Nevertheless, the critical distance, which they kept from these parties during the last years of their life, reflects their inner belief that the formation of a proletarian collective-educator is a highly complicated matter. Actually, Marxism's life and adventures, from Western to Eastern Europe, to which we now turn, seem to verify the hypothesis that the intellectual question – a problem which Marx and Engels confronted inadequately – constitutes one of the most controversial issues of their own theory of revolution, deserving a far more detailed consideration.

Chapter 14
Intelligentsia: an Attempt to a Definition

In fact, one of the most interesting aspects of the intellectual question is its further study in comparison with the intelligentsia phenomenon, which appeared in Russia during the nineteenth century. Before proceeding, however, to this analysis, it is necessary to define, as accurately as possible, the historical and socio-political content of the term 'intelligentsia'.

According to Martin Malia, 'the term intelligentsia was introduced into the Russian language in the 1860's by a minor novelist named Boborykin and became current almost immediately'.[1] As Aleksander Gella confirms, however, this term was born in Poland in 1844 and used in Russian literature by Belinsky in 1846.[2] Finally, following Richard Pipes' analysis, 'the Russians [...] adopted [the term] from France and Germany, where 'intelligence' and 'Intelligenz' had gained currency in the 1830s and 1840s to designate educated and 'progressive' citizens.'[3]

Apart from the historical origin of the term, however, what really matters is the *sociological* definition of the concept 'intelligentsia' itself. In regard to this issue, political thinkers converge over the view that *ideology* constitutes the determinant element of the intelligentsia; in Malia's own words, 'the primacy of the ideological is

---

[1] M. Malia, 'What is the Intelligentsia' in R. Pipes (ed.), *The Russian Intelligentsia*, New York, Columbia University Press, 1961, p.1.
[2] A. Gella, 'An Introduction to the Sociology of the Intelligentsia' in A. Gella (ed.), *The Intelligentsia and the Intellectuals, Theory, Method and Case Study*, California, SAGE Publications, 1976, p.12.
[3] R. Pipes, *The Russian Revolution, 1899-1919*, London, Fontana Press, 1992, p.122.

fundamental to the group as a whole'.[4] From a similar point of view, Alain Besançon points to the role of ideology in cementing the cohesion of the intelligentsia group[5] and proposes three more crucial criteria as far as the intelligentsia's birth is concerned:[6]

1. The existence of a national educational system under the direction of the state.
2. The inability of civil society to incorporate its younger and more or less educated members within its ranks and institutions.
3. The social and political crisis of the *ancien régime*.

At this point, however, it is worth commenting on the significant distinction between *intellectuals* and *intelligentsia*. According to Isaiah Berlin, who confronts the intelligentsia phenomenon as the most eminent Russian contribution to social change in the world,

> the concept of intelligentsia must not be confused with the notion of intellectuals. Its members thought of themselves as united by something more than mere interest in ideas; they conceived themselves as being a dedicated order, almost a secular priesthood, devoted to the spreading of a specific attitude to life, something like a gospel.[7]

From another point of view, Richard Pipes reaches the following conclusion:

> The popularity of the word [intelligentsia] derived from the fact that it made it possible to distinguish social 'activists' from passive 'intellectuals'. However, we shall use the two terms interchangeably [concludes

---

[4] M. Malia, op. cit., p.2.
[5] A. Besançon, *Les origines intellectuelles du Leninisme*, Paris, Editions Agora, 1977, pp.122-127.
[6] op. cit., pp.118-121.
[7] I. Berlin, *Russian Thinkers*, Harmondsworth, Penguin Books, 1978, p.117; in a similar direction:
  a) N. Berdyaev, *The Origin of Russian Communism*, Ann Arbor Paperbacks, The University of Michigan Press, 1960, pp.19, 60
  b) A. Gella, op. cit., p.19 ff.

Pipes] since in Western languages the distinction has not been established.[8]

Nevertheless, from our own point of view, such an interchangeable use of the terms 'intelligentsia' and 'intellectual', though acceptable on a general level of analysis, should not lead to the conclusion that every intellectual is, because of this social identity, a member of the intelligentsia. In fact, what actually characterises the Russian intelligentsia is not a common shared class origin,[9] but a 'sense of guilt' and, consequently, a sense of moral debt towards the (Russian) people,[10] due to which its distinguished members decide to intervene in the social and political process in order to teach or, rather, be taught by the masses and promote the people's own emancipation.

Hence, the intelligentsia can be defined as a special group of more or less educated persons highly motivated by moral and ideological principles and devoted to serve the cause of the people's social and political liberation. In Nikolai Berdyaev's own words,

> the intelligentsia reminds one more of a monastic order or sect, with its own very intolerant ethics, its own obligatory outlook on life, with its own manners and customs and even its own particular physical appearance, by which it is always possible to recognise a member of the intelligentsia and distinguish him from other social groups [...]. Intelligentsia was not a function of the life of the people, it was broken off from that life, and felt guilty in relation to the people [...]. *The intelligentsia was always in debt to the people and had to pay its debt.*[11] (our emphasis)

---

[8] R. Pipes, *The Russian Revolution, 1899–1919*, p.123; from his own point of view, Richard Pipes proposes the distinction between the intelligentsia *in the objective sense* and the intelligentsia *in the subjective sense*. (R. Pipes, 'The Historical Evolution of the Russian Intelligentsia', in R. Pipes (ed.), op. cit., p.48).

[9] According to Martin Malia, op. cit., p.5, 'the intelligentsia were the *raznochintsy*, that is 'people of diverse rank' or 'people of no estate in particular'.' (Malia's emphasis).

[10] The *locus classicus* of this argument is the well-known work of the Russian thinker Pëtr Lavrov, *Historical Letters*.

[11] N. Berdyaev, op. cit., pp.19, 58.

In relation to the intelligentsia's social identity, however, a few further remarks should be made: firstly, and contrary to the typical case of the Western intellectual, official education and, especially, university education is not a necessary requisite for adherence to the intelligentsia. According to Richard Pipes,

> although in fact most of those regarded as *intelligenty* had a superior education, education in itself was not a criterion: thus a businessman or a bureaucrat with a university degree did not qualify as a member of the intelligentsia [...]. Only those qualified who committed themselves to the public good, even if they were semiliterate workers or peasants.[12] (Pipes' emphasis)

Secondly, the social composition of the intelligentsia differs from time to time; it is this historical variation as regards the class origin of its members, however, which supplies the group with a special vitality and dynamism. More specifically, according to Malia the Russian intelligentsia's social composition altered in time, as follows:

> Although in the 1840's the intelligentsia included men from all classes, it was in fact dominated by those who came from the gentry. By the 1860's the center of gravity had shifted to the *raznochintsy* [people's of diverse rank]. It was the universities, moreover, that brought *raznochintsy* together with the young gentry into the 'circle' or discussion group of the 1830's and 1840's, and the 'student commune' or co-operate living group, of the 1860's and 1870's.[13] (Malia's emphasis)

Thus, it is beyond doubt that the intelligentsia, being a minority group which developed in nineteenth century Russia, must be considered as the explosive outcome of a *class renegade association,* since its members belonged to a quite broad spectrum of classes and strata of the Russian society.

Given such a high degree of social diversity, however, it becomes evident that the cohesion of the intelligentsia was achieved mainly on the basis of ideological and moral standards. In regard to ideology, it

---

[12] R. Pipes, *The Russian Revolution, 1899–1919*, p.123.
[13] M. Malia, op. cit., pp.12–14.

is worth arguing that the Enlightenment, on the one hand, and Romanticism, on the other, exerted a special influence on the intelligentsia's formation and action. As a matter of fact, the French *philosophes* and the German Romantics are two intellectual groups worth remembering when talking about the philosophical origins of the Russian intelligentsia.[14]

Following Richard Pipes' analysis, for example, it is worth noting that, as long as the theory of knowledge was based on the concept of 'innate ideas', the immutability of human nature and, consequently, the immutability of social and political institutions seemed beyond doubt. During the years of the Enlightenment, however, the above situation changed. Firstly by John Locke's *Essay on Human Understanding* (1690) and some decades later by Helvétius', anonymously published, *De l'Esprit* – a work drawing political conclusions from Locke's sensualistic theory of knowledge – human beings were analysed in a direct interrelationship with their natural and social environment. According to Helvétius, education and legislation are the most effective means to reshape both social and political institutions and people themselves.

The most interesting conclusion of this analysis, however, vividly described by Pipes himself, is the following:

> A life ruled by 'reason' is a life ruled by intellectuals: it is not surprising, therefore, that intellectuals want to change the world in accord with the requirements of 'rationality' [...]. Democracy is, of course, mandatory, but preferably interpreted to mean the 'rational' rather than the actual will of the people: Rousseau's 'general will' instead of the will made manifest through elections or referenda.[15]

Thus we approach once again the central point of our analysis, i.e. the pivotal and, at the same time, controversial role of intellectuals in the emancipatory cause. Through reforms or by revolution, intellectuals, or rather a part of them, often tried to change the world.

---

[14] op. cit., p.5; in special regard to the German Romantics, see Peter Ludz's analysis on Fichte and the *Bund der freien Männer* in his 'Methodological Problems in Comparative Studies of the Intelligentsia', as included in A. Gella (ed.), op. cit., pp.37–45.

[15] R. Pipes, op. cit., p.127.

In fact, the young Marx himself did not hesitate to reject contemplative philosophy and unreservedly adopted a *philosophy of praxis,* as – for example – his own *Theses on Feuerbach* clearly illustrate. It is, nevertheless, this turning point in the intellectual/praxis relationship, which leads Pipes to argue that

> the moment a thinker begins to conceive his mission to be not only observing the world and adapting to it, but changing it, he ceases to be a philosopher and turns into a politician with his own political agenda and interests.[16]

From our point of view, however, it is worth underling that the intellectual's more or less direct intervention in the realm of politics constitutes a long-lasting process, the philosophical origin of which – as has already been mentioned – can be traced in Plato's theory and practice. This process was promoted even further through the most radical versions of European Enlightenment and German Idealism, with Fichte and Hegel as his chief representative, some decades before Marx himself presented his own positions on the philosopher/politics relationship.

In fact, Fichte and Hegel's Romanticism should be regarded as the most significant influence on the intelligentsia's activity as the Russian case proves,

> The basic Western influence, by which Russian nineteenth century thought and culture were moulded to a remarkable degree [argues Berdyaev], was the influence of German romanticism and idealism at the beginning of the century.[17]

It was, indeed, under the influence of a specific version of Romanticism that not only individuals, but social groups as well 'come to be possessed by a 'spirit' of which they themselves might well be

---

[16] op. cit., p.136.
[17] N. Berdyaev, op. cit., p.27; notice, however, the following interesting remark made by E. Lampert in his *Studies in Rebellion,* Routledge and Kegan Paul, London 1957, p.33: 'Romanticism is a hydra-headed word: it cannot be equated with any one intellectual principle, however broad. [...] It is in the *moral* or *psychological* sense that romanticism must be rescued in order to understand the attitude of the Russian revolutionary thinkers'. (our emphasis)

unaware'.[18] Hence, a new kind of religion began to take shape. The 'priests' of this new religion, often sons of priests and students of theology themselves, were actually possessed by the passion of Truth, the Truth which might be traced in people's life itself, though still in an embryonic form.

Within this philosophical framework, Fichte's already quoted declaration of the scholar's vocation offers a particular opportunity to compress into few words what has already been noted and discussed in regard to the socially and politically active intellectual.

> I am called [declares Fichte] to testify to the truth. I am a priest of truth. I am in its pay, and thus I have committed myself to do, to risk, and to suffer anything for its sake. If I should be pursued and hated for the truth's sake, or if I should die in its service, what more would I have done than what I simply had to do?[19]

On this ground, the active intellectuals of Western Europe and the intelligentsia of Eastern Europe, as defined above, actually meet. As a matter of fact, it can be argued that the dialectical transition from the philosophical world of the Enlightenment to the world of German idealism and Romanticism signifies that a number of radical intellectuals of the West think and act as *intelligenty*.[20]

It is, therefore, necessary to proceed to a more detailed examination of the way in which the intelligentsia/people relation was formed within the Russian populist tradition. Through this approach the Russian intelligentsia's vanguard role will be directly connected with the intellectual question, as this was confronted no only by Marx and Engels, but also by their Russian (and Western European) followers en route to the October Revolution.

---

[18] I. Berlin, op. cit., p.119; in a further reference to romantic philosophers, Berlin argues as follows: '[T]heir fervid vision, which remained mystical and irrationalist no matter how heavily disguised in quasi-scientific or quasi-lyrical terminology, captivated the imagination of the young Russian intellectuals of the 30s and 40s and seemed to open a door to a nobler and calmer world from the sordid reality of the Empire ruled by Tsar Nicholas I'.

[19] J. Fichte, 'Some lectures concerning the Scholar's Vocation', op. cit., p.176.

[20] It is only in this philosophical context that the terms 'intellectual' and 'intelligentsia' may be used interchangeably as Richard Pipes suggests.

Chapter 15
Intelligentsia, Emancipation and Russian Populism

It is widely admitted that the study of the intelligentsia's itinerary in nineteenth century Russia should be firmly connected with an analysis of the multidimensional philosophical and political movement of the Russian populism. On the other hand, it is beyond doubt that the origins of so-called Russian Marxism cannot be observed without previous reference to the revolutionary tradition of the Russian populism. Hence, it is necessary to proceed to a brief discussion of the populist movement in connection with the intelligentsia's social and political mission.

According to Herzen, 'the true founder of Populism',[1] the 1848–49 revolutions, which broke out all over Europe, represent the turning point, after which new ideas on revolution begin to surface, especially in Russia. More specifically, distrust of parliamentarianism, belief in the autonomous development of Russian society based on the institution of the 'obschina', and recognition of the need for a group of enlightened revolutionaries dedicated to the people's cause, determine the populist revolutionary tradition in nineteenth century Russia.

Alexander Herzen, who was neither Slavophile, nor Westerniser, 'combined the idea of national road, or 'mission', for Russia with a Westerniser's attachment to political freedoms'.[2] In his view, the intelligentsia/people relationship proves of special importance as far as the future social change in Russia is concerned. Indeed this 'stricken Voltaire' – as Lampert calls him[3] – is fully convinced that suffering people 'are not waiting for books but for apostle-men who combine

---

[1] F. Venturi, *Roots of Revolution*, p.1.
[2] D.W. Lovell, *From Marx to Lenin*, p.122.
[3] For Herzen's comparison with Voltaire, see E. Lampert, op. cit., pp.189–192.

faith, will, conviction and energy; men who will never divorce themselves from them; who do not necessarily spring from them, but who act within them and with them, with a dedicated and steady faith.'[4]

It is exactly these new 'apostle-men', argues Herzen, who should inspire the masses with passion for liberation, a liberation even from their own liberators and their authoritarian political dogmas as well.[5] Nevertheless, Herzen himself does not fail to note the unwillingness of the people to emancipate themselves. In a way reminiscent of Voltaire's own mistrust of the populace's ability to be enlightened and liberated, the Russian thinker argues as follows:

> The masses want to stay the hand which impudently snatches from them the bread which they have earned. They are indifferent to individual freedom, liberty of speech; *the masses love authority*. They are still blinded by the arrogant glitter of power, they are offended by those who stand alone. By equality they understand equality of oppression... they want a social government to rule for their benefit, and not, like the present one, against it. But *to govern themselves doesn't enter their heads*.[6] (our emphasis)

In other words, under the influence of the inglorious end of the 1848 French Revolution, as far as the working class is concerned, Herzen appears very pessimistic in regard to people's self-emancipation. Besides, he does not hesitate to mention that 'truth belongs to the minority'.[7] In fact, knowledge, truth, sense of justice and morality are privileges of a 'small group of people'.[8] These gifted persons are the agents of a historical mission; knowledge and justice should be diffused by the 'apostle-men' all over society. It is the fact that this vanguard enjoys intellectual and moral superiority over common people which makes its members to act in favour of the masses by

---

[4] Quoted in F. Venturi, op. cit., p.35.
[5] See I. Berlin, *Russian Thinkers*, pp.200–201.
[6] Quoted in I. Berlin, op. cit., p.88.
[7] Quoted in E. Lampert, op. cit., p.230.
[8] 'I see, in the present and the past [argues Herzen in his *From the Other Shore*], knowledge, truth, moral vigour, striving for independence, love of beauty vested in a small group of people, who are lost in an unsympathetic hostile environment.' (Quoted in E. Lampert, op. cit., p.230).

making them conscious of their own social position and revolutionary perspectives as well.

Thus Lampert's conclusion seems accurate and justifiable here as well:

> For Herzen, the idea of true aristocracy was, in fact, inseparable from his socialism [...]. It contained a challenge to the attitude of the privileged social groups, struggling to protect themselves against the violent hand of those whom they have deprived of their humanity. The 'few' are nothing without reference to their responsibility towards the 'many'. The few ought not to justify themselves by means of the many, by turning other men into the objects of their own power and self-interest.[9]

From this aristodemocratic point of view, the intelligentsia - faithful to the Kantian imperative and contrary to any version of political instrumentalism - should avoid confronting their fellow citizens as mere means or instruments in their struggle to achieve their end. On the other hand, the members of such a vanguard group should respond to what Plato asked from the philosopher-rulers of his *Republic;* they must return to the dark cave where common people are imprisoned, live with them and prepare them for emancipation.

Nevertheless, according to Herzen, emancipation should not be achieved by violating people's own political rights or by *forcing them to be free.* It is, in fact, this strong belief in the priority of the individual personality, which brings Herzen nearer to Voltaire's than to Rousseau's social philosophy. Within the context of his analysis of the intelligentsia/people relation, Herzen points to a *libertarian socialism,* that is to say a socialism based upon respect for personal freedom.[10]

---

[9] E. Lampert, op, cit., p.232.
[10] For Herzen's libertarian socialism as opposed to Bakunin's authoritarianism, see:
   a) I. Berlin, 'Herzen and Bakunin on Individual Liberty', in I. Berlin, op. cit. pp.82-113.
   b) N. Pirumova, 'Bakunin and Herzen: An Analysis of their Ideological Disagreements at the end of the 1860s.' *Canadian American Slavic Studies*, vol. 10, 4, pp.552-567.

To this end, the Russian thinker becomes one of the most eminent precursors of the 'go-to-the-people' movement, as his *quasi* Fichtean call[11] to the students expelled from the Saint Petersburg University clearly shows:

> Go among the people! Go to the people! That is your place, outcasts of learning. Show the Bistroms [Tsarist generals] that you will become not Government clerks, but soldiers; not mercenaries without a country, but soldiers of the Russian people![12]

'Go among the people', however, in Herzen's political theory and practice, means enlightenment and moral regeneration of the masses through the intelligentsia's intervention in the socio-political process. In opposition to Bakunin's urgent call to revolt, Alexander Herzen proceeds, therefore, to the following assessment of the tactics of a future revolution in Russia.

> Ours is a time of definitive study, which must *precede* the work of implementation.[13] (our emphasis)

In other words, authoritarian leadership and conspiratorial action without the people's direct commitment to the revolutionary process are means unsuitable to bring both the vanguard and the masses closer to the communist ideal; on the other hand, the intelligentsia's educational activity is, according to Herzen, the most effective way in order to make the masses theoretically and politically mature for a successful transition to a new communal life.

Thus, it may be argued that Herzen's approach to the intelligentsia question is philosophically determined by a mixture of a Voltairean

---

[11] It is worth underlining Herzen's dictum: 'Action itself is personality' (quoted in E. Lampert, op. cit., p.207), through which Herzen is directly connected with Fichtean activism and Voltairean philosophy of action as well.

[12] Quoted in E. Lampert, op. cit., p.253 (Compare with *Fichte's Lectures Concerning the Scholar's Vocation*).

[13] Quoted in N. Pirumova, op. cit., p.561; it is worth mentioning however that, contrary to Herzen and in defence of Bakunin, Herzen's own collaborator Ogarev argues as follows: 'For people to know where they are going is impossible, just as prophecies are impossible... To await the implementation of a theory without doing anything and without taking any risk is even more impossible, for theory itself... can arise only *after*... a revolution has taken place and circumstances demand the establishment of new relations between people, on a new basis.' (our emphasis – ibid).

Enlightenment and a Fichtean Romanticism, though a certain flavour of Slavonic temperament and mentality should be noted as well.

Following Herzen's philosophical path, two other representatives of Russian populism, Peter Lavrov and Nikolai Mikhailovsky, focus their arguments on the intelligentsia's debt to the people. Especially Lavrov, in his well-known *Historical Letters,* points to the fact that it is 'at the price of the others' tireless labour and struggle for existence' that a social minority has the privilege 'to observe, to reflect, to calculate – without having to worry about food, shelter and the simplest comfort'.[14]

Consequently, according to Lavrov's philosophical approach to history, the members of this *educated minority,*[15] these 'critically thinking individuals', as he himself calls them,[16] are morally obliged to repay their debt to the people and lead to the further progress of society.

> [I]t is upon them [argues Lavrov] that the moral duty to repay the cost of this progress is incumbent. This repayment [...] consists in the greatest possible extension of material comforts and intellectual and moral development to the majority, and in the introduction of scientific understanding and of justice into social institutions.[17]

On the basis of this position a delicate interrelation between the cultivated minority and the masses is formed. According to Lavrov and Mikhailovsky, the guiding role of the intelligentsia in the struggle for truth and justice should not be denied. The masses themselves need such an intellectual leadership and moral regeneration in order to achieve their emancipation. On the other hand, no critically thinking individual has the right to force the people to follow his (or her) own ideas.

> Perhaps a moment will come [assumes Lavrov] when [the critically thinking individual] can take part in social

---

[14] P. Lavrov, *Historical Letters*, Berkeley, University of California Press, 1967, p.133.

[15] op. cit., p.135; Lavrov also uses the terms 'cultivated minority' and 'civilised minority' interchangeably.

[16] op. cit., p.141.

[17] ibid.

life. If it does not come, he will transmit to the next generation the tradition of truth and justice which for him existed only in the realm of consciousness, and which he could not actualise or did not know how to actualise. In such a case, even the fact that he did not bow to the universal evil, did not become its tool, constitutes a service.[18]

Hence, Lavrov endorses the aristodemocratic concept of the intelligentsia/people relationship, since he neither bows to the people's spontaneous will, nor disregards it;[19] on the contrary, he tries to confront social reality as critically as possible in order to promote its radical transformation through the enlightenment of the masses.[20]

The effectiveness, however, of those tactics based on the education and persuasion of the masses depends upon the collective action of critically thinking individuals being united in the form of a *party*. More concretely, it is worth noting that, from Lavrov's point of view, there is no unresolved contradiction between the independence of a critical intellectual, on the one hand, and collective action, on the other:

> Yet it is precisely these people, who think and act independently and are accustomed to moral solitude [Lavrov suggests], who now must come together, unite, think together, act together and organise something

---

[18] op. cit., p.154.

[19] Mikhailovsky himself endorses the aristodemocratic position, since, while admitting his debt to the people, nevertheless proceeds to arguments like the following: 'If Russian life with all its ordinary practices breaks into my room, destroys my bust of Belinsky, and burns my books, I will not submit to the people from the village; I will fight.' (Quoted in D.W. Lovell, op. cit., p.127).

[20] It is, from this point of view, that Berdyaev, op. cit., p.70, comes closer to Lavrov's and Mikhailovsky's *aristodemocratic* populism: 'The narodnichestvo of Lavrov and Mikhailovsky belongs to the type which regards itself as *bound by the interests of the people but not by their opinions*. They thought that true enlightened opinions are to be found among the intelligentsia and not among the people. It was the duty of the intelligentsia to give the people knowledge, to serve the interests of the people and work for their freedom, but to preserve its own independence in opinions and ideas.' (our emphasis)

strong and single, but strong as a collective force and single as an abstract unity.[21]

As becomes obvious, what Lavrov proposes, in fact, is the creation of a *collective educator*, composed mainly of critically thinking individuals, who are intellectually and morally ready to repay their historical debt to their fellow citizens. Furthermore, in a way which reminds us of Marx and Engels' critical comment on German social democracy, Lavrov insists that such a social party should not be 'a party of armchair scholars'.[22] Fighting for truth is inseparable from fighting for justice, just as 'critical thinking is inseparable from action'.[23] In other words, in a way which echoes Marx's *Thesis XI on Feuerbach*, Lavrov believes that observation and mere interpretation of reality are useless when not combined with the action to change it.

At this point, Mikhailovsky's confession is worth mentioning:

> Only in Russian, it seems, are 'truth' and 'justice' designated by the same word ['pravda'], fusing as it were in one great whole. *Pravda* - in his vast meaning of the word - has always been *the goal of my searchings*. To gaze without fear into the eyes of reality and its reflection in objective truth, and at the same time to preserve its subjective justice - such is the task of my whole life... Everything has occupied me exclusively from the point of view of this great unity of truth-justice.[24] (Mikhailovsky's emphasis)

It is on this philosophical and moral basis, that Lavrov's and Mikhailovsky's views on the intelligentsia question converge with Herzen's positions, conforming therefore to what may be defined as the *culturalist* aristodemocratic current of the Russian populism. From this point of view, it is worth mentioning as well that Russian populists, like Herzen, Lavrov and Mikhailovsky, despite their love for humanities and science, declined to succumb to the cult of positive science, which, on the contrary, attracted other eminent

---

[21] P. Lavrov, op. cit., p.174.
[22] op. cit., p.178.
[23] op. cit., p.179.
[24] Quoted in V.V. Zenkovsky, *A History of Russian Philosophy*, London, Routledge and Kegan Paul, 1953, vol. 1, p.364.

representatives of Russian populism, such as the so-called nihilists, Nikolai Tsernyshevsky and Dimitry Pisarev.

At this point, it is worth noting that this passionate love for positive science led thinkers like Tsernyshevsky and Pisarev to contribute, though unintentionally, to the formation of a new religion, the real goddess of which was science itself. In other words, it can be argued that even the intellectual-scientist who devotes his (or her) life to the promotion of technical knowledge and positive science, while living in the cultural milieu of nineteenth century Russia, cannot avoid acting, to a certain degree, like an intellectual-priest.

From this particular point of view, Zenkovsky rightly argues that

> the primacy of ethics over 'pure' science was essential for Chernyshevsky. He had a genuine *faith* in science [...]. But it would be wrong to conclude that romanticism disappeared entirely from this new generation; a genuine romantic basis was retained under the cover of realism. Hence the 'scientism' of the Russian radicals was really a naive *faith* in the 'power' of science. But in its ultimate foundation this unquenched romanticism manifested itself in a 'secular religiosity' which flourished under the cover of realism and even materialism.[25] (Zenkovsky's emphasis)

In other words, even in this *positivistic* version of the Russian populism, the intelligentsia/people relationship retains its moral feature. In their fight 'to increase the number of men who think, [which is] the alpha and omega of social development',[26] the Russian nihilists combined technical scientism with social moralism, serving what they themselves considered to be public utility and the common good.

Needless to say that, for the Russian nihilists faith in the critically thinking individual does not contradict, in the last analysis, the collective fight for the people's benefit. As a matter of fact, Pisarev's cult of the individual scientist is likely to upset the delicate balance of the intelligentsia/masses relation as presented above. Even in Pisarev's short life as a writer, however, 'we can discern a shift of

---

[25] op. cit., pp.326–327.
[26] Quoted in F. Venturi, op. cit., p.327.

emphasis from the individual to society, from the emancipation of the human being from old traditions and beliefs, from all that is not supported by science, to the positive promotion of the common good'.[27] Thus even Pisarev's 'New Men', as he himself calls them in *The Thinking Proletariat* (1865), are fighting for the people's interest and not for personal benefit.[28]

As far as Russian nihilism is concerned, it can be argued, therefore, that the difference between thinkers like Herzen, Lavrov and Mikhailovsky, on the one hand, and Chernyshevsky and Pisarev, on the other - with regard to the intelligentsia question - is not so obvious. In fact, their difference lies not in the way the educated minority forges its relation with the people, but in the content of the educational process as such. Thus, the first group of thinkers mentioned above gives special emphasis to the *culturalist* content of education, while for the Russian nihilists, knowledge is actually synonymous with positive science.[29] From this point of view, the ideological tension between Romanticism and positivism is reproduced within the ranks of Russian populism itself without shattering, however, the aristodemocratic basis of the intelligentsia/people relationship as defined and discussed above.

In opposition to the aristodemocratic version of the intelligentsia/people relation as conceived by both the culturalist and positivist representatives of the Russian populism, two further versions can be identified within the same movement; an ultra-libertarian/ spontaneist version and an authoritarian/elitist one, mainly represented by Bakunin's analysis in the Appendix A of his *Statism and Anarchy* and by Tkachev's positions respectively.

According to Bakunin's views as expressed in the Appendix mentioned above, 'no scholar can reach the people or even define for himself how they will and must live on the morrow of the social revolution'.[30] Thus, the Russian anarchist is naturally drawn to the

---

[27] F.C. Copleston, *Philosophy in Russia*, Notre Dame, Search Press, 1986, From Herzen to Lenin and Berdyaev, p.115.

[28] At this point, it is worth noting that, despite his severe critique of Plato's political philosophy, Pisarev converges with the ancient Greek philosopher with regard to the philosopher's duty towards his (her) fellow citizens. (For Pisarev's critique to Plato, see F.C. Copleston, op. cit., p.112).

[29] Chernyshevsky and Pisarev's critical approach to arts and culture constitutes another point of similarity with Plato's views, as expressed in his *Republic*.

[30] M. Bakunin, *Statism and Anarchy*, pp.198-199.

rhetorical question, which actually addresses the *educationalist* trend of the populist movement:[31]

> What are you going to teach the people? [Bakunin asks]. Is it not what you yourselves do not know and cannot know, and must first learn from the people?[32]

As becomes obvious, therefore, Bakunin argues that the intelligentsia itself has nothing to teach the masses. Hence, although he gives the impression that he follows the young Marx's minimalistic tendency, as far as the intellectual/proletarian relationship is concerned,[33] Bakunin moves far beyond this position by ultimately endorsing the spontaneist position, within the limits of which the role of the intelligentsia is *de facto* nullified.

> [T]he most renowned geniuses [Bakunin insists] have done nothing or very little, specifically for the people, for the many millions of laboring proletarians. Popular life, popular development, popular progress belong *exclusively* to the people themselves. That progress is achieved, of course, not by book learning but by the natural accumulation of experience and thought, transmitted from generation to generation and necessarily broadening and deepening its content and perfecting itself and assuming its forms very slowly.[34] (our emphasis)

In this context of Bakunin's spontaneism, it is worth identifying as well the role of this social group, which he himself calls 'intellectual proletariat' and which he urges to 'go to the people, because today [...] outside of the people there is neither life, nor cause, nor future'.[35]

---

[31] Bakunin's question is probably addressed to the so-called Ruble Society, the goal of which was to send educators to the villages. (See note 138, in M. Bakunin, op. cit., p.236).

[32] op. cit., p.199.

[33] op. cit., p.204: 'If the people do not develop this ideal themselves, of course, no one can give it to them. In general, it must be noted that nobody – neither an individual, a society, nor a people – can be given what does not already exist within him, not just in embryonic form but at a certain level of development.'

[34] op. cit., p.205.

[35] op. cit., p.212.

It is in regard to this question, that he suggests that the intellectual proletariat should become the docile executant rather than the educational transformer of the people's will. It is within such an approach that Bakunin appears to be a passionate supporter of ultra-libertarian views, in the sense that the labouring masses have no need – not even transitionally – of the intelligentsia's vanguard activity in their effort to emancipate themselves.[36] As a result, the intellectual proletariat proves nothing more than a mere instrument to unleash the people's instinct to revolt.

From this point of view, therefore, Bakunin seems to reject not only Rousseauist state worship, but also the educational and moral lessons of the 'Geneva Citizen',[37] whose influence, however, upon the 1873–1874 'go-to-the-people' movement was so significant that Professor Venturi does not hesitate to characterise the whole process as 'a collective act of Rousseauism'.[38]

In opposition to the aristodemocratic trend of the populist movement and to Bakunin's apparent anti-authoritarianism as well, Tkachev proceeds to his own Blanquist/elitist approach to the intelligentsia/people relation.[39]

According to Tkachev – who shared, however, with the culturalist representatives of the Russian populism the rejection of the mechanistic transfer of positive science to the field of society[40] – the exploited masses are unable to emancipate themselves, which is why the social and political role of the intelligentsia proves so decisive.[41]

---

[36] For the complementary relation of Bakunin's manifest libertarianism with his latent authoritarianism, see Chapter 10 of this study.

[37] For Rousseau's influence, however, on the main stream of Russian populism, see Berlin's general assessment in I. Berlin, op. cit., p.214.

[38] F. Venturi, op. cit., p.503.

[39] According to Lovell, op. cit., pp.127–128, 'with his emphasis on organising a revolutionary elite, and his unbounded contempt for the masses, Tkachev gave the traditional problem of the relations between intelligentsia and masses a new direction. If Lavrov and Mikhailovsky had looked to the masses for ultimate regeneration, for the source of ultimate truth, Tkachev believed that it was the masses themselves who needed regeneration.'

[40] See:
   a) F. Venturi, op. cit., p.392.
   b) I. Berlin, op. cit., p.220: 'The new class of technical specialists, [...], were for the Jacobin Tkachev 'worse than cholera or typhus', for by applying scientific methods to social life they were playing into the hands of the new, rising capitalist oligarchs and thereby obstructing the path to freedom.'

[41] F. Venturi, op. cit., pp.405–406.

On the other hand, following Tkachev's analysis, the masses constitute the raw material of the revolution, while the intelligentsia's educative role is transmitted and confined to the *post*-revolutionary phase of the process.

It is at this point, indeed, that Lovell's following remark is worth noting:

> Tkachev's transition period [argues Lovell] was an extension of the pre-eminent, pre-revolutionary role of the radical intelligentsia. It was the product of the concern that the people would halt or reverse the transformation of society. Marx was concerned, on the contrary, that the bourgeoisie would obstruct the transformation of society.[42]

Nevertheless, from our point of view, what actually lies behind Marx and Tkachev's difference of approach is a philosophical conflict with regard to the way the two thinkers evaluate enlightenment as a means to effective revolutionary action. While Marx and his followers confront the political education of the people as a *conditio sine qua non* for a successful revolution, Tkachev – faithful in the tradition of Babeuf, Buonarroti and Blanqui – believes that a determined political minority may prove capable of overthrowing the *ancien régime* by *using* the 'tempestuous force' of the masses for its own ends.

> The minority [argues Tkachev] will impart a considered and rational form to the struggle leading it towards determined ends, directing this coarse material element towards ideal principles. In a true revolution the people acts as a tempestuous force of nature which destroys and ruins everything in its way, always acting outside all calculations and consciousness.[43]

In this context, the political vanguard, the Apollonean element of the revolution, takes the place of the masses, the Dionysiac element of the same process, while using their destructive power to achieve its political goal. For their part, the masses act as the mere supporters and executants of the vanguard's revolutionary will.

---

[42] D.W. Lovell, op. cit., p.129.
[43] Quoted in F. Venturi, op. cit., pp.413–414.

Given the fact, however, that such a leading minority should be hierarchically organised in order to reach its end, Tkachev – in a way reminiscent of Engels' critique of Bakunin and his followers – does not hesitate to admit that as a natural consequence 'any [revolutionary] organisation is always authoritarian and therefore anti-anarchist'.[44]

On the basis of these positions, therefore, no doubt remains that the Russian Blanquist comes in direct conflict not only with Bakunin's anti-authoritarian version of the intelligentsia/people relationship,[45] but also with the aristodemocratic approach to the same issue within the broad ideological context of Russian populism. In fact, Tkachev believes that the masses should neither elect, nor control the leading minority en route to the revolution. On the other hand, the members of the vanguard group should not derive their power from an *intellectual* leadership and *moral* influence over the masses; their primary interest – at least during the pre-revolutionary period – should be strictly *political*. In other words, the real concern of such a vanguard must be not to *prepare* but to *make* a revolution. Thus, due to a very naive and simplistic juxtaposition of thought and action, Tkachev reaches the following conclusion:

> Revolutionaries do not prepare; they make a revolution. Make it then; make it faster! Every indecision, every procrastination, is criminal... That is why we say: do not carry your thoughts too far ahead; stand firmly on the basis of a sober, thought-out realism. Do not dream, but act! Make a revolution and make it as fast as possible.[46]

Consequently it can be argued that there is, in fact, an extreme political activism, which clearly separates Tkachev's views on the intelligentsia question not only from the Enlightenment tradition, but even from the Fichtean romantic activism. Moreover, it is

---

[44] Quoted in F. Venturi, op. cit., p.422.

[45] It is worth noting that Tkachev makes the following comment on Bakunin's latent, though indisputable, authoritarianism: 'The authority of the State demands the submission of only the outer manifestations of man's activities; but the authority that you want (if you really want it) subjects not only man's actions but his intimate convictions, his most hidden feelings, his mind and his will, and also his heart.' (Quoted in F. Venturi, op. cit., p.422).

[46] Quoted in L.H. Haimson, *The Russian Marxists and the Origins of Bolshevism*, Cambridge, Massachusetts, Harvard University Press, 1955, p.17.

self-evident that such a passionate expression of political voluntarism[47] could not but result in an authoritarian/quasi-dictatorial version of the intelligentsia/people relation, an authoritarianism which is likely to determine not only the pre-revolutionary but the post-revolutionary socio-political process as well.[48]

Finally, it is worth mentioning that distinguished thinkers like Nikolai Berdyaev, Isaiah Berlin and Alain Besançon suggest that Tkachev should be regarded as the intellectual and political precursor of Lenin.[49] More concretely, by focusing their analysis on the elitist conception of the intelligentsia as expressed by Tkachev in the field of political theory, they support the hypothesis that his views had a significant impact upon Lenin's political practice.

Nevertheless, a detailed evaluation of this hypothesis cannot be made, unless this analysis is extended to the well-known controversy over the intellectual question, which took place between the leading representatives of Russian and Western European Marxism during the last decades of the nineteenth and the first years of the twentieth century up to the Revolution of October 1917.

---

[47] Tkachev's political voluntarism is undoubtedly connected with the fact that the Russian bourgeoisie was unable to play a revolutionary role and, consequently, socialism, according to Tkachev himself, could be *immediately* reached through the determined action of a political minority; contra F. Engels, 'On Social Relations in Russia' in K. Marx and F. Engels, *Collected Works*, vol. 24, pp.39–50.

[48] *Contra* Tkachev: 'What are you frightened of? What right have you to think that this minority [...] by taking power into its hands will suddenly change itself into a tyrant? You say: Any power corrupts men. But on what do you base such a strange idea? On the examples of history?... Read biographies and you will be convinced of the contrary.' (Quoted in F. Venturi, op. cit., p.427).

[49] See:
a) N. Berdyaev, op. cit., pp.71–73.
b) I. Berlin, op. cit., pp.236–237.
c) A. Besançon, op. cit., pp.196–198.

Chapter 16
Intellectuals, Emancipation and Russian Marxism

From within the ranks of the Russian populism, and especially through the revolutionary organisation *Zemlia i Volia* (Land and Freedom), a new generation of political thinkers and activists was born. The most distinguished figure among the representatives of this generation was the founder of the so-called Russian Marxism, Georgi Plekhanov. After rejecting terrorism, Plekhanov and his followers formed a small organisation of their own named *Cherny Peredel* (Black Repartition), which aimed at the political education of the masses. Nevertheless, *Cherny Peredel* soon collapsed due to the political persecution which followed Czar Alexander II's assassination, organised and executed by the terrorists of the *Narodnaya Volia* (People's Will) in 1881. Two years later, while living in Switzerland and under the influence of Marxism, Plekhanov and three of his comrades – Axelrod, Zasulich and Deich – founded the *Osvobozhdenie Truda* (Emancipation of Labour), i.e. the first Russian Marxist organisation.[1]

It is often suggested that the Russian Marxists endorsed an elitist approach as far as the intelligentsia/proletarian relation is concerned.[2] As Reidar Larsson characteristically argues, for example,

---

[1] For a historical presentation of the above revolutionary organisations, see:
a) L.H. Haimson, op. cit., p.17 ff.
b) J.L.H. Keep, *The Rise of Social Democracy in Russia*, Clarendon Press, Oxford 1963, p.15 ff.
c) F. Venturi, op. cit., p.558 ff.

[2] Talking about Russian Marxism, Samuel H. Baron in his *Plekhanov, The Father of Russian Marxism*, Stanford, Stanford University Press, 1963, p.129 argues as follows: 'In essence, [the Russian Marxists] mistrusted numbers and insisted upon a kind of elite leadership of the Marxian movement.'

it must be concluded that the first Russian Marxists allocated to the intelligentsia the role of a temporary elite vis à vis the workers.[3]

To what extent, however, is this hypothesis justifiable? Did the Russian Marxists really face the intelligentsia as an elite group in relation to the labour movement as a whole? In order to confront such a question, Plekhanov's ideas, as expressed in the founding documents of the Russian Marxism under the titles *Socialism and Political Struggle* (1883) and *Our Differences* (1884), need to be analysed.

Given the fact that 'without revolutionary theory there is no revolutionary movement in the true sense of the word'[4] – a position repeated word for word by Lenin twenty years later in his *What is to be Done?* – the founder of the Russian Marxism was led to defend the vanguard role of the intelligentsia in the proletarian movement itself.

> The strength of the working class [argues Plekhanov] depends among other things on the clarity of its political consciousness, its cohesion and its degree of organisation. It is these elements of its strength that must be influenced by our socialist intelligentsia. The latter must become the leader of the working class in the impending emancipation movement, *explain* to it its political and economic interests and must prepare it to play an independent role in the social life of Russia [...]. The detailed elaboration of the [social and political] programme must, of course, be left to the workers themselves, but the intelligentsia must elucidate for them its principal points [...][5] (our emphasis)

As becomes obvious from Plekhanov's point of view, the Russian intelligentsia should by no means play the role of a mere executant of the people's will. The members of this vanguard group should take advantage instead of the socialist instincts of the working masses in order to make them conscious of their revolutionary perspective. To

---

[3] R. Larsson, *Theories of Revolution, From Marx to the First Russian Revolution*, Stockholm, Almavist and Wiksell, 1970, p.133.
[4] G. Plekhanov, 'Socialism and the Political Struggle' in G. Plekhanov, *Selected Philosophical Works*, Moscow, Progress Publishers, 1977, vol. I, p.90.
[5] G. Plekhanov, op. cit., p.102.

this end, the theoretical and political preparation of the proletariat under the intelligentsia's leading activity proves absolutely necessary *before* the workers' self-emancipation becomes achievable.[6] By drawing, therefore, a clear demarcation line between his own critical approach to the intelligentsia/people relation and the populist idealisation of the people, Plekhanov attacks the spontaneist/workerist interpretation of the self-emancipation principle.

> The fact that this basic principle of the General Rules of the International Working Men's Association had another, so to speak philosophico-historical meaning [writes Plekhanov] that the emancipation of a definite class can be its own affair only when an independent emancipation movement arises within that class – all this partly did not occur at all to our [populist] intelligentsia, or partly conception of it was a very strange one.[7]

In other words, according to Plekhanov, the working class' emancipation presupposes an independent workers' movement; nevertheless, such a movement cannot be developed, unless the intelligentsia plays its vanguard role.[8] Thus, it must be admitted that the intelligentsia should *transitionally* direct the proletariat towards its transformation from class in itself to a class for itself.

At this point, the time has come, however, to investigate even further the crucial question of this study in relation to Plekhanov's own analysis: Is there an immanent and, ultimately, unresolved contradiction between the proletarian self-emancipation, on the one hand, and the intellectual leadership, on the other?

From our point of view, there is no doubt that Plekhanov's position in this issue lies within the aristodemocratic approach as defined in our previous chapters. Hence, Georgi Plekhanov of the 1880s seems deeply convinced that there is no contradiction between

---

[6] G. Plekhanov, 'Programme of the Social Democratic Emancipation of Labour Group' in G. Plekhanov, *Selected Philosophical Works*, vol. 1, p.362.

[7] G. Plekhanov, 'Our Differences' in G. Plekhanov, *Selected Philosophical Works*, vol. I, p.147.

[8] G. Plekhanov, 'Programme of the Social Democratic Emancipation of Labour Group', p.363: 'The *Emancipation of Labour* group is convinced that not only the success but even the mere possibility of such a purposeful movement of the Russian working class depends in a large degree upon the work [...] being done by the intelligentsia among the working class.'

the intelligentsia's vanguard activity and the workers' self-emancipation.

In his own words,

> [the members of the Emancipation of Labour] do not believe in that peculiar theory according to which the cause of a certain class can be accomplished – 'to a greater or lesser degree' – by a small group. [They] only say that the emancipation of that class *must be its own work* and that in order to carry it out the class must acquire political education and must understand and assimilate the ideas of socialism [...]. Our socialist intelligentsia, for whom it would be childish even to think of carrying out the economic upheaval by their own forces, can however render inestimable services to the workers by preparing them to put into effect 'the general idea of the worker estate'. (Plekhanov's emphasis)[9]

This means that Plekhanov's conception of the intelligentsia/ proletarian relation is opposed not only to the spontaneist/libertarian, but also to the elitist/ authoritarian version of this relation. As a matter of fact, he openly refutes the idea that the intelligentsia should act as a substitute for the ignorant masses in the revolutionary process itself. On the other hand, by focusing his attention on the leading character of the intelligentsia's educational activity, Plekhanov extends the central line of the Russian aristodemocratic populism into the field of the newly founded Russian Marxism.

> [The Social Democrat] will bring consciousness [argues Plekhanov] into the working class, and without that it is impossible to begin a serious struggle against capital.[10]

It is exactly at this point, however, that Plekhanov's biographer Samuel Baron suggests that 'a major inconsistency entered into his system'.[11] From Baron's point of view, although Plekhanov's philosophical analysis points towards a *natural* formation of the proletarian (revolutionary) consciousness on the basis of capitalist

---

[9] G. Plekhanov, 'Our Differences', p.179.
[10] op. cit., p.340.
[11] S. Baron, op. cit., p.103.

development, nevertheless Plekhanov himself insisted that '[the] proletarian consciousness has to be aroused by the socialist intelligentsia [...]. Plekhanov's system, [concludes Baron], counted on the awakening of the proletarian consciousness in the proletariat by a non-proletarian element!'[12]

What Baron regards as a 'major inconsistency' into Plekhanov's system, however, constitutes a fruitful contradiction which can be noticed within Marx's own political theory as well. As a matter of fact, the role of revolutionary class-renegade intellectuals, as conceived by Marx and Engels, runs parallel to the intelligentsia's role, as described by Plekhanov and his comrades. Both Marx and Plekhanov reject spontaneism and substitutism, while they also argue that the working class is *objectively* driven towards its self-emancipation. Nevertheless, from their point of view, the indisputable fact of the proletariat's natural attraction to socialism is not enough *per se* to guarantee its self-emancipation. That is why Plekhanov, faithful to Marx and Engels' positions, insists so passionately on the importance of knowledge, without which the masses are doomed to exploitation and misery.

At this point, attention should be drawn, therefore, to what may be called 'diffusion of knowledge' from the intelligentsia to the workers. It is in relation to this issue that Plekhanov himself develops the critical distinction between *propaganda* and *agitation*.

> [T]he propagandist conveys *many* ideas to a single person or to a few people, whereas the agitator conveys *only one or a few* ideas, but he conveys them to a *whole mass of* people, sometimes to almost the entire population of a particular locality. But history is made by the mass. Consequently, agitation is the aim of propaganda: I conduct propaganda so that I shall have the opportunity to transfer to agitation.[13] (Plekhanov's emphasis)

---

[12] ibid.

[13] G. Plekhanov, 'The Tasks of the Social Democrats to the Struggle against the Famine in Russia' in N. Harding (ed.), *Marxism in Russia, Key Documents 1871–1906*, Cambridge, Cambridge University Press, 1983, p.104.

From this point of view, propaganda and agitation constitute the two stages of a single process, i.e. of the diffusion of knowledge, and especially political knowledge, to the workers.

It was actually in its first phase of development that the Russian social democratic intelligentsia approached the proletarians by propaganda, which was mainly promoted through the so-called *Kzuzhkovschina* (circle work). The specific aim of this work was the formation of future agitators through recruiting and educating the most talented members of the working class itself.

According to Baron,

> instead of addressing themselves to the mass, the Marxists were simply drawing from it the most intelligent and able of the literate workers. In concentrating upon the education of a minority, [however], the propagandist left the mass of workers untouched.[14]

It is due to this lack of contact with the working masses that the members of the 'circles' gave the impression of an *intellectual elite*[15] more or less indifferent to the workers' need for struggle and liberation. More concretely, the newly born worker-intelligentsia, which eminent social democrats like Plekhanov and Axelrod saw as the future leader of the proletarian movement,[16] seemed very satisfied within the selfish world of their circle education.

Under these circumstances the transition from propaganda to agitation, which Plekhanov constantly suggested and supported, appeared to be blocked until Kremer and Martov wrote their brochure entitled *On Agitation* in 1896,[17] a pamphlet which illustrates in fact the

---

[14] S. Baron, op. cit., p.148.

[15] According to L.H. Haimson, op. cit., p.57, 'so great and so rapid had been the triumph of Social Democracy that its young champions appeared satisfied to view it (as they viewed themselves) as an *aristocracy at the intellect*.' (our emphasis)

[16] See:
   a) G.W. Plekhanov and P. Axelrod, 'From the Publishers of the *'Workers' Library'* in N. Harding (ed.), op. cit., especially pp.70–71.
   B) P. Axelrod, 'The Tasks of the Worker Intelligentsia in Russia' in N. Harding (ed.), op. cit., pp.113–119.

[17] According to Israel Getzler, *Martov, A Political Biography of a Russian Social Democrat*, Cambridge, Cambridge University Press, 1967, p.22; 'there can be no two opinions [...] that Kremer and Gozhansky formulated what came to be known

delicate, though essential, difference between elitism and aristodemocratism as far as the intelligentsia/worker relationship is concerned.

At this point, it is worth commenting on the way in which Kremer and Martov describe the real motive, which lies behind the publication of this handbook:

> What has been the result of this kind of propaganda? The best, most able men have received theoretical evidence that is only very superficially connected with real life, with the conditions in which these people live. The worker's desire for knowledge, for an escape from his darkness, has been exploited in order to accustom him to the conclusions and generalisations of scientific socialism. The latter has been taken as something mandatory, immutable and identical for all [...]. On the one hand, with this system of propaganda the mass have remained completely on the one side, being regarded as material to be tapped, and tapped as much as possible [...]. On the other hand, these best elements of the proletariat have formed a special group of people with all the traits that characterise our revolutionary intelligentsia doomed to everlasting circle life and activity with the results that flow inevitably from that.[18]

Hence, according to the authors of *Ob Agitatsii,* the desired transition from propaganda to agitation is actually impossible without a bipolar rupture with dogmatism and elitism at the same time. Knowledge must be diffused to the masses and respond to their needs. In other words, knowledge must not be the 'private capital' of an intellectual elite; knowledge should be regarded as a common good, that is why the social democratic intelligentsia – following their aristodemocratic populist predecessors and contrary to the authoritarian/Blanquist trend of Russian populism, represented by Tkachev – needs to overcome its separation from the masses and

---

[18] as the Vilno Program, and that Martov wrote it up in 1894 in the form of the pamphlet *Ob agitatsii (On Agitation)* [...]'
A. Kremer and Yu., Martov, 'On Agitation', in N. Harding (ed.), op. cit., pp.201–202.

become the collective educator and agitator of the proletarian movement.

It is from this point of view, therefore, that a crucial change arises with regard to the intelligentsia/people relationship. According to *On Agitation,* the intellectual-agitator should become conscious not only of socialist theory, but especially of the workers' living conditions; otherwise he (or she) would prove unable to play his (or her) vanguard role. On the other hand, the masses themselves should not be treated as if they were the passive element of the forthcoming revolution. Thus, the proletarian movement itself becomes the 'school' for the working class' educators. Factory-centred agitation particularly helps to bridge the gap between the intelligentsia and the workers, a gap which was actually enlarged during the Kzuzhkovschina/propaganda period. It is extremely important to note, however, that this worker-oriented philosophy, as expressed in *On Agitation,* does not render intellectual leadership as such superfluous; though the educator should himself (or herself) be educated, he (or she) is still regarded as the guide of the workers. Nevertheless, this fragile relation of the intelligentsia, on the one hand, with the workers, on the other, is shattered under the critical impact of theoretical and political trends like economism, revisionism etc. It was against these trends that the most controversial figure of the Russian social democracy, Lenin, becoming the leader of the so-called Iskra group, launched his own criticism seven years later.

Before proceeding to the discussion of the intellectual/proletarian relation during the Iskra period, however, a brief reference to the Russian economism, as this developed in the turn of the nineteenth century is necessary.[19]

It is beyond doubt that the *anti-intellectualism,* commonly shared by the various groups of Russian economism,[20] actually determined the theoretical and political distance separating the economists from (Russian) Marxism as represented by Plekhanov and his group. More specifically, while the Emancipation of Labour and its successors

---

[19] As J.L.H. Keep, op. cit., p.58 informs us, 'in April 1900, when the League [of Russian Social Democrats Abroad] held its second congress, partisans of the rival factions almost came to blows. Accompanied by a few loyal followers, Plekhanov walked out of the meeting and set up a new body, which he christened "The Revolutionary Organisation 'Social Democrat'".'

[20] For the various trends of Russian Economism, see J.L.H. Keep, op. cit., pp.58-66.

regarded the intelligentsia's leading activity as a necessary condition for the development of proletarian consciousness, the Russian economists opposed the intelligentsia's leadership by insisting that life itself would teach the workers how to reach their own self-emancipation. Consequently, according to the economist analysis, workers should confine their action to economic agitation up to the time that they would be mature enough to act politically, relying exclusively on their own forces.

As Kuskova characteristically argues in her well-known *Credo* (1899) – the manifesto of the Russian economism – just one year after the founding congress of the Russian Social Democratic Labour Party (RSDRP) in Minsk,[21]

> talk of an independent workers' political party is nothing but the result of transplanting alien aims and alien achievements on to our soil [...]. Clearly the absence in every Russian citizen of a feeling for, and a sense of, politics cannot be compensated by the discussion of politics or by appeals to a non-existent force. This feeling for politics can only be acquired through education, i.e., through participation in the life (however un-Marxian it may be) offered by Russian conditions.[22]

What Yekaterina Kuskova suggested, in fact, was the position, which her husband Sergei Prokopovich openly declared when writing that the Socialists must wait patiently until 'the workers themselves, of themselves, begin to struggle against autocracy, *without the revolutionary bacillus – the intelligentsia*'[23] (our emphasis)

Nevertheless, Kuskova and Prokopovich were not the only opponents to the intelligentsia's interference in the proletarian movement. The editors of the *Rabochaya Mysl*[24] and the moderate

---

[21] For the foundation of the Russian Social Democratic Labour Party, see J.L.H. Keep, op. cit., pp.49–53; it is worth noting, moreover, that following J.L.H. Keep, op. cit., p.53, 'a majority of delegates opposed the inclusion of the word *Rabochaya* (Labour) on the grounds that Party should not pretend to be what it was not.' (Keep's emphasis)

[22] E. D. Kuskova, 'Credo' in N. Harding (ed.), op. cit., pp.252-253.

[23] Quoted in R. Larsson, op. cit., pp.152-153.

[24] See L.H. Haimson, op. cit., p, 79.

economists of *Rabochee Delo*[25] also supported the view that the working class must be left undisturbed in its spontaneous approach to socialism: 'Regardless of the success of social science, regardless of the growth of conscious fighters the appearance on this earth of a new social order will be primarily the result of spontaneous outbreaks.'[26]

As is obvious, therefore, it is basically the intelligentsia/proletarian relation which divides the Russian revolutionaries into the camps of the Russian economism, on the one hand, and Russian Marxism, on the other.[27] From this point of view, the two poles of the contradiction upon which Martov and Kremer built their pamphlet *On Agitation* – spontaneity and consciousness – were ultimately separated, giving rise to a direct conflict between the supporters of workerist spontaneism and the defenders of intellectual vanguardism.

Furthermore, it is worth noting that this schism within the Russian labour movement was not the result of a mere theoretical conflict. Revisionism in the West combined with immense agitating activity in the East directly challenged the ideological identity and radically altered the social composition of Russian revolutionary forces. In fact, agitation as such opened the way for the transformation of Russian social democracy from an intellectual sect to a proletarian party. On the other hand, workers themselves proved rather reluctant to accept the growth of the intelligentsia's 'revolutionary bacillus' within their ranks.

As Baron argues, for example,

> confronted with a worker psychology of this kind, a majority of the Social Democratic intelligentsia capitulated. In taking the existing level of worker consciousness as the touchstone, they demonstrated their willingness to yield to the workers themselves the ultimate determination of the direction of the movement. The relationship which resulted [concluded Baron] mirrored the altered composition of Russian Social

---

[25] op. cit., pp.121–122.
[26] Quoted in op. cit., p.123.
[27] See P.B. Axelrod, *On the Question of the Present Tasks and Tactics of the Russian Social Democrats (Draft Programme)* in N. Harding (ed.), op. cit., pp.236–237.

Democracy, with the working class increasingly dominant and the intelligentsia less and less in control.[28]

Such a concession to the workers' spontaneity, however, was completely rejected by Plekhanov and his fellow intellectuals. Following the aristodemocratic line of approach, these Russian Marxists decided neither to ignore, nor to bow to the workers' instinct and the majority's spontaneous will. On the contrary, Plekhanov himself – in order to counteract revisionism and economism's influence on the proletarian movement – was led to attribute an even greater responsibility to the intelligentsia as the *transitional* leader of the forthcoming revolution.[29] Hence, the Russian Marxist intelligentsia appeared as the collective guardian of this theoretical and political milieu, within the limits of which the proletarian instinct could flourish and finally ripen, taking the form of revolutionary consciousness. To this end, the members of the social democratic intelligentsia decided to take the lead in the struggle for the education and organisation of the working class.

At this point, actually, the organisational dimension of the intelligentsia/worker relationship becomes crucial. The question whether or not intellectual leadership is compatible indeed with the proletarian party's independence and, ultimately, with proletarian self-emancipation – a question already confronted by Marx and Engels during the last years of their life and the first years of the German social democracy – comes back again bringing us up against the critical point of this analysis. Thus, it is now the time to consider the intelligentsia question in the light of the organisational debate which took place during the first years of the twentieth century.

It was in August 1900 when Lenin, a young revolutionary who had already departed from his ideological – rather economistic – past,[30]

---

[28] S. Baron, op. cit., p.199.

[29] For Plekhanov's reaction against revisionism and economism in connection with his views on the intelligentsia's role, see S. Baron, op. cit., especially pp.183-185.

[30] For the various stages of development of Lenin's views on the vanguard/masses relation see:
  a) R. Larsson, op. cit., pp.196-202.
  b) P. LeBlanc, *Lenin and the Revolutionary Party*, New Jersey, Humanities Press International, 1990, pp.9-13.

  For the young Lenin's economistic approach to the party/masses relation, see V.I. Lenin, 'Draft and Explanation of a Programme for the Social Democratic Party' in N. Harding (ed.), op. cit., pp.153-171 and, especially, pp.165, 168.

arrived in Geneva and negotiated with Plekhanov the establishment of a political newspaper as the most effective means to propagate socialist ideas and organise a strong political movement all over Russia. In December 1900 the first issue of *Iskra* was published under the editorial leadership of three young revolutionaries – Lenin, Martov, Potresov – and three eminent figures of the Emancipation of Labour Group, i.e. Plekhanov, Axelrod and Zasulich.

There is no need to point out, of course, the well-known fact that the editorial board of *Iskra* believed that the intelligentsia itself had to play a vanguard role within the newly born Russian proletarian movement. Both the old and the young generation of the Russian revolutionaries, as represented in the *Iskra's* staff, were convinced that the working class was in urgent need of a transitional intellectual leader in order to achieve its emancipatory end.

> The proletariat [argues Axelrod] grows and develops at the bottom of the social pyramid, without air, light and sun, in an atmosphere of absolute lack of legal rights [...]. In its political development, the proletariat must therefore, in the first moment of its political awakening to historic life, be dependent on the radical intelligentsia.[31]

For his own part Yuli Martov as well expressed similar views on the intelligentsia/proletarian relation in his article 'Always in a Minority',[32] while Vera Zasulich did not miss the opportunity to highlight the fact that Western European intellectuals – contrary to the Russian intelligentsia – are characterised by 'aggressive individualism, social indifference and contempt for the 'masses'.'[33] At the same

---

[31] Quoted in R. Larsson, op. cit., pp.163-164.
[32] See I. Getzler, op. cit., p.52, 220: '"Always in a Minority" [argues Getzler] clearly appeals to a minority, to an *elite*, and calls upon it to join *Iskra*, "the regiment of the Guards", in an admittedly unpopular battle to capture the movement from its existing leaders and majorities. Had Martov become an elitist? The sort of boss he was later to denounce when Lenin assumed the role? I do not think so. In "Always in a Minority" the elitism is tactical and temporary, never ideological [...]. Even during the *Iskra* period when, in his "Always in a Minority" he had come closest to Lenin's elitism, he never went as far as Lenin in making a virtue out of necessity of that conspiratorial party which tsarist conditions had imposed.' (Getzler's emphasis)
[33] Quoted in R. Larsson, op. cit., p.166.

time, Martov and Potresov argue that it is Russian social reality as such which drives the already marginalised intellectuals of their country towards the proletarian movement.[34]

Thus on the grounds of this analysis the following conclusion can be reached: Plekhanov's central positions on the intelligentsia/worker relation, as expressed in his 1880s writings, still remain unchallenged. From this point of view, *Iskra's* leading article, written by Lenin himself in the first issue of the journal under the distinctive title 'Our urgent tasks', is revealing indeed:

> Social democracy [says Lenin] is the fusion of the workers' movement with socialism. Its task *is not to serve the workers' movement passively at each of its separate stages* but to *represent* the interests of the movement as a whole, to *direct* this movement towards its ultimate goal, its political tasks, and to *safeguard* its political and ideological independence. Divorced from social democracy, the workers' movement degenerates and inevitably becomes bourgeois: in carrying on the purely economic struggle, the working class loses its independence, becomes an appendage of the other parties and betrays the great principle that the emancipation of the workers should be a matter for the workers themselves [...]. The task that Russian social democracy is called upon to fulfil is to instil socialist ideas and political self-consciousness into the mass of the proletariat and to organise a revolutionary party that is inseparably linked to the spontaneous workers' movement.[35] (our emphasis)

Hence *Iskra's* approach to the workers' movement, as expressed by Lenin, constitutes in fact an extension of and not a divergence from Plekhanov's criticism of economistic spontaneism and Blanquist

---

[34] See:
  a) I. Getzler, op. cit., pp.50–51.
  b) Potresov's position as quoted in R. Larsson, op. cit., p.166: 'Free from attention to career and placed on a relatively low social level, all of these intellectuals and semi-intellectuals are drawn like plants to the light... to the emancipation movement of the proletariat.'

[35] V.I. Lenin, 'The Urgent Tasks of Our Movement' in N. Harding (ed.), op. cit., pp.260–261.

substitutism as well; the social democratic party should neither serve passively nor break away from the spontaneous workers' movement. Thus, *Iskra's* editors, and especially Lenin, supported the aristodemocratic version of the intellectual/proletarian relationship, as already suggested by Marx and Engels and developed further by Russian populists and the founder of Russian Marxism, Plekhanov himself.

At this point, however, it is worth returning to the distinction between aristodemocratism, on the one hand, and elitism, on the other, as far as the intellectual/proletarian relationship is concerned. To this end, it must be noted that even a political theorist like Reidar Larsson – who, believes that the *Iskra* editors endorse a temporary elite theory – makes the following assessment:

> The Iskra staff obviously felt that it was questionable that they should have to appeal to the intelligentsia as an 'external force'. They did everything possible to reduce the impression of an elite concept and make special efforts to mark the close social relationship of the revolutionary intelligentsia and the working class.[36]

From our point of view, it is worth repeating that the young Marx himself, long before *Iskra's* publication, made exactly the same attempt to *minimise,* without annihilating however, the distance between the radical intellectuals and the workers themselves. Besides, it should be remembered that this *minimalistic* tendency has been linked – from the first part of this study – to what Jean-Jacques Rousseau defined as the *negative education,* i.e. an education aimed at removing (negating) the obstacles blocking the student's *natural* march towards his (her) self-knowledge.

As a matter of fact, it is in the same theoretical context that the following comment proves worth mentioning indeed:

> Even to Plekhanov even to Martov and Axelrod, concerned as they were with the development of the workers' own independent initiative [comments Haimson], it had seemed imperative that Social Democracy should do everything in its power to *remove*

---

[36] R. Larsson, op. cit., p.165.

> *the obstructions* that stood in the way of the workers' recognition of their true identity (our emphasis).[37]

To what extent such an overall assessment remained valid, however, with regard to the further evolution of Russian Marxism and especially to Lenin's theory and practice in the 1900s en route to the October Revolution remains to be examined.

It is in Lenin's W*hat is to be Done?*, where both the tendency to minimise the intelligentsia/proletarian distance and the model of negative education, i.e. two crucial criteria of aristodemocratism, *seem* to be challenged the most.

According to Lenin's well-known position,

> *there could not have been* Social Democratic consciousness among the workers. It would have to be brought to them from without. The history of all countries shows that the working class, exclusively by its own effort, is able to develop only trade-union consciousness [...]. The theory of socialism, however, grew out of the philosophic, historical and economic theories elaborated by educated representatives of the propertied class, by intellectuals. By their social status the founders of modern scientific socialism, Marx and Engels, themselves belonged to the bourgeois intelligentsia. In the very same way in Russia, the theoretical doctrine of Social Democracy arose altogether independently of the spontaneous growth of the working-class movement; it arose as a natural and inevitable outcome of the development of thought among the revolutionary socialist intelligentsia.[38] (Lenin's emphasis)

It is clear, therefore, that Lenin's main argument, while reminiscent of Plekhanov's similar remark,[39] leads to a clear-cut demarcation between the intelligentsia's theoretical work, on the one hand, and the spontaneous proletarian movement, on the other. In

---

[37] L.H. Haimson, op. cit., p.214.
[38] V.I. Lenin, 'What is to be Done?' in V.I. Lenin, *Selected Works*, Moscow, Progress Publishers, 1977, vol. I, p.114.
[39] See note 10 of this chapter.

fact, Lenin chooses to overemphasise what distinguishes the one pole of the intellectual/proletarian relation from the other, instead of stressing their organic unity. As a matter of fact, he has been driven to this position by his critique of the self-emancipation ideology of economism,[40] while finding valuable support in the writings of Karl Kautsky, the leader of the German social democracy.

Hence, according to Kautsky's analysis, quoted *verbatim by* Lenin in his *What is to be Done?*,

> modern socialist consciousness can arise only on the basis of profound scientific knowledge [...]. The vehicle of science is not the proletariat, but the *bourgeois intelligentsia;* it was in the minds of individual members of this stratum that modern socialism originated, and it was they who communicated it to the more intellectually developed proletarians who, in their turn, introduce it into the proletarian class struggle where conditions allow to be done. Thus, consciousness is something introduced into the proletarian class struggle from without [von Aussen Hineingetragenes] and not something that arose within it spontaneously [urwüchsig].[41] (Kautsky's emphasis)

At this point, however, the crucial question arises: what did Lenin (and Kautsky) really mean when talking about the introduction of socialist consciousness into the proletarian movement *from without?*

In relation to this question, it may be argued that Lenin vacillates between Blanquist elitism, on the one hand, and aristodemocratic vanguardism, on the other. More concretely, it is worth noting that,

---

[40] See, especially, V. Akimov, *On the Dilemmas of Russian Marxism, 1895–1903*, Cambridge, Cambridge University Press, 1969, pp.112-125. (From *The Second Congress of the Russian Social Democratic Labour Party*).

For the economistic approach to proletarian self-emancipation, see also Martynov and Ryazanov's positions as described in R. Larsson, op. cit., pp.186-190.

[41] V.I. Lenin, op. cit., p.121; see, however, Adler's critique of Kautsky, as included in Akimov's, *The Second Congress of the Russian Social Democratic Labour Party*, pp.117-118. According to Adler, 'the socialist idea is the product of the working class... Social Democracy is its brain... The birthplace of Social Democratic thought is the proletariat; Social Democracy is the product of this thought, and it brings the proletariat to self-knowledge.'

although extracts from *What is to be Done?*, such as those quoted above, point directly towards an elitist version of the intellectual/proletarian relation, the Russian revolutionary does not hesitate to admit that 'the 'spontaneous element', in essence, represents nothing more nor less than consciousness in an *embryonic form*'[42] (Lenin's emphasis). From this point of view the following comment proves worth mentioning as well:

> It is often said [argues Lenin] that the working class *spontaneously* gravitates towards socialism. This is perfectly true in the sense that socialist theory reveals the causes of the misery of the working class more profoundly and more correctly than any other theory, and for that reason the workers are able to assimilate it so easily, *provided,* however, this theory does not itself yield to spontaneity, provided it subordinates spontaneity to itself. Usually, this is taken for granted, but it is precisely this which *Rabocheye Dyelo* forgets or distorts. The working class spontaneously gravitates towards socialism; nevertheless, most wide spread [...] bourgeois ideology spontaneously imposes itself upon the working class to a still greater degree.[43] (Lenin's emphasis)

Within such a frame of analysis, therefore, Lenin does not call into question the working class' gravitation towards socialism; on the other hand, contrary to the Russian economists,[44] and in apparent agreement with the aristodemocratic version of the intelligentsia/proletarian relation, he lays special emphasis on the need for socialist theory's *resistance* to bourgeois ideology, which dominates the workers' spontaneous will. It should be admitted, however, that under the influence of his political conflict with economism, Lenin seems to

---

[42] V.I. Lenin, op. cit., p.113; at this point it is worth comparing Lenin's analysis with Michels' approach to the intellectual/proletarian relation as expressed within the latter's elite theory. (R. Michels, op. cit., p.229 ff.)

[43] op. cit., p.123.

[44] At this point, it is worth noting that Lenin gives the expression 'from without' or 'from outside', used against the economists, another meaning as well: 'Class political consciousness [says Lenin] can be brought to the workers only from without, that is only from outside the economic struggle, from outside the sphere of relations between workers and employers.' (Lenin's emphasis, op. cit., p.152).

confront socialist theory as if it were a *ready-made* system of ideas, which should be imposed upon or assimilated by the working masses. From this point of view, the working class itself risks becoming the object of history, while the social democratic intelligentsia appears to be the revolutionary subject.[45] Furthermore, it may be argued that Lenin's rather disjunctive confrontation of the socialist theory-proletarian movement relation gives the impression of a certain shift from aristodemocratism and negative education to elitism and positive education.

Before reaching such a misleading conclusion, however, and before taking into consideration subsequent 'moments' of Lenin's theory and practice as well, it is worth mentioning that Lenin, in his effort to reduce the overall political significance of the distance between the intelligentsia and the workers, makes an interesting distinction. According to Lenin's analysis, as long as the socialist movement is still in its embryonic phase, the guiding role of the intelligentsia seems indisputable. The further development of the revolutionary process, however, leads to the formation of a political vanguard – this was actually the case of the Russian social democracy in the early 1900s – within which, Lenin believes, the division between workers and intellectuals should and would be, finally, overcome.

> The organisation of the revolutionaries must consist first and foremost of people who make revolutionary activity their profession [...]. In view of this common characteristic of the members of such an organisation, *all distinctions as between workers and intellectuals [...] must be effaced.* [46] (Lenin's emphasis)

---

[45] According to Plekhanov, 'excluding socialism from the mass and the mass from socialism, Lenin proclaimed the socialist intelligentsia the demiurge of the socialist revolution.' (Quoted in S. Baron, op. cit., p.250).

From this point of view, the Russian economist Vladimir Akimov reaches a similar conclusion: 'Comrade Lenin [...] regards the proletariat as a passive medium in which the bacillus of socialism, introduced from without, can develop.' (V. Akimov, op. cit., p.115).

Finally Potresov, through his study on the Russian intelligentsia, argues in the same way, pointing out the intelligentsia's cult of itself. (See R. Larsson, op. cit., pp.237–238).

[46] V.I. Lenin, op. cit., p.178.

Paradoxical though it may appear, it is exactly at the point where Lenin argues in favour of the transcendence of the intellectual-worker distinction within the organisational framework of the revolutionary party, that he appears to approximate closely to the elitist version of Russian populism, and more specifically to Tkachev's ideas on the intelligentsia/masses relation.[47] Nevertheless, at least as far as his theoretical analysis in *What is to be Done?* is concerned, such a convergence cannot be defended. It is beyond doubt that Lenin's political vanguard, as presented in this specific work, does not act *on behalf* of the masses; it is rather the collective educator and organiser of the mass movement, which opens the way to proletarian self-emancipation. From this point of view, it can be argued that during his theoretical and political conflict with the Russian economists and their spontaneist and ultra-libertarian interpretation of the self-emancipation principle, Lenin avoids surrendering to elitism and substitutism. In fact, the final outcome of his intellectual and political vacillation between aristodemocratism and elitism en route to the Second Congress of the RSDLP is well illustrated by his frontal attacks on the economists, like the one that follows just below, where, though special emphasis is put upon the vanguard's activity, the masses as such are neither treated with contempt nor replaced by a revolutionary minority in the emancipatory process.[48] On the contrary, the activity of the intellectual and political vanguard, as conceived by Lenin and expressed in *What is to be Done?*, aims at the further

---

[47] A common feature of Tkachev's elite and Lenin's professional revolutionaries is the minor importance attributed to the social origin of the vanguard.
For Tkachev's position on this issue, see F. Venturi, op. cit., p.426; compare V.I. Lenin, op. cit., pp.187-188.

[48] See for example the following extract from Lenin's 'What is to be Done?', p.126, where he rejects actually both elitism and economism and develops a rather aristodemocratic version of the vanguard/masses relation: 'That the mass movement [argues Lenin] is a most important phenomenon is a fact not to be disputed. But the crux of the matter is, how is one to understand the statement that the mass working-class movement will 'determine the tasks'? It may be interpreted in one of two ways. *Either* it means bowing to the spontaneity of this movement, i.e. reducing the role of Social Democracy to mere subservience to the working-class movement as such [...] *or* it means that the mass movement places before us new theoretical, political, and organisational tasks, far more complicated than those that might have satisfied us in the period before the rise of the mass movement.' (Lenin's emphasis)

development of the recently born mass movement without which society cannot change.⁴⁹

> The Germans [the Social Democrats] only smile with contempt at these *demagogic* attempts to set the 'masses' against the 'leaders', to arouse bad and ambitious instincts in the former, and to rob the movement of its solidity and stability by undermining the confidence of the masses in their 'dozen wise men'. Political thinking is sufficiently developed among the Germans [argues Lenin] and they have accumulated sufficient political experience to understand that without the 'dozen tried and talented' leaders (and talented men are not born by the hundreds), professionally trained, schooled by long experience, and working in perfect harmony, no class in modern society can wage a determined struggle.⁵⁰ (our emphasis)

It was within this theoretical and political milieu, therefore, that the various trends of the Russian revolutionary movement proceeded to the Second Congress of the Russian Social Democratic Labour Party, which ended with the historical split between Bolshevism and Menshevism.

It was on 30 July 1903, when Georgi Plekhanov opened the proceedings of the Congress, in the course of which leading members of the *Iskra* group were embroiled in one of the most crucial ideological controversies of recent political history.⁵¹ The spark which set off the process of conflict was Lenin and Martov's disagreement as regards Article 1 of the party's rules, the object of which consisted of the definition of the qualifications required for party membership. According to Lenin's draft of the Rules, a party member could be one 'who accepts its programme and who supports

---

⁴⁹ It is for this reason that Alain Besançon, op. cit., pp.197–198, because of admitting the divergence between Tkachev's and Lenin's theoretical positions, chooses to draw the line of convergence between Tkachev's *theory*, on the one hand, and Lenin's *practice*, on the other.
⁵⁰ V.I. Lenin, op. cit., p.185.
⁵¹ For a historical presentation of the works of the Second Congress of the RSDLP and the final split of the party, see:
 a) J.L.H. Keep, op, cit., p.107 ff.
 b) L.H. Haimson, op. cit., p.171 ff.

the Party both financially and by *personal participation* in one of the Party organisations'[52] (our emphasis); following Martov's formulation, however, such a personal participation in a party organisation was not necessary: 'A member of the Russian Social Democratic Labour Party [proposed Martov] is one who accepts its programme, supports the Party financially, and renders it regular, personal assistance *under the direction* of one of its organisations'[53] (our emphasis).

It is hard to believe that a disagreement about an organisational question was the real crux of the matter; it appears that under the pretext of an argument about the qualifications for party membership, there was an *ideological* dispute, which was determined by the intellectual/proletarian relationship.

In fact, it was Lenin himself who linked his organisational views with his own approach to the intelligentsia question:

> In words [argues Lenin], Martov's formulations [concerning a looser type of organisation] defends the interests of the broad strata of the proletariat, but *in fact* it serves the interests of *bourgeois intellectuals,* who fight shy of proletarian discipline and organisation. No one will venture to deny that *the intelligentsia, as a special stratum* of modern capitalist society, is characterised, by and large, *precisely by individualism* and incapacity for discipline and organisation (cf. for example, Kautsky's well-known articles on the intelligentsia). This, incidentally, is a feature which unfavourably distinguishes this social stratum from the proletariat; it is one of the reasons for the flabbiness and instability of the intellectual, which the proletariat so often feels [...].[54] (Lenin's emphasis)

According to Lenin, therefore, a looser organisational framework, like the one proposed by Martov, will inevitably lead to the domination of the intellectuals' individualism over the proletariat's indisputable drive towards organised life and collectivism. Quoting

---

[52] V.I. Lenin, 'One Step Forward, Two Steps Back' in V.I. Lenin, *Selected Works*, vol. 1, p.274.
[53] ibid.
[54] op. cit., pp.293-294.

Kautsky word for word, as he had already done in *What is to be Done?*, Lenin clarifies his position as follows: 'the individual intellectual, like the individual capitalist, may identify himself with the proletariat in its struggle. When he does, he changes his character too. It is not *this type* of intellectual, who is still an exception among his class, that we shall mainly speak of in what follows'.[55] (Kautsky's emphasis)

Given this clarification, however, most of the intelligentsia, for both Lenin and Kautsky, proves to be more or less *antagonistic* to the working class. It is at this same point that Plekhanov also does not hesitate to take Lenin's side and defend his formulation of Article 1 of the party's rules. Within the context of this discussion, Plekhanov's argument is worth quoting:

> I also do not understand why people think that Lenin's draft, if adopted, would close the doors of our party to a large number of workers. Workers who want to join the party are not afraid to join an organisation. But that is a good thing. These bourgeois individualists usually also emerge as the representatives of all kinds of opportunism. We must keep them at arm's length. Lenin's draft [concludes Plekhanov] may serve as a bulwark against their penetration of the party and, for that reason alone, all those who are opposed to opportunism should vote for it.[56]

As becomes obvious, therefore, Lenin finds a fervent ally in his effort to link the organisational with the intellectual question. Besides, it should be noted that Karl Kautsky hastens to provide a *philosophical* screening for the defenders of this new version of anti-intellectualism:

---

[55] op. cit., p.339; for Kautsky's sociological views on the intelligentsia/proletarian relation, see K. Kautsky, *Selected Political Writings*, P. Goode (ed.), The Macmillan Press, London, 1983, pp.18-24.

[56] See 'Second Party Congress: The Debate on Clause I of the Party Rules, Russian Social Democratic Labour Party (1903)' in N. Harding (ed.), op. cit., pp.280-281. For his part, Trotsky reacted as follows to Plekhanov's view: 'I was very surprised when Comrade Plekhanov proposed that we should vote for Lenin's formulation as a reliable defence against opportunism. [T]he point is that Lenin's formulation, directed against intelligentsia's individualism, hits a quite different target. It is much easier for intelligentsia youth, organised in one way or another, to enrol in the party.' (N. Harding (ed.), op. cit., pp.282-283).

'Nietzsche's philosophy [argues Kautsky and quotes Lenin], with its cult of the superman, for whom the fulfilment of his own individuality is everything and any subordination of that individuality to a great social aim is vulgar and despicable, is the real philosophy of the intellectual; and it renders him totally unfit to take part in the class struggle of the proletariat'.[57]

In fact, it is worth asking what kind of an intellectual Kautsky has in mind, when suggesting such a position, and indeed Lenin, when he transfers this position from Western European to Russian social reality.[58] Neither the passive, very conformist, academic intellectuals of the West, nor the active western and eastern intelligentsia with their developed sense of collective action may find their philosophical archetype in Nietzsche's cult of the superman.

In our opinion therefore, Lenin's pseudo-philosophical attack on the intelligentsia can be accurately interpreted only within the strict limits of the *political* conflict which took place in the ranks of the Russian social democracy among various groups, mainly composed of intellectuals, fighting for the leadership of the forthcoming revolution. It is because of this fight that the political discourse of the opposing sides became highly *ideological* – in the negative and polemical sense of the term – constantly taking the illusory form of a proletarian self-emancipation theory, while concealing the intelligentsia's leading role in the proletarian movement.

In this context, it is worth noting that both Martov[59] and Trotsky,[60] who opposed Lenin's positions in the Second Congress of the RSDLP, laid special emphasis on Lenin's shift from enthusiastic support for the revolutionary intelligentsia's vanguard role in *What is to be Done?* to condemnation for individualism in his *One Step Forwards, Two Steps Back*.[61]

---

[57] V.I. Lenin, op. cit., p.340.
[58] op. cit., pp.340-341.
[59] See: I. Getzler, op. cit., pp.85-86.
[60] L. Trotsky, *Nos tâches politiques*, Paris, Éditions Pierre Belford, 1970, p.160.
[61] For his part, Eduard Bernstein as well – in his *Evolutionary Socialism, A Criticism and Affirmation*, Schocken Books, New York, 1961, p.216 – makes the following comment: 'We come across passages in (Marxist) publications where the maturity of the workers is emphasised with an acuteness which differs very little from the doctrinairism of the early Utopian socialists, and soon afterwards we come across passages according to which we should assume that all culture, all intelligence, all virtue, is only to be found among the working class [...]'.

Nevertheless, Lenin does not hesitate to support his new approach to the intelligentsia/proletarian relation with indisputable determination, deriving his central argument directly from the organisational model of capitalist production:

> It is not the proletariat [insists Lenin] but certain *intellectuals* in our Party who lack *self-training* in the spirit of organisation and discipline, in the spirit of hostility and contempt for anarchistic talk [...]. And Marxism, the ideology of the proletariat trained by capitalism, has been and is teaching unstable intellectuals to distinguish between factory as a means of exploitation [...] and the factory as a means of organisation [...]. The discipline and organisation which come so hard to the bourgeois intellectual are very easily acquired by the proletariat just because of this factory 'schooling'.[62] (Lenin's emphasis)

There is no doubt that Lenin leans to this argument in order to point out that the workers themselves must become the organised leaders and members of the RSDLP, while the vast majority of intellectuals should be kept out of or in the margin of such an organisation. From this point of view, Lenin seems to express a *quasi* economistic optimism as regards the working class' self-emancipatory capacities; nevertheless, contrary to the economists who insist that the workers must temporarily confine themselves to the economic struggle, Lenin insists on the workers' urgent task to extend their action to the political field under the leading banner of the Russian social democracy. Hence, the need to construct an independent workers' party which would act as the political vanguard of the whole proletarian movement.

It is at this point, however, that Lenin's position becomes the object of a severe critique, especially from Luxemburg's ideological point of view.

According to Rosa Luxemburg, who strikes directly at Lenin's argument, Lenin misuses words and deceives himself when he refers to the factory discipline and organisation in order to exalt the workers' revolutionary perspectives and capacities:

---

[62] V.I. Lenin, 'One Step Forward, Two Steps Back', pp.392, 394.

> What is there in common [asks Luxemburg] between the regulated docility of an oppressed class and the self-discipline and organisation of a class struggle for emancipation?
> The self-discipline of social democracy is not merely the replacement of the authority of bourgeois rulers with the authority of a socialist central committee.[63]

In other words, according to Luxemburg's criticism, despite his distinction between the factory as an exploitative institution and the factory as a model of organisation, Lenin fails to confront the political consequences of the fact that 'factory schooling' not only does not promote the workers' critical thinking, but even tends to suppress this critical ability, which is nevertheless a *conditio sine qua non* for proletarian self-emancipation.

Thus, Lenin's attack on the intelligentsia – as Luxemburg in *Organisational Question of Russian Social Democracy* and Trotsky in *Our Political Tasks* argue[64] – does not lead to proletarian liberation from an alleged intellectual tutelage, but, on the contrary, risks making the workers even more susceptible to an ideological and political elite, which acts on behalf of the working masses and dominates them.

In regard to this specific issue, Luxemburg lays special emphasis on the distinction between Western and Eastern intellectuals, following at this point the already cited example of Vera Zasulich and that of Pavel Axelrod as well,[65] while rejecting Lenin's mechanistic transfer of Kautsky's analysis of the intellectual question to Russian social reality.

> The milieu where intellectuals are recruited for socialism in Russia [argues Luxemburg] is much more

---

[63] R. Luxemburg, 'Organizational Question of Social Democracy' in M-A. Waters (ed.), *Rosa Luxemburg Speaks*, New York, Pathfinder Press, 1986, p.119.

[64] See:
  a) R. Luxemburg, op. cit., pp.117–118.
  b) L. Trotsky, op. cit., pp.158–160.

[65] For Axelrod's use of the distinction between Eastern and Western Europe in relation to the intellectual question, see R. Larsson, op. cit., pp.238–239; according to Axelrod, while in Western Europe the working class is capable of self-emancipation, in Russia the guiding role of the intelligentsia still proves absolutely necessary.

> declassed and by far less bourgeois than in Western Europe [...]. The Western intellectual who professes at this moment the 'cult of the ego' and colours his socialist yearnings with an aristocratic morale is not the representative of the bourgeois intelligentsia 'in general'. He represents only a certain stage of social development. He is the product of bourgeois decadence [...].
> On the other hand, the utopian or opportunist dreams of the Russian intellectual who has joined the socialist movement tend to nourish themselves on theoretic formulas in which the 'ego' is not exalted but humiliated.[66]

Given this distinction, Luxemburg seems to suggest that the intelligentsia and the workers, having come together in pre-revolutionary Russia, had the opportunity to form a political vanguard organisation which should have led the labouring masses to self-emancipation. Nevertheless, the actual relation of this vanguard – within which the distinction between workers and intellectuals should be effaced – with the working class as a whole, remained problematic and constituted the central question around which the Bolshevik/Menshevik controversy developed.

More concretely, Luxemburg seems justified in pointing to the possibility that Lenin's version of the intelligentsia/proletarian relation, as expressed in *One Step Forward, Two Steps Back,* would turn out to be definitely elitist *in practice.*

> Nothing will more surely enslave a young labour movement to an intellectual elite hungry for power [says Luxemburg] than this bureaucratic straitjacket, which will immobilise the movement and turn it into an automaton manipulated by a central Committee. On the other hand, there is no more effective guarantee against opportunist intrigue and personal ambition than the independent revolutionary action of the proletariat, as a

---

[66] R. Luxemburg, op. cit., p, 125.

result of which the workers acquire the sense of political responsibility and self-reliance.[67]

At this point, it is worth noting that Luxemburg's attack on what she defines as Lenin's intellectual elitism converges not only with the young Trotsky's analysis, but also – paradoxical though it may sound – with Plekhanov's positions as developed after the Second Congress of the RSDLP.

As Baron mentions,

> having earlier remained silent about *What is to be Done?*, having collaborated intimately in the effort to implement its central ideas at the Congress, in 1904 Plekhanov at last subjected this key work to a searching examination.[68] (Baron's emphasis)

Actually, in his effort to counteract the Leninist concept of vanguard, Plekhanov shifted the emphasis of his analysis from the intelligentsia's guiding role to the proletarian instinctive predisposition towards socialism.[69] In fact, this shift of emphasis was so great that Plekhanov, as well as Luxemburg, came very close to the economists' ultra-libertarian and spontaneist version of the intellectual/proletarian relationship.

According to the ex-defender of the intelligentsia,

> if the socialist revolution is a necessary consequence of the contradictions of capitalism, then it is clear that at a certain stage of social development the workers of capitalist countries would come to socialism *even if 'left to themselves'*. (our emphasis)[70]

From this point of view, however, the intellectual vanguard becomes the mere *accelerator* – i.e. a *quantitative* factor – of a process which may well unfold without the 'revolutionary bacillus' of

---

[67] op. cit., pp.126–127.
[68] S. Baron, op. cit., p.249.
[69] See the analysis of S. Baron, op. cit., pp.250–251.
[70] Quoted in S. Baron, op. cit., p.251; it is, moreover, worth comparing Plekhanov's position with Akimov's analysis of the same issue as expressed in V. Akimov, op. cit., p.122 ff. and especially p.122: 'Social Democracy [writes Akimov] has no need to "*divert*" the proletariat from its path; it can and must seek only to accelerate its movement.' (Akimov's emphasis).

the intelligentsia.[71] Thus, the criticism of elitism and substitutism as well, directed against Lenin by thinkers like Luxemburg, Trotsky and Plekhanov,[72] proves equally damaging for what has hitherto been defined as the aristodemocratic relation of intellectuals and proletarians. Especially Luxemburg's critique of Lenin's positions on the organisational question opens the way to a workerist spontaneism.

> The nimble acrobat [says Luxemburg] fails to perceive that the only 'subject' which merits today the role of director is the collective 'ego' of the working class. The working class demands the right to make its mistakes and learn in the dialectic of history.
> Let us speak plainly. Historically, the errors committed by a truly revolutionary movement are infinitely more fruitful than the infallibility of the cleverest Central Committee.[73]

What Luxemburg neglects, however, is the fact that learning in the dialectic of history is a *mediated* process. Without the mediative role of the intellectual vanguard the transformation of the proletariat from a class in itself to a class for itself becomes highly debatable.[74] The 'collective ego' of the working *class* is not *a priori* given; in order to form its revolutionary 'collective ego', the working class must be prudent enough to profit by a special type of intellectual leadership

---

[71] According to Akimov, 'anyone who says that Social Democracy accelerates the development of the proletariat's class consciousness obviously expresses an idea diametrically opposed to the idea of the man who finds it necessary to bring socialist consciousness to the proletariat 'from without' and who feels that 'by its own efforts alone the working class is able to develop only trade-union consciousness'. Under such conditions, it is natural that Plekhanov wants to 'accelerate' the development of the proletariat's self-awareness, while Lenin wants to 'divert' the proletariat from its path. Both are right from their respective points of view. But the points of view are poles apart.' (V. Akimov, op. cit., p.123).

[72] The most critical attacks to Lenin's so-called elitism and substitutism were launched by:
  a) R. Luxemburg, op. cit., pp.116–122.
  b) G. Plekhanov, 'Centralism or Bonapartism'. (See the extract quoted in S. Baron, op. cit., p.248).
  c) L. Trotsky, op. cit., p.148 ff.

[73] R. Luxemburg, op. cit., p.130.

[74] *Contra* V. Akimov, op. cit., p.120: 'The proletariat's philosophy is thus created by the conditions of its existence. As the proletariat evolves into an independent class, its ideas form themselves into an orderly theory.'

without becoming a mere instrument in the hands of class renegade intellectuals.[75] Needless to say that the ultra-libertarian conception of the masses' *self*-education, which Luxemburg so passionately defends, seems far away from the aristodemocratic version of the intellectual/proletarian relation. Democracy, however, in the sense of popular self-determination, cannot be reached if a transitional stage of aristodemocratic leadership, exerted by the 'best' in terms of knowledge and virtue with the approval of the masses, is neglected or underestimated.

In fact, due to the political controversy which took place among the most distinguished Russian and Western European socialists, the frail thread of aristodemocratism which should have connected the intelligentsia with the workers was finally lost en route to the October Revolution or, rather, cut off during the difficult years 1902-1904 under the ideological pretext or the historically unjustified argument that the proletarian self-emancipation was *ante portas*.

---

[75] According to Plekhanov, 'in the view of Lenin [...] we see not Marxism but [...] a new edition of the theory of the hero and the crowd [...]. Since he declares himself to be the only active element in history, he considers the masses as only [...] strong but obedient tools.' (Quoted from G. Plekhanov, 'The Working Class and the Social Democratic Intelligentsia', as included in T.T. Hammond, 'Leninist Authoritarianism before the Revolution', in E.J. Simmons (ed.), *Continuity and Change in Russian and Soviet Thought*, Cambridge, Harvard University Press, 1955, p.147.)

Conclusion
Intellectual Leadership and Proletarian Self-Emancipation from the 1905 to the 1917 Russian Revolution

There is no doubt that the 1905 Revolution had a special impact on the development of the Russian proletarian movement and the historical events of 1917 as well. On the other hand, it is during this period that the intellectual/proletarian relationship seems to lose a great part of its overall significance as regards the theory and the practice of a forthcoming socialist revolution.

It has been argued, however, that, as far as Lenin is concerned,

> if one only read what [he] wrote during the years of the [first Russian] revolution, the question would arise if there was anything left in Bolshevism of the typical Leninist distrust of the working class' own capacity [...]. After 1905, he swung so far in the positive direction that he must be said to have abandoned his former elite theory.[1]

Nevertheless, according to our analysis, Lenin – as far as his political theory is concerned – never endorsed an elitist approach to the intellectual question, despite a certain vacillation in this direction. His *What is to be Done?* tends towards a more balanced aristodemocratic version of the intelligentsia/masses relation, given the fact that it was his own attack on the spontaneist/workerist position of the Russian

---

[1] R. Larsson, op. cit., pp.322, 328.
  For the same argument see also:
  a) N. Geras, *Literature of Revolution, Essays on Marxism*, Verso, London 1986, pp.138, 186.
  b) T.T. Hammond, op. cit., p.149

economists, as he himself asserted, which provoked the special shift of emphasis on the intelligentsia's vanguard role in the proletarian movement.²

On the basis of this assessment, it should be stated that, although the 1905 Russian Revolution allowed Lenin to emphasise the proletarian gravitation towards socialism, he nevertheless remained faithful to his original position:

> The relation between the functions of the intellectuals and the proletariat (workers) in the Social Democratic working class movement can probably be expressed [argues Lenin in November 1905] with a fair degree of accuracy, by the following general formula: the intelligentsia is good at solving problems 'in principle', good at drawing plans, good at reasoning about the need for action – while the workers act, and transform drab theory into living reality.³

This means that, 'although the working class is instinctively, spontaneously Social Democratic, and more than ten years of work put in by Social democracy has done a great deal to transform this spontaneity into consciousness',⁴ the time for a *stricto sensu* proletarian self-emancipation has not come yet. As a matter of fact, the revolutionary intelligentsia, following Lenin's analysis, still has a vanguard role to play within the Social Democratic party and the proletarian movement as well.

It was from this point of view that not only Lenin, but the Mensheviks as well rejected Axelrod's proposal for a workers' congress. As Reidar Larsson informs us,

> Axelrod was extremely bitter and denied that the Party was a class organisation, even after the membership figures had increased enormously as compared with 1905. The intelligentsia were still, he said, the Party's

---

² See Lenin's analysis in his 'Preface to the Collection Twelve Years', as included in V.I. Lenin, *Collected Works*, Moscow, Progress Publishers, 1972, vol. 13, pp.100–108.
³ V.I. Lenin, 'The Reorganisation of the Party' in V.I. Lenin, *Collected Works*, vol. 10, p.38.
⁴ op. cit., p.32.

aristocrats, its patrician class, while the workers had to be satisfied with being plebeians.[5]

Within such an intellectualist atmosphere, therefore, Lenin's effort to change the intellectual/worker proportion in favour of the workers did not result in the intelligentsia withdrawal from their leading activity after the 1905 Russian Revolution. In the final analysis, as it has already been suggested, the leadership of a revolutionary movement is not chiefly a matter of quantitative criteria. The question 'who is holding the reins of the revolutionary movement?' cannot be answered by the power of numbers. Such a quantitative logic, characteristic of a rather naive conception of democracy (exclusive use of equality of numbers), is totally unsuitable to express the inner structure of what has been defined as aristodemocracy (combined use of equality of numbers and value), mainly determined by the answer to the question 'who enjoys intellectual and moral superiority within the ranks of the movement?'

As a matter of fact, the intellectual leadership of the proletarian movement, often undervalued or even bypassed in the field of theory, proved indisputable in the Russian historical practice. In regard to this issue therefore – although a detailed historical analysis lies beyond the boundaries of this study – the following data are worth noting indeed: according to Richard Pipes' documented research, 'during and immediately after the revolutionary year 1905, the ranks of social democracy increased manifold, with ten of thousands of new adherents signing up, a *high proportion of them intellectuals*'.[6] (our emphasis). Furthermore Pipes' position converges in fact with Krupskaia's – Lenin's wife – assessment as well; as she herself argues,

> at the Third Congress [of the RSDLP in April 1905] there were no workers at any rate, there was not one remotely noticeable worker. But there were at the congress many 'committee men'. Whoever ignores the structure of the Third Congress will not understand much in its minutes.[7]

---

[5] R. Larsson, op. cit., p.350.
[6] R. Pipes, op. cit., p.364.
[7] Quoted in op. cit., pp.363-364.

As becomes obvious, therefore, just before and after the 1905 Russian Revolution the proletarian movement was basically directed by party intellectuals. Not only the political organisations, however, but the newly born Soviets as well do not make any exception to the rule; thus, it is worth mentioning that the socialist intellectuals who took part in the Executive Committee of the 1905 Soviet of Workers' Deputies in Saint Petersburg were not even elected by the Soviet, but appointed by their parties and, although their vote was merely consultant, their leading role in the Committee is hardly disputable. In the same way, the Executive Committee of the 1917 Petrograd Soviet also consisted exclusively of intellectuals appointed again by the socialist parties.[8]

In this context, Pipes' conclusion, referring especially to the 1905 Revolution, proves interesting as well:

> Since the emergence of Social Democracy in Russia in the 1880s, the workers treated the socialist intelligentsia with ambivalence. The unskilled and semi-skilled workers shunned them altogether, because they viewed intellectuals as gentlemen ('white hands') who used them to settle private scores with the Tsar. They remained immune to the influence of the Social Democratic Party. The better educated, more skilled and politically conscious workers often regarded the Social Democrats as friends and supporters, without being prepared to be led by them: as a rule they preferred trade unionism to party politics [...]. As a consequence, the number of workers in Social Democratic organisations remained minuscule [...]. In effect, therefore, both the Menshevik and Bolshevik fractions [concludes Pipes] were organisations of intellectuals.[9]

Consequently, to the extent that such a description proves accurate, there is no doubt that the political vanguard, at least as far as its social composition is concerned, can hardly be characterised a workers' party. On the other hand, it is not accidental that even Martov himself, from whom Pipes mainly derives his arguments, reaches the

---

[8] See Richard Pipes' analysis, op. cit., p.41.
[9] op. cit., p.365.

conclusion – finally published in 1914 – that the 'politically more mature worker element remained formally outside the organisation or was only counted as belonging to it, which has the most deleterious effect on the relations of the organisation and its centres with the masses. At the same time, the mass influx of the intelligentsia into the party [...] resulted in all the higher cells of the [Social Democratic] organisation... being filled by the intelligentsia, which in turn led to their psychological isolation from the mass movement'.[10]

Given this analysis, therefore, it seems beyond doubt that the course of the historical events leading to the 1917 Revolution was determined by a number of intellectual groups confronting each other in order to obtain the leadership of the newly arising mass movement. Furthermore, within such an ideological and historical milieu, the intellectual and, ultimately, the political asymmetry among the intelligentsia and the workers proved impossible to bridge. On the other hand, in the years which followed the 1905 Russian Revolution, despite or because of the removal of press restrictions, a dramatic fragmentation of the intelligentsia took place and led to severe internal controversies, controversies remarkably different from these of the years 1902–1904. As Jane Burbank argues,

> disputes were nothing new, of course, since ideological controversy had always been the sustenance and substance of intelligentsia politics. Yet in the past the factions, and schools within the opposition had at least agreed that their major target was the autocracy, while after 1905 a part of the intelligentsia turned its weapons against itself.[11]

From this point of view, the collection of articles, published in 1909 by distinguished ex-Marxist intellectuals, like Struve, Berdyaev, Bulgakov and others, under the title *Vekhi [Landmarks]*, is worth

---

[10] Quoted in op. cit., p.366.
Nevertheless, according to Paul LeBlanc, op. cit., pp.197–198, the situation in Moscow seems rather different: 'Statistics on the Moscow Bolsheviks indicate that about 60 percent were workers, that over 49 percent of their leadership cadres were also workers, and that the overwhelming majority of these were either second-generation workers or urbanised and proletarianised first-generation workers.'

[11] J. Burbank, *Intelligentsia and Revolution, Russian Views of Bolshevism 1917–1922*, Oxford, Oxford University Press, 1986, p.9.

mentioning. The *Vekhovtsy* actually launched the first frontal attack against the members of the revolutionary intelligentsia and their basic ideological principles as well. In the *Vekhovtsy's* opinion, the revolution of 1905 proved the intelligentsia's inability to change society; a genuine reform of Russia should be achieved only through a moral regeneration of the Russian people, a regeneration which presupposes a deep faith in the ideals of state, justice and religion.

Within the context of such an ideological fragmentation, however, it seems quite natural that

> in the years between 1905 and 1917, the intelligentsia had little success in bringing its vision – new and old – to life. After their initial strident call for different and positive ideas, the *vekhovtsy* failed to produce a concrete program for moral transformation. Their opponents among the overtly political intellectuals did no better.[12]
> (Burbank's emphasis)

Hence, en route to the October 1917 Revolution the intelligentsia/proletarian organic unity could barely be achieved. Not only a divided intelligentsia, but also the great mass of the workers continued to remain outside the main political vanguard organisations,[13] and this leads to the well-founded hypothesis that proletarian self-emancipation was still far away. Although the working class appeared to take part in a well organised trade union movement, nevertheless the vast majority of the workers did not take the initiative as far as political practice is concerned.[14] Thus, given

---

[12] op. cit., p.10.

[13] Following R. Pipes, op. cit., p.365 and according to Martov's estimation, 'in the first half of 1905, when the Revolution was already well underway, the Mensheviks had in Petrograd some 1,200 to 1,500 active worker supporters and the Bolsheviks 'several hundred' – and this in the Empire's most industrialised city with over 200,000 industrial workers. At the end of 1905, the two factions had between them in St. Petersburg a total of 3,000 members'.

Carmen Sirianni in his *Workers Control and Socialist Democracy, The Soviet Experience* (New Left Books, London 1982, p.93), shows that things have not changed so much during the February 1917 Revolution: 'At the time of February revolution (Bolsheviks and their allies] numbered perhaps as few as 23,000 in a country of 160 million, with only 2,000 or so in the capital.'

[14] However, it is worth mentioning that the trade unions are not separated from the political parties by the Chinese Wall. According to Paul LeBlanc, op. cit., p.196, 'by the summer of 1914, the Bolsheviks controlled fourteen and one-half out of

their class identity, both the Bolshevik and the Menshevik faction of the RSDLP could not constitute in themselves a reliable means to proletarian self-emancipation. Besides, it is because of the class identity of the so-called proletarian vanguard that Alvin Gouldner proceeds to the following quite unbalanced formulation:

> As the Jesuits purported to act in the interests of the church, so too, does the proletarian vanguard purport to act in the interests of 'its' class. But the proletariat is 'its' class only in the way a tribe 'belongs' to the anthropologist who studies it and calls them 'my people'.[15]

From our point of view, the highly complicated and fragile relation between the political and, in fact, the intellectual vanguard, on the one hand, and the proletarian masses, on the other, can neither be illustrated, nor interpreted through the 'anthropologist-tribe' image proposed by Gouldner. At the same time, we concede that the problem of the proletarian self-emancipation acquires a treatment which is much more sensitive than the one Gouldner gives. To this end, it is worth following, for example, once again Richard Pipes' analysis, which places, however, Lenin's approach to the intellectual/proletarian relationship in the elite camp:

> In the spirit of Mosca and Pareto, whose theories of political elites were there in vogue, Lenin asserted that the proletariat, for its own sake, had to be led by a minority of the elect [...]. Now, in as much as workers have to earn a living, they cannot devote 'their entire lives' to the revolutionary movement, which means that it follows from Lenin's premise that the leadership of the workers' cause has to fall on the shoulders of the socialist intelligentsia. This notion subverts the very principle of democracy: the will of the people is not

---

eighteen governing boards of trade unions in Petersburg and ten out of thirteen in Moscow.'

[15] A.W. Gouldner, *The Future of Intellectuals and the Rise of the New Class*, p.79; see also Michael Levin's comments on Gouldner's position as expressed in M. Levin, op. cit., pp.155-156.

what the living people want but their 'true' interests, as defined by their betters, are said to be.[16]

At this point, it is worth returning to the concept of aristodemocracy, as opposed to the concept of elitism. It is important to repeat that the 'vanguard' and the 'elite' are by no means identical. In particular, the aristodemocratic vanguard differs from the elite as far as its relation with the people is concerned. Contrary to the intellectual or the political elite, the aristodemocratic vanguard neither ignores nor feels contempt for the people's will; the aristodemocratic vanguard sees the masses' spontaneity as the *embryonic* expression of their true interests and works upon this spontaneous element by removing all the obstacles to its further development and fulfilment. Contrary to the elitists, the intellectual and political aristodemocrats refuse to act *on behalf* of the masses. On the other hand, they constantly aim at an organic unity between themselves and the people; such a unity is *a conditio sine qua non* for a successful approach to the people's self-emancipation. To this end, the aristodemocratic vanguard focuses its attention on the enlightenment of the masses and not on their, more or less, immediate manipulation, as is the case with the elitists. As a matter of fact, the members of an aristodemocratic intelligentsia fight to shape their relation with the proletarians in agreement with Parvus' categorical imperative: 'Act so that the workers can manage without you.'[17]

Consequently, to return to Pipes' position, the following comment must be made: the notion of aristodemocracy, as far as it is clearly distinguished from elitism, does not subvert the principle of democracy; it serves the cause of people's self-determination by pointing to the intellectuals' debt to the people, on the one hand, and the people's capacities for self-transformation, on the other. From our point of view, therefore, it is worth recalling that Lenin's *theoretical* positions of the early 1900s, especially before the Second Congress of the RSDLP, belong to an aristodemocratic tradition,[18] a

---

[16] R. Pipes, op. cit., pp.357–358.

[17] Quoted in R. Larsson, op. cit., p.282; it is worth mentioning as well that, according to Larsson, *ibid*, 'Parvus not only accused Lenin of not believing in the capacity of the working class. The Menshevik faction leaders were also told that they had acted exactly the same way as Lenin.'

[18] *Contra* J.V. Femia, *Marxism and Democracy*, Oxford, Clarendon Press, 1993, especially p.118 ff., who insists that Lenin not only subverts democracy, but

tradition which arises from the works of the young Marx and Engels and was promoted even further through the writings of Russian populists and Marxists as well.

Nevertheless, as has already been mentioned, the frail thread of aristodemocracy was cut off not in theory but in the battlefield of political practice, especially during the Second Congress of the RSDLP (1903). Nothing can illustrate better such an overall assessment than Plekhanov's thesis on democracy as presented by the founder of Russian Marxism in the above congress. Far away from his aristodemocratic theoretical background, and mesmerised by the political conflicts which dominated the party congress, Georgi Plekhanov did not hesitate to argue as follows:

> Every democratic principle must be considered not by itself, abstractly, but in relation to that which may be called the fundamental principle of democracy, namely, *salus populi suprema lex*. Translated into the language of the revolutionist, this means that the success of the revolution is the highest law. And if the success of the revolution demanded a temporary limitation on the working of this or that democratic principle, then it would be criminal to refrain from such a limitation.[19]

To what extent was Lenin himself against this position? It is beyond doubt that, as he became more and more involved in the political movement, he gradually departed from his aristodemocratic theoretical positions. From this point of view, it is not accidental that in both practice and theory the intellectual/proletarian relationship is hardly tackled by Lenin especially after the unofficial Third Congress of the RSDLP which took place in the spring of 1905. This highly complicated relationship was finally replaced in practice by the party/masses relation, within the framework of which the 'committee men' tend to become an elite group using the physical power of the masses in order to achieve its revolutionary goal.

Under these conditions, therefore, the rule 'salus populi suprema lex', as translated by Plekhanov into the language of the revolutionary, does not sound so strange when compared with Lenin's political

---

Leninism as well 'is a lineal descendant of Platonism' (op. cit., p.127); from our point of view, Femia misinterprets both Lenin and Plato.

[19] Quoted in S. Baron, op. cit., p.242.

practice; it is, in fact, a tragic irony of history that Plekhanov himself came to realise the further consequences of his argument through Bolshevik political action just after the October 1917 Revolution. On the other hand, it is under the impact of the oncoming revolutionary process that Lenin and his followers were to make a crucial tactical change as far as their relation with the working masses is concerned. They proceeded to a gradual shift of emphasis from the *intellectual* and *moral* regeneration of the people towards the *organisational* shaping of the mass movement itself. In other words, the Social Democratic vanguard, and more specifically its Bolshevik faction, focused its attention not on the educational preparation of the proletarian masses for their ultimate self-emancipation, but on the formation of an organisational structure suitable to lead the workers towards revolutionary ends. Between the 1905 and the 1917 Revolution, the political vanguard played the role of the *army commander* rather than that of the *collective educator,* as had been the initial objective of Russian Marxists in the early 1900s.

The consequences of this change for proletarian self-emancipation were by no means negligible. From this point of view, it is worth noting that 'some 60 per cent of the population in 1917 did not have even basic literacy skills, though peasants, women, and older people were disproportionately deficient'.[20] It seems, however, that the Bolsheviks had no time to lose in the education of the masses; what actually mattered for them was the political conflict *stricto sensu*. As a result, Lenin and his followers came closer to the Blanquist model, according to which the outbreak of revolution should precede the enlightenment of the masses. Under these circumstances, Lenin's appeal for the transmission of all power to the Soviets, 'the only possible form of revolutionary government', (April 1917 Theses), could not guarantee by itself an authentic proletarian self-emancipation. It was in fact the constantly unchallenged intellectual and political asymmetry between the vanguard, on the one hand, and the masses, on the other, which *de facto* undermined the workers' self-emancipatory perspectives.

Given, moreover, the absence of a mature proletarian *ecclesia militans,* the Russian revolutionary intelligentsia could not be confined to the role of the scientific adviser of the masses. They were

---

[20] C. Sirianni, op. cit., p.72.

inevitably led to become the political leaders of the proletarian movement.

Finally, from our point of view, special attention should be given as well to the fact that the tempo of history proved remarkably faster in Russia than that required for the achievement of an organic aristodemocratic relation between the intelligentsia and the workers. Under these conditions, therefore, the Russian revolutionaries were obliged to lean either towards political or towards ethical Socialism.[21] Unity of politics and ethics finally proved a mere utopia, while Lenin's reference to the revolutionary party as 'the vanguard of the proletariat, capable of assuming power and leading the whole people to socialism, of directing and organising the new system, of being the teacher, the guide, the leader of all the working and exploited people in organising their social life'[22] proved out of date as well.

At this point, Bernstein's argument seems much more convincing:

> We cannot demand from a class the great majority of whose members live under crowded conditions, are badly educated, and have an uncertain and insufficient income, the high intellectual and moral standard which the organization and existence of a socialist community presupposes.[23]

It is exactly this kind of argument that makes the leadership of the 'aristoi' and the 'gnorimoi', i.e. the 'best' in terms of moral virtue and knowledge, the most decisive prerequisite for proletarian self-emancipation. On the road to the October Revolution, however, such an aristodemocratic transition to the people's self-determination

---

[21] From this point of view, it is worth mentioning that while Bolsheviks lean, especially after the 1917 Revolution, towards political socialism, Plekhanov represents actually a more general tendency towards what may be defined 'Ethical Socialism', inspired mainly by Kant's political and moral philosophy. As S. Baron, op. cit., p.330 suggests, 'whereas he had once seen in Kantianism a philosophy inimical to the interests of the proletariat, [Plekhanov] now envisaged a kind of synthesis between it and Marxism. It was Kantian ethics in particular that now exercised a strong attraction on him'.

[22] V.I. Lenin, 'The State and Revolution' in V.I. Lenin, *Collected Works*, vol. 25, p.404.

[23] E. Bernstein, op. cit., p.218.

and government, proved to be a chimera for intellectuals and proletarians alike.

Bibliography

Akimov, V., *On the Dilemmas of Russian Marxism, 1895–1903*, Cambridge, Cambridge University Press, 1969

Aristotle, *The Politics*, Harmondsworth, Penguin Books, 1974

Avineri, S., 'Marx and the intellectuals', *Journal of the History of Ideas*, April–June 1967, vol. XXVIII, pp.269–278

Bakunin, M., *Statism and Anarchy*, Cambridge, Cambridge University Press, 1990

Bakunin, M., *God and the State*, New York, Dover Publications, 1970

Bambrough, R., 'Plato's Political Analogies' in G. Vlastos (ed.), *Plato II, Ethics, Politics and Philosophy of Art and Religion*, USA, Doubleday Anchor, 1971, pp.187–206

Baron, S.H., *Plekhanov, The Father of Russian Marxism*, Stanford, Stanford University Press, 1963

Berdyaev, N., *The Origin of Russian Communism*, Ann Arbor Paperbacks, The University of Michigan Press, 1960

Berlin, I., *Karl Marx*, Oxford, Oxford University Press, 1978

Berlin, I., *Russian Thinkers*, Harmondsworth, Penguin Books, 1978

Bernstein, E., *Evolutionary Socialism, A Criticism and Affirmation*, New York, Schocken Books, 1961

Besançon, A., *Les Origines Intellectuelles du Leninisme*, Paris, Éditions Agora, 1977

Blanqui, A., *Textes Choisis*, Paris, Éditions Sociales,

Burbank, J., *Intelligentsia and Revolution, Russian Views of Bolshevism, 1917-1922*, Oxford, Oxford University Press, 1986

Carr, E.H., *Michael Bakunin*, London, The Macmillan Press, 1937

Carver, T., *Friedrich Engels, His Life and Thought*, London, The Macmillan Press, 1989

Cassirer. E., *The Question of Jean-Jacques Rousseau*, Yale University Press, New Haven, 1989

Clark, J., 'Marx, Bakunin and the problem of social transformation', *Telos*, 42, Winter 1979-1980, pp.80-97

Cole, G.D.H., *A History of Socialist Thought, Marxism and Anarchism 1850-1890*, London, The Macmillan Press, 1954

Copleston, F.C., *Philosophy in Russia, From Herzen to Lenin and Berdyaev*, Notre Dame, Search Press, 1986

Cranston, M., *The Noble Savage, Jean-Jacques Rousseau 1754-1762*, Harmondsworth, Allen Lane, 1991

Crowder, G., *Classical Anarchism, The Political Thought of Godwin, Proudhon, Bakunin and Kropotkin*, Oxford, Clarendon Press, 1991

Dolgoff, S.(ed.), *Bakunin on Anarchism*, , Montreal, Black Rose Books, 1980

Draper, H., 'The Principle of Self-Emancipation in Marx and Engels', *The Socialist Register*, 1971, pp.81-109

Draper, H., *Karl Marx's Theory of Revolution*, New York, Monthly Review Press

Femia, J.V., *Marxism and Democracy*, Oxford, Clarendon Press, 1993

Fernbach, D. (ed.), *Karl Marx: The First International and After*, Harmondsworth, Penguin Books, 1974

Feuer, L.S., *Marx and the Intellectuals, A Set of Post-Ideological Essays*, New York, Anchor Books, 1969

Feuerbach, L., *Principles of the Philosophy of the Future*, Indianapolis, Hackett Publishing Company, 1986

Fichte, *Early Philosophical Writings*, D. Breazeale (ed. and trans.), Ithaca, Cornell University Press, 1988

Fichte, *The Vocation of Man*, Indianapolis, Hackett Publishing Company, 1987

Gay, P., *Voltaire's Politics, The Poet as Realist*, New York, Vintage Books, 1965

Gella, A., 'An Introduction to the Sociology of the Intelligentsia' in A. Gella (ed.), *The Intelligentsia and the Intellectuals, Theory, Method and Case Study*, California, SAGE Publications, 1976

Geras, N., *Literature of Revolution, Essays on Marxism*, London, Verso, 1986

Getzler. I., *Martov, A Political Biography of a Russian Social Democrat*, Cambridge, Cambridge University Press, 1967

Gouldner, A.W., *The Future of Intellectuals and the Rise of the New Class*, London, The Macmillan Press, 1979

Gouldner, A.W., *Against Fragmentation, The Origins of Marxism and the Sociology of Intellectuals*, Oxford, Oxford University Press, 1985

Grandjonc, J., *Marx et les communistes allemands á Paris,* Paris, François Maspero, 1974

Guérin, D., 'Marxism and Anarchism' in D. Goodway (ed.), *For Anarchism, History, Theory and Practice,* London, Routledge, 1989

Haimson, L.H., *The Russian Marxists and the Origins of Bolshevism,* Cambridge, Massachusetts, Harvard University Press, 1955

Hammond, T.T., 'Leninist Authoritarianism before the Revolution' in E.J. Simmons (ed.), *Continuity and Change in Russian and Soviet Thought,* Cambridge, Harvard University Press, 1955

Harding, N.(ed.), *Marxism in Russia, Key Documents 1879-1906,* Cambridge, Cambridge University Press, 1983

Hegel, G.W.F, *Logic,* Oxford, Oxford University Press, 1975

Hegel, G.W.F, *Philosophy of Right,* Oxford, Oxford University Press, 1967

Hegel, G.W.F, *Lectures on the Philosophy of World History: Introduction,* Cambridge, Cambridge University Press, 1975

Helvétius, *De I' Esprit,* Paris, Éditions Sociales, 1968

Hobbes, T., *Leviathan,* London, Dent, 1973

Hoffman, J., *Marxism and the Theory of Praxis,* London, Lawrence and Wishart, 1975

Hoffman, J., *State, Power and Democracy,* Sussex, Wheatsheaf Books, 1988

Hoffman, J., 'The Tension between Democracy as a Form of the State and Democracy as a Self-Government' (unpublished paper)

Hook, S., *From Hegel to Marx: Studies in the Intellectual Development of Karl Marx*, Ann Arbor Paperbacks, The University of Michigan Press, 1962

Hunley, J.D., *The Life and Thought of Friedrich Engels, A Reinterpretation*, New Haven, Yale University Press, 1991

Hunt, R.N., *The Political Ideas of Marx and Engels*, London, The Macmillan Press, , 1984

Johnstone, M., 'Marx and Engels and the Concept of the Party', *The Socialist Register*, 1967, pp.121-158

de Jouvenel, B., 'Rousseau's Theory of the Forms of Government' in M. Cranston and R.S. Peters (eds), *Hobbes and Rousseau: A Collection of Critical Essays*, New York, Anchor Books, 1972, pp.484-497

Kamenka, E.(ed.), *Ideas end Ideologies, Intellectuals and Revolution*, London, Edward Arnold, 1979

Kant, *Political Writings*, H. Reiss (ed.), Cambridge, Cambridge University Press, 1991

Kautsky, K., *Selected Political Writings*, P. Goode (ed. and trans.), London, The Macmillan Press, 1983

Keep, J.L.H., *The Rise of Social Democracy in Russia*, Oxford, Clarendon Press, 1963

Kelly, A., *Mikhail Bakunin, A Study in the Psychology and Politics of Utopianism*, New Haven, Yale University Press, 1987

Kolakowski, L., *Main Currents of Marxism*, Oxford, Oxford University Press, 1981

Lampert, E., *Studies in Rebellion*, London, Routledge and Kegan Paul, 1957

Lapassade, G., 'Rousseau et les encyclopédistes', *Arguments*, No. 20, 1960, pp.14-21

Larsson, R., *Theories of Revolution, From Marx to the First Russian Revolution*, Stockholm, Almavist and Wiksell, 1970

Lavrov, P., *Historical Letters*, Berkeley, University of California Press, 1967

LeBlanc, P., *Lenin and the Revolutionary Party*, New Jersey, Humanities International, 1990

Lehning, A., 'Bakunin's conceptions of Revolutionary Organisations and their Role: A Study of his Secret Societies' in *Essays in Honour of E.H. Carr*, C. Abramsky (ed.), London, The Macmillan Press, 1974, pp.57-81

Lenin, V.I., *Collected Works*, Moscow, Progress Publishers,

Lenin, V.I., *Selected Works*, Moscow, Progress Publishers, 1977

Levin, M., *Marx, Engels and Liberal Democracy*, London, The Macmillan Press, 1989

Lichtheim, G., *From Marx to Hegel*, New York, The Seabury Press, 1974

Lovell, D.W., *From Marx to Lenin, An evaluation of Marx's responsibility for Soviet authoritarianism*, Cambridge, Cambridge University Press, 1984

Lovell, D.W., *Marx's Proletariat: The Making of a Myth*, London, Routledge, 1988

Löwy, M., *La théorie de le révolution chez le jeune Marx*, Paris, François Maspero, 1970

Ludz, P., 'Methodological Problems in Comparative Studies of the Intelligentsia' in A. Gella (ed.), *The Intelligentsia and the Intellectuals, Theory, Method and Case Study,* California, SAGE Publications, 1976

Luxemburg, R., 'Organisational Question of Social Democracy' in M.A. Waters (ed.), *Rosa Luxemburg Speaks,* New York, Pathfinder Press, 1986

Malia, M., 'What is the Intelligentsia?' in R. Pipes (ed.), *The Russian Intelligentsia,* New York, Columbia University Press, 1961

Mannheim, K., *Ideology and Utopia,* New York, Harvest, 1936

Marcuse, H., *Soviet Marxism: a critical analysis,* New York, Vintage Books, 1961

Marx, K., *Capital,* London, Lawrence and Wishart, 1954

Marx, K. and Engels, F., *Collected Works,* Moscow, Progress Publishers,

Marx, K. and Engels, F., *Selected Works,* V. Adoratsky (ed.), New York, International Publishers,

Marx, K. and Engels, F., *Selected Correspondence,* Moscow, Progress Publishers, 1955

Maximoff, G.P.(ed.), *The Political Philosophy of Bakunin: Scientific Anarchism,* Glencoe, Illinois, The Free Press, 1953

McLellan, D., *The Young Hegelians and Karl Marx,* London, The Macmillan Press, 1969

Mészáros, I., *Marx's Theory of Alienation,* London, Merlin Press, 1975

Michels, R., *Political Parties, A Sociological Study of the Oligarchical Tendencies of Modern Democracy*, New York, The Free Press, 1962

Miliband, R., *Marxism and Politics*, Oxford, Oxford University Press, 1977

Molyneux, J., *Marxism and the Party*, London, Bookmarks, 1978

Namier, L.B., '1848: The Revolution of the Intellectuals', *Proceedings of the British Academy* (July 12, 1944), vol. XXX, pp.3-124

Nicolaievsky, B. and Maenchen-Helfen, O., *Karl Marx: man and fighter*, Harmondsworth, Penguin Books, 1976

Noyes, P.H., *Organization and Revolution, Working-Class associations in German Revolutions of 1848-1849*, Princeton, Princeton University Press, 1966

Ober, J., *Mass and Elite in Democratic Athens, Rhetoric, Ideology and the Power of People*, Princeton, Princeton University Press, 1989

Oizerman, T.I., *The Making of the Marxist Philosophy*, Moscow, Progress Publishers, 1981

O'Malley, J. and Algozin, K. (eds and trans.), *Rubel on Karl Marx, Five Essays*, Cambridge, Cambridge University Press, 1981

Parekh, B., *Marx's Theory of Ideology*, London, Groom Helm, 1982

Pipes, R., 'The Historical Evolution of the Russian Intelligentsia' in R. Pipes (ed.), *The Russian Intelligentsia*, New York, Columbia University Press, 1961

Pipes, R., *The Russian Revolution, 1899-1919*, London, Fontana Press, 1992

Pirumova, N., 'Bakunin and Herzen: An Analysis of their Ideological Disagreements at the end of the 1860s', *Canadian American Slavic Studies*, vol. 10, 4, pp.552–567

Plato, *The Republic*, Harmondsworth, Penguin Books, 1974

Plekhanov, G., *Selected Philosophical Works*, Moscow, Progress Publishers, 1977

Proudhon, P.J., *Textes et débats*, P. Ansart (ed.), Paris, Librairie Générale Française, 1984

Rigby, S.H., *Engels and the formation of Marxism, History, Dialectics and Revolution*, Manchester, Manchester University Press, 1992

Rihs, C., *La Commune de Paris, Sa Structure et ses Doctrines*, Paris, Éditions de Seuil, 1973

Rockmore, T., *Fichte, Marx and the German Philosophical Tradition*, Corbondale, Southern Illinois University Press, 1980

Rousseau, J.J., *The Social Contract and Discourses*, G.D.H. Cole (introd. and trans.), London, Dent, 1975

Rousseau, J.J., *Political Writings*, A. Ritter and J. Conaway Bondamella (eds), New York, Norton Critical Editions, 1988

Rousseau, J.J., *The Social Contract*, Harmondsworth, Penguin Books, 1968

Rousseau, J.J., *Confessions*, Harmondsworth, Penguin Books, 1953

Rousseau, J.J., *Emile*, Harmondsworth, Penguin Books, 1991

Schwarzschild, L., *The Red Prussian, The Life and Legend of Karl Marx*, London, Pickwick Books, 1986

Seliger, M., *The Marxist conception of ideology,* Cambridge, Cambridge University Press, 1977

Shklar, J.N., 'Rousseau's Images of Authority' in M. Cranston and R.S. Peters (eds), *Hobbes and Rousseau: A Collection of Critical Essays,* New York, Anchor Books, 1972, pp.333-365.

Sirianni, C., *Workers' Control and Socialist Democracy, The Soviet Experience,* London, New Left Books, 1982

Stepelevich, L.S.(ed.), *The Young Hegelians, An Anthology,* Cambridge, Cambridge University Press, 1983

Strauss, L., 'On the Intention of Rousseau' in M. Cranston and R.S. Peters (eds), *Hobbes and Rousseau: A Collection of Critical Essays,* New York, Anchor Books, 1972, pp.255-290

Taylor, A.E., *Socrates,* Westport, Connecticut, Greenwood Press Publishers, 1975

Teeple, G., *Marx's Critique of Politics, 1842-1847,* Toronto, University of Toronto Press, 1984

Therborn, G., *Science, Class and Society,* London, Verso, 1980.

Thomas, P., 'Marx and Science', *Political Studies,* vol. xxiv, No. 1 (1976), pp.1-23.

Thomas, P., *Karl Marx and the Anarchists,* London, Routledge and Kegan Paul, 1980

Trotsky, L., *Nos tâches politiques,* Paris, Editions Pierre Belford, 1970

Venturi, F., *Roots of Revolution, A History of the Populist and Socialist Movements in Nineteenth-Century Russia,* Chicago, The University of Chicago Press, 1983.

Vlastos, G., *Platonic Studies,* Princeton, Princeton University Press, 1973

Voegelin, E.J., 'The Formation of the Marxian Revolutionary Idea', *The Review of Politics,* July 1950, vol. 50, No. 3, pp.275-302

Wittke, C., *The Utopian Communist: A Biography of Wilhelm Weitling, Nineteenth-Century Reformer,* Louisiana State University Press, 1950

Woodcock, G., *Anarchism, A History of Libertarian Ideas and Movements,* Harmondsworth, Penguin Books, 1986

Zenkovsky, V.V., *A History of Russian Philosophy,* London, Routledge and Kegan Paul, 1953